Communications in Computer and Information Science 1346

More information about this series at http://www.springer.com/series/7899

Alvaro David Orjuela-Cañón ·
Jesus Lopez · Julián David Arias-Londoño ·
Juan Carlos Figueroa-García (Eds.)

Applications of Computational Intelligence

Third IEEE Colombian Conference, ColCACI 2020
Cali, Colombia, August 7–8, 2020
Revised Selected Papers

 Springer

Editors
Alvaro David Orjuela-Cañón (i)
Universidad del Rosario
Bogotá, Colombia

Jesus Lopez (i)
Universidad Autónoma de Occidente
Cali, Colombia

Julián David Arias-Londoño (i)
Universidad de Antioquia
Medellín, Colombia

Juan Carlos Figueroa-García (i)
Universidad Distrital Francisco José
de Caldas
Bogotá, Colombia

ISSN 1865-0929   ISSN 1865-0937 (electronic)
Communications in Computer and Information Science
ISBN 978-3-030-69773-0   ISBN 978-3-030-69774-7 (eBook)
https://doi.org/10.1007/978-3-030-69774-7

This Springer imprint is published by the registered company Springer Nature Switzerland AG
The registered company address is: Gewerbestrasse 11, 6330 Cham, Switzerland

Preface

The computational intelligence (CI) area is increasingly employed in engineering problems in the Latin America (LA) region. LA scientists have focused their efforts on the CI field as a way to deal with problems of interest for the international community but also of great impact in the LA region. Many different areas including optimization of energy and transportation systems, computer-aided medical diagnoses, bioinformatics, mining of massive data sets, robotics and automatic surveillance systems, among many others, are commonly addressed problems from this part of the world, because of the great potential those applications could also have in developing countries.

In its third edition, the IEEE Colombian Conference on Computational Intelligence (IEEE ColCACI 2020) was fortified with contributions from scientists, engineers and practitioners working on applications/theory of CI techniques. In this version of IEEE ColCACI, we received 65 papers by authors from 8 countries, and accepted 28 oral presentations in virtual mode due to the COVID-19 pandemic. In this way, the conference was an international forum for CI researchers and practitioners to share their recent advancements and results. The present proceedings include the best 12 papers presented as extended versions of the works exhibited at the conference, attending to this call for extended selected versions in these difficult times. We will continue working on offering an excellent IEEE ColCACI in future editions.

Finally, we would like to thank the IEEE Colombia Section, the IEEE Computational Intelligence Colombian Chapter, the IEEE Computational Intelligence Society, the Universidad Autónoma de Occidente, the Universidad del Rosario, the Universidad Distrital Francisco José de Caldas and the Universidad de Antioquia. Also, special thanks to all volunteers, participants, and the whole crew that worked together to have a successful conference. See you at IEEE ColCACI 2021!

November 2020

Alvaro David Orjuela-Cañón
Julián David Arias Londoño
Jesus Lopez
Juan Carlos Figueroa-García

Organizers

General Co-chairs

Jesus Lopez — Universidad Autónoma de Occidente, Colombia
Alvaro David Orjuela-Cañón — Universidad del Rosario, Colombia

Technical Co-chairs

Julián David Arias Londoño — Universidad de Antioquia, Colombia
Juan Carlos Figueroa-García — Universidad Distrital Francisco José de Caldas, Colombia

Publication Chairs

Alvaro David Orjuela-Cañón — Universidad del Rosario, Colombia

Diana Briceño — Universidad Distrital Francisco José de Caldas, Colombia

Financial Chair

José David Cely — Universidad Distrital Francisco José de Caldas, Colombia

Webmaster

Fabian Martinez — IEEE Colombia, Colombia

Program Committee

Alvaro David Orjuela-Cañón — Universidad del Rosario, Colombia

Jesus Lopez — Universidad Autónoma de Occidente, Colombia
Julián David Arias Londoño — Universidad de Antioquia, Colombia
Juan Carlos Figueroa-García — Universidad Distrital Francisco José de Caldas, Colombia

Danton Ferreira — Universidade Federal de Lavras, Brazil
Efrén Gorrostieta — Universidad Autónoma de Querétaro, Mexico
Cristian Rodríguez Rivero — UC Davis Center for Neuroscience, USA
José Alfredo Costa — Universidade Federal do Rio Grande do Norte, Brazil
Javier Mauricio Antelis — Instituto Tecnológico de Monterrey, Mexico

Leonardo Forero Mendoza	Universidade do Estado do Rio de Janeiro, Brazil
Carmelo Bastos-Filho	Universidade de Pernambuco, Brazil
Edgar Sánchez	CINVESTAV, Unidad Guadalajara, Mexico
Guilherme de Alencar Barreto	Universidade Federal do Ceará, Brazil
Gonzalo Acuña Leiva	Universidad de Santiago de Chile, Chile
Carlos Alberto Cobos Lozada	Universidad del Cauca, Colombia
Juan Bernardo Gómez Mendoza	Universidad Nacional de Colombia - Sede Manizales, Colombia
Diego Peluffo-Ordóñez	Universidad Técnica del Norte, Ecuador
Gerardo Muñoz Quiñones	Universidad Distrital Francisco José de Caldas, Colombia
Alvaro David Orjuela-Cañón	Universidad del Rosario, Colombia
Jorge Eliécer Camargo Mendoza	Universidad Antonio Nariño, Colombia
Claudia Victoria Isaza Narváez	Universidad de Antioquia, Colombia
Sandra Esperanza Nope-Rodríguez	Universidad del Valle, Colombia
Jesus Lopez	Universidad Autónoma de Occidente, Colombia
Cesar Hernando Valencia Niño	Universidad Santo Tomás - Sede Bucaramanga, Colombia
Miguel Melgarejo Rey	Universidad Distrital Francisco José de Caldas, Colombia
Wilfredo Alfonso Morales	Universidad del Valle, Colombia
Diana Consuelo Rodríguez	Universidad del Rosario, Colombia
Oscar Julián Perdomo Charry	Universidad del Rosario, Colombia
Humberto Loaiza-Correa	Universidad del Valle, Colombia
Eduardo Francisco Caicedo Bravo	Universidad del Valle, Colombia
Alexander Molina Cabrera	Universidad Tecnológica de Pereira, Colombia
Luiz Pereira Caloba	Universidade Federal do Rio de Janeiro, Brazil
Alvaro Gustavo Talavera	Universidad del Pacífico, Peru
Efraín Mayhua-López	Universidad Católica San Pablo, Peru
Yván Túpac	Universidad Católica San Pablo, Peru
Ana Teresa Tapia	Escuela Superior Politécnica del Litoral, Ecuador
Miguel Núñez del Prado	Universidad del Pacífico, Peru
Heitor Silvério Lopes	Universidade Tecnológica Federal de Paraná, Brazil
Waldimar Amaya	ICFO-The Institute of Photonic Sciences, Spain
Leonardo Franco	Universidad de Málaga, Spain
Carlos Andrés Peña	University of Applied Sciences and Arts of Western Switzerland, Switzerland
Edwin Alexander Cerquera	University of Florida, USA

Nadia Nedjah	Universidade do Estado do Rio de Janeiro, Brazil
María Daniela López De Luise	CI2S Lab, Argentina
Gustavo Eduardo Juárez	Universidad Nacional de Tucumán, Argentina

Contents

Earth Sciences Applications

Understanding the Cotopaxi Volcano Activity
with Clustering-Based Approaches 3
Adrián Duque, Kevin González, Noel Pérez, and Diego S. Benítez

Seismic Event Classification Using Spectrograms and Deep Neural Nets 16
Aaron Salazar, Rodrigo Arroyo, Noel Pérez, and Diego S. Benítez

An Android App to Classify *Culicoides Pusillus* and *Obsoletus* Species..... 31
*Sebastián Gutiérrez, Noel Pérez, Diego S. Benítez, Sonia Zapata,
and Denis Augot*

Hammerhead Shark Species Monitoring with Deep Learning 45
Alvaro Peña, Noel Pérez, Diego S. Benítez, and Alex Hearn

Towards Automatic Comparison of Online Campaign Versus
Electoral Manifestos 60
*Daniel Riofrío, Pamela Almeida, José Dávalos, Ricardo Flores Moyano,
Noel Pérez, Diego S. Benítez, and Pablo Medina-Pérez*

Biomedical and Power Applications

Time and Frequency Domain Features Extraction Comparison for Motor
Imagery Detection.. 77
Alvaro D. Orjuela-Cañón and Juan Sebastian Ramírez Archila

Automatic Classification of Diagnosis-Related Groups Using ANN
and XGBoost Models 88
*Angelower Santana-Velásquez, John Freddy Duitama M.,
and Julián D. Arias-Londoño*

Power Management Strategies for Hybrid Vehicles: A Comparative Study... 103
*Fernanda Cristina Corrêa, Jony Javorski Eckert,
Fabio Mazzariol Santiciolli, Marcella Scoczynski Ribeiro Martins,
Cristhiane Gonçalves, Virgínia Helena Varoto Baroncini,
Ludmila Alckmin e Silva, and Franco Giuseppe Dedini*

Alternative Proposals and Its Applications

FCM Algorithm: Analysis of the Membership Function Influence
and Its Consequences for Fuzzy Clustering.   119
   Luis Mantilla and Yessenia Yari

Echo State Network Performance Analysis Using Non-random Topologies. . .   133
   *Diana Roca, Liang Zhao, Alex Choquenaira, Daniela Milón,
and Roselli Romero*

Deep Learning-Based Object Classification for Spectral Images   147
   Román Jácome, Carlos López, Hans Garcia, and Henry Arguello

Transfer Learning for Spectral Image Reconstruction from RGB Images   160
   Emmanuel Martínez, Santiago Castro, Jorge Bacca, and Henry Arguello

Author Index   175

Earth Sciences Applications

Understanding the Cotopaxi Volcano Activity with Clustering-Based Approaches

Adrián Duque, Kevin González, Noel Pérez(iD), and Diego S. Benítez(✉)(iD)

Colegio de Ciencias e Ingenierías "El Politécnico", Universidad San Francisco de Quito USFQ, Quito 170157, Ecuador
{aduque,kgonzalezc}@alumni.usfq.edu.ec, {nperez,dbenitez}@usfq.edu.ec

Abstract. We explored four different clustering-based classifiers to categorize two different volcanic seismic events and to find possible overlapping signals that could occur at the same time or immediately after seismic events occurrence. The BFR classifier with $k = 2$ was chosen as the best out of 36 explored models statistically ($p < 0.05$), reaching a mean of accuracy score of 88%. This result represents a satisfactory and competitive classification performance when compared to the state of art methods. The CURE classifier with $k = 3$ achieved a mean of accuracy value of 87% at $p < 0.05$, allowing it to be the only model capable of detecting seismic events with overlapping signals. Therefore, the proposed clustering-based exploration was effective in providing competitive models for seismic events classification and overlapped signal detection.

Keywords: Volcanic seismic event categorization · k-means · Agglomerative · BFR · CURE · Clustering methods · Unsupervised learning

1 Introduction

Volcanic eruptions have been responsible for thousands of deaths since the year 1500 [34]. Historical records show that between 1986 and 2019, approximately 7670 deaths were reported from direct and indirect volcanic activity worldwide. There are many highly populated cities around the world where people reside within a 30 km radius to volcanoes [26,32] such as Quito (Ecuador) near to Cotopaxi (last active in 2012), Guagua Pichincha (last active in 2000), and Reventador (last active in 2002) volcanoes, Mexico City (Mexico) near to Popocatepetl volcano, Tokyo (Japan) near to Mt. Fuji, Naples (Italy) close to Vesuvius, Seattle (USA) close to Mount Rainier among others [30]. Currently, volcanic observatories worldwide use seismic monitoring as the most effective tool for forecasting eruptions [30]. However, most of these methods involve manual seismic events classification which could lead to errors due to human subjectivity.

Work funded by Universidad San Francisco de Quito (USFQ) through the Poli-Grants Program under Grants no. 10100, 12494, and 16916.

A. D. Orjuela-Cañón et al. (Eds.): IEEE ColCACI 2020, CCIS 1346, pp. 3–15, 2021.
https://doi.org/10.1007/978-3-030-69774-7_1

Machine learning classifiers with supervised or unsupervised learning have been employed during the last decade to different application contexts. Successfully supervised learning approaches used to tackle the problem of seismic events classification include artificial neural networks (ANN) [15], random forest [29], hidden Markov models [4], Gaussian mixture models [36] and support vector machine methods [6]. On the other hand, unsupervised learning methods intend to form structured groups or clusters in datasets without prior knowledge of any class labels [37].

The majority of previously developed approaches have been applied to different problems. Some studies reported in the literature include: principal component analysis (PCA) [35], mixtures of Gaussian [9], hidden Markov models [3] and self-organizing map (SOM) [14]. However, approaches focusing on volcanoes and their seismic activities have been less explored, but the SOM models seeing to be the most popular. In [12], a SOM model focused on volcanic wavefield patterns was used to analyze the Mount Merapi (Indonesia), classification errors of 6% and 26% were obtained for volcano-tectonic and rockfall events, respectively. However, when both events were combined into one cluster class, the error value was significantly reduced to 12%. In [28], SOM and k-means models were used to classify volcanic signals recorded from the Tungurahua volcano (Ecuador), attaining accuracy (ACC) values of 91% and 86% for noise and infra-sound signals, respectively. In [17], SOM and clustering-based models were integrated to built the KKAnalysis software, a tool that takes less than a minute to classify events, reaching an ACC value of 90%.

Despite the several developed approaches, the problem of volcano seismic event classification remains as an interesting and important challenge. This paper aims to explore four different clustering-based classifiers in the context of volcano seismic events classification and overlapped signals detection. The employed models belong to the unsupervised learning type of machine learning algorithms. They have the advantage of being trained without knowing the output label of input instances, making it a real-life problem application. The main drawback is that they are less accurate than supervised learning models.

2 Materials and Methods

2.1 Volcano Seismic Event Dataset

This work used a public dataset (*SeisBenchV1*) of the ESeismic[1] repository, which contains several seismic event samples recorded at the Cotopaxi volcano [25]. Each event sample is described by an 84-dimensional feature vector, including 13 features from time-domain, 21 features from frequency-domain, and 50 features from scale-domain. More detailed information about these features and their calculation can be found in [25].

---

[1] ESeismic repository was provided by courtesy of the Instituto Geofísico of Escuela Politécnica Nacional (IGEPN) and collaborators, and it is available at http://www.igepn.edu.ec/eseismic_web_site/index.php. Please note that you must register and complete a disclaimer agreement to obtain the data.

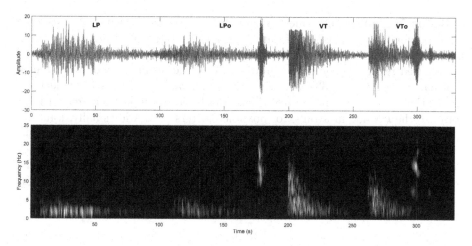

Fig. 1. Example of LP, LPo (LP with overlapped signal), VT, and VTo (VT with overlapped signal) seismic event in time-domain signals (top) and their respective spectrogram (bottom) from the *MicSigV1* dataset. The time signals were normalized by their maximum absolute value.

We formed an experimental dataset by extracting a subset of the *Seis-BenchV1* dataset, containing 668 feature vectors distributed in 587 samples of LP and 81 samples of VT event classes. Since this dataset comes from a real-life scenario, there are some samples with overlapped signals of non-volcanic origin events, e.g., rockfalls or icequakes that occurred at the same time or immediately after volcanic origin seismic events occurrence. This situation produces a mixed signal in the seismometer used to record the event. Figure 1 shows examples of LP and VT seismic signals, without and with overlapped waveform signatures on non-volcanic origin, respectively.

2.2 Clustering-Based Classifiers

As mention before, clustering methods have been effectively applied in a variety of engineering and scientific disciplines [13]. Clustering is a term used for the process of data grouping. Data are represented as points in a multidimensional space and are placed in different clusters according to a given metric, commonly, distance measures [22]. We considered three different clustering-based models instead of PCA or factor analysis, which are unsupervised learning models as well, since clustering-based models are not sensitive to the internal data correlation as could be the others. In real-life data, the correlation of features is an inherited problem; thus, the use of non-sensitive models are preferred to avoid data preprocessing steps. A brief description of the selected models are presented below:

k-Means Method: The k-means algorithm partitions the whole dataset into small number (k) of clusters of data in a way that the resulting intra-cluster similarity is high, but the inter-cluster similarity is low. The cluster similarity is measured regarding the euclidean distance to the mean value of the samples in a cluster (centroid) [33]. Selecting the right value of k is a hard decision due to the unknown class number. Thus, the basic in the k-means model is to optimize the k value in a range of possible clusters [22]. Additionally, k-means is mainly based on the distance computation using (1) between the randomly selected sample (instance to be assigned) and the centroid (cluster mean) of the considered clusters [21]. In the last step, the model recomputes the cluster centroid in which the sample was assigned [31]. The process is repeated until all the samples are analyzed.

$$S = \sum_{j=1}^{k} \sum_{i=1}^{n} ||x_i^j - c_j||^2 \qquad (1)$$

where $||x_i^j - c_j||^2$ is the distance from any sample x_i^j to the centroid c_j; k is the total number of clusters; n is the number of samples in the dataset and S is the similarity value of the ith sample respect to the k clusters.

BFR Method: BFR stands for Bradley, Fayad, and Reina, who developed a variant of the k-means algorithm, which is mainly used for clustering large amounts of data [22]. The BFR algorithm assumes that clusters are typically distributed around centroids in a euclidean space. On its first iteration, the whole data is read and loaded to memory. Then, it computes some simple statistic variables such as the number of points N, vector SUM and $SUMSQ$ [7] that will serve to avoid memory full-load in the next iterations. The initial k centroids are also estimated in the first iteration, usually by taking a random sample, picking up random points (instance of data), and then taking $k - 1$ more points (far as possible from the previous ones). There are three classes of points that are using to represent the data and to perform the inclusion of a given point to a cluster [7]:

- Discard set (DS): the points that are close to a known centroid can be discarded for further iterations.
- Compression set (CS): the points that are close together, but not really close to any k centroid, are summarized but not assigned to any existing cluster.
- Retained set (RS): the isolated points are the set of data points that are not recognized to belong to any cluster and need to be retained in the buffer, waiting to be assigned.

Once the DS, CS, and DS sets are conformed (in the first iteration), the BFR iterates over the CS and RS to assign their points to a specific cluster. Before each inclusion, the data dispersion (using the Mahalanobis distance) is calculated among the internal elements of the cluster with the highest probability of hosting the new point [2]. After a new point was included, the internal distances of the cluster are recalculated.

CURE Method: CURE (clustering using representatives) is a specialized model used to cluster the data in non-spherical shapes [8], usually ring or S-shape, and its main application is related to process large amounts of data (big data). The clusters formation starts by considering a group of representative points instead of centroids like the other methods do [22]. CURE treats each sample in the data as an individual class. Then, the closest samples (without taking into consideration the class) are merged until reach the number of desired clusters. After that, the samples are multiplied by an appropriate shrinkage factor to make them closer to the center of the cluster and to diminish the misleading effect of noise [18]. CURE is the most robust model for outliers and size variances.

Agglomerative Method: The Agglomerative clustering method is the most common Hierarchical clustering algorithm. It starts by splitting the data set into individual singleton nodes, treating each object as an independent cluster. In each subsequent step, the two 'closest' clusters are merged until only one cluster remains. To define the agglomerative strategy properly, we have to specify a distance measure between clusters [20]:

– Single linkage strategy: the distance between two clusters is defined as the distance between their closest pair of data objects.
– Complete linkage strategy: the distance between two clusters is defined as the distance between their farthest pair of data objects
– Average linkage strategy: the distance is defined as the average distance between data objects from the two clusters.

This agglomerative clustering can be shaped like a 'dendrogram', a continuous tree that starts with all the nodes as branches and ends with 'n' branches, depending on the desired number of clusters [1].

2.3 Experimental Setup

This section outlines the experimental evaluation carried out with the selected three clustering-based models using the *SeisBenchV1* dataset containing feature vectors of LP and VT seismic events. Dataset normalization, model configuration, assessment metrics, and selection criteria are important aspects that are described next.

Dataset Normalization: All the values of the dataset were normalized using the min-max method [11] for bringing them into the range between 0 to 1 and thus, avoiding data dispersion.

Model Configuration: For all models, the k parameter was optimized in the range from 2 to 10 (empirically selection). Other hyperparameters, e.g., the random seed was tuned from 0 to 10000 units; the children per node varied from 0 to the number of instances in the dataset (688), and the threshold value was set from 10^{-8} to 10^{-1}. All of then were estimated using a brute force-based approach. A brief description of the individual optimal settings for each clustering method are:

- *K-means:* the initialization algorithm for centroid selection and the maximum of iterations for each run were set to *k-means++* method and 1000 units, respectively.
- *BFR:* the merge threshold, which determines the approximation of two clusters, was set to 2 units. The Mahalanobis factor, which measures the closeness between points and clusters, was tuned to 3 units. The euclidean threshold, which determines the closeness of two points in the retained set, was tuned to 3 units, and the initial number of iterations was set to 40 units.
- *CURE:* the affinity metric used to compute the distance between sets was set to the *euclidean distance* algorithm.
- *Agglomerative:* the linkage criterion between sets was set to use the maximum distances. Also, the affinity metric used to compute the distance between sets was the *l1*-norm (Manhattan distance).

Assessment Metrics: The classification performance of all employed models was based on the mean of accuracy (ACC) metric over 25 runs (the minimum sample needed for accomplishing the statistical test). Also, for supporting the obtained ACC results, the true-positive rate (TPR) and true-negative rate (TNR) metrics of a single class were computed. It is worth noting that in binary classification tasks, the TPR and TNR metrics of a one-class complement the other. The *SeisBenchV1* used in this work is a benchmarking dataset and provides all the needed information about the samples, including the class labels required to assess classification performance.

We used the Wilcoxon statistical test with a significance decision value of 5% ($\alpha = 0.05$) for a two-tailed test [10] to conduct the ACC-based statistical comparison between clustering methods. This test provides a fair comparison among them, and therefore a reasonable selection of the best classification model.

Selection Criteria: Since the considered classifiers explore several k values, it was mandatory to select the best model using the following criteria: (1) the highest statistically ACC score and, (2) if there is a tie rating in performance, the one with less algorithmic complexity is preferred. Despite not existing a universal rule to select the best classifier, we stated the "rule of gold" for the selection based on the particularity of the experimental *SeisBenchV1* dataset. Thus, we ranked the model complexity in an ordered sequence of k-means, Agglomerative, BFR, and CURE classifiers.

We used the t-SNE (t- Distributed Stochastic Neighbor Embedding) technique [16] to visualize the multidimensional feature space presented in the *SeisBenchV1* dataset into a bi-dimensional one. It was always applied after the classification process to avoid transforming the data before feeding the classifiers.

Table 1. Classification performance based on the TPR, TNR and the mean of ACC metrics for the explored models

Model	LP classification																	
	$k=2$		$k=3$		$k=4$		$k=5$		$k=6$		$k=7$		$k=8$		$k=9$		$k=10$	
	TPR	TNR	TPR	TNR	TPR	TNR	TPR	TNR	TPR	TNR	TPR	TNR	TPR	TNR	TPR	TNR	TPR	TNR
k-means	0.58	0.56	0.74	0.38	0.39	0.64	0.36	0.32	0.11	0.30	0.35	0.27	0.09	0.09	0.28	0.09	0.13	0.7
BFR	0.88	0.37	0.83	0.21	0.64	0.25	0.85	0.30	0.26	0.28	0.47	0.34	0.62	0.27	0.48	0.40	0.10	0.15
CURE	0.94	0.19	0.81	0.47	0.90	0.25	0.85	0.31	0.86	0.27	0.14	0.25	0.16	0.22	0.80	0.18	0.87	0.15
Agglomerative	0.89	0.33	0.76	0.33	0.12	0.42	0.10	0.26	0.10	0.17	0.08	0.23	0.13	0.27	0.70	0.07	0.55	0.10
	Binary classification																	
	ACC	STD	ACC	STD	ACC	STD	ACC	STD	ACC	STD	ACC	STD	ACC	STD	ACC	STD	ACC	STD
k-means	57	0.02	56	0.07	56	0.09	33	0.08	15	0.07	31	0.07	10	0.04	24	0.03	12	0.03
BFR	**88**	**0.03**	71	0.06	61	0.08	78	0.05	28	0.02	43	0.05	57	0.03	46	0.04	6	0.04
CURE	87	0.01	87	0.02	84	0.05	83	0.03	82	0.02	16	0.05	16	0.03	78	0.07	80	0.05
Agglomerative	82	0.01	70	0.03	16	0.07	10	0.08	8	0.05	4	0.06	15	0.03	60	0.02	40	0.03

TPR - true positive rate; TNR - true negative rate; ACC - accuracy values rounded to the closest integer and are represented in percent (%); STD - standard deviation

The implementation of all classifiers was done in Python language version 3.7.4 [27] with the *scikit-learn (Sklearn)* library [23] and the BFR implementation posted at [5].

3   Results and Discussion

According to the experimental setup section, a total of 36 clustering-based models were evaluated on the experimental dataset which contains 668 features vectors. The straightforward statistical comparison based on the mean of ACC performance highlighted interesting results for the classification of LP and VT seismic events, as are described next:

3.1   Performance of Explored Models

Regarding the first selection criteria, only one out of 36 models were obtained after exploring the whole classification space. Table 1 shows the obtained results based on the mean of ACC metric for the binary classification of both types of seismic events and in terms of TPR and TNR of the LP samples. From this table, the BFR classifier with $k = 2$ was able to reach the highest ACC value of 88%. This result was statistically superior at $p < 0.05$ against the rest of the models. The CURE with $k = 2$ and $k = 3$ accomplished the same ACC value of 87%. The agglomerative method obtained a reasonable ACC score of 82% for $k = 2$, but a poor ACC value of 70% for $k = 3$. The k-means classifier obtained the worst performance, but the ACC value attained with $k = 2$ was the higher among all the presented results of this classifier. Concerning the TPR and TNR metrics, the CURE method reached the highest TPR score of 0.94 when compared to the remaining methods, but, the TNR score of 0.19 was the lowest among the rest. The agglomerative method was slightly better than the BFR method in terms of TNR scores, reaching 0.89 against 0.88. But, a bit worst in terms of TNR scores, obtaining 0.33 versus 0.37. Thus, the BFR method better compensated

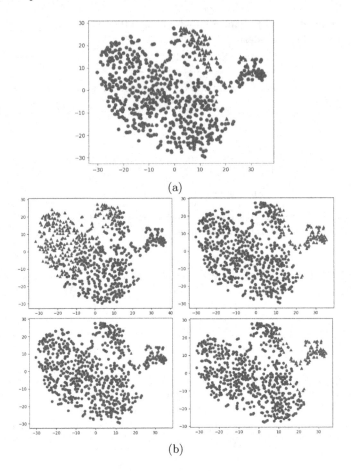

Fig. 2. Data visualization using the t-SNE technique for $k = 2$ clusters. The LP (red circles) and VT (green triangles) seismic events in the (a) original space and (b) as clusters obtained by the k-means, BFR (top row) and CURE, Agglomerative (button row) classifiers. (Color figure online)

both metrics. That means it was able to successfully classified the predominant class (LP events) and overcome the CURE method in the classification of the less represented class (VT events) in the dataset. Once again, the k-means method touched a limited score on both metrics.

Overall, the better performances was obtained with $k = 2$ for all classifiers, this was expected since the experimental dataset contains only LP and VT seismic events. Beyond this fact, the CURE classifier still assigned the same ACC value of 87% to a new cluster ($k = 3$). This value was statistically superior at $p > 0.05$ when compared to the remaining methods. This situation is related to the internal configuration of the *SeisBenchV1* dataset, in which some samples of LP or VT have signals overlapped. Eventually, this situation leads to

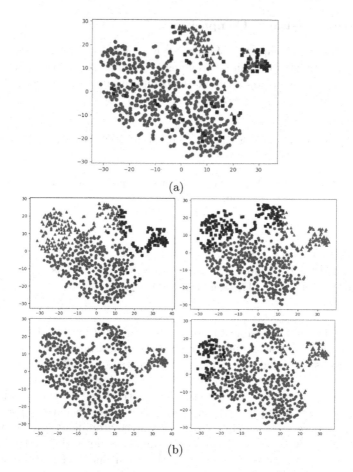

Fig. 3. Data visualization using the t-SNE technique for $k = 3$ clusters. The LP (red circles), VT (green triangles) and LP or VT (blue squares) seismic events in the (a) original space and (b) as clusters obtained by the k-means, BFR (top row) and CURE, Agglomerative (button row) classifiers. (Color figure online)

an incorrect classification when using supervised learning models due to the inaccurate event segmentation and, therefore, the calculation of the wrong features used to feed the classifiers [24]. However, the unsupervised learning CURE classifier was able to categorize and understand this particular data behavior. Figures 2 and 3 show an approximation of the data clustering at $k = 2$ and $k = 3$ using the t-SNE technique. From this figure, it is possible to corroborate that the CURE classifier was able to detect most of those samples with overlapped signals, enabling it as a non-sensitive model to be use in real-life environments. However, the BFR classifier with $k = 2$ constituted the best model selection for the problem under analysis.

3.2   State of Art-Based Comparison

Concerning the classification performance, it is not possible to make a statistically direct comparison against previously developed methods in the literature. However, we aimed to carry out the comparison based on the ACC scores reported by the state of art methods, as shown in Table 2.

Table 2. Comparison based on the ACC between previous works available in the literature and the selected best model

Method	Number of samples	Balanced dataset	Number of features	ACC* (%)
PCA [35]	672	Yes	57	99
SOM [12]	40	No	26	88
KKAnalysis [17]	5465	Yes	62	90
BFR ($k = 2$)	**668**	**No**	**84**	**88**

ACC - accuracy; *values rounded to the closest integer

From Table 2 it is possible to notice that the ACC value of 88% reached by the BFR classifier was similar to the SOM [12] and inferior to the PCA [35] and KKAnalysis [17]. The superior performance demonstrated by the PCA and KK Analysis methods could be linked to the employed datasets; while more and better distributed are the samples, better intraclass variation will have the model during the training process and, therefore, a more accurate classification can be achieved. Nevertheless, in volcano real-life environments, the likelihood of having balanced datasets is very low. For example, although LP and VT are the main type of events recorded at Cotopaxi, the occurrence of LP events is higher than VT events [19]. The ACC performance score of 88% reached by the SOM model in [12] was similar to our best model. However, it is impossible to draw comparative conclusions since in [12] the model was validated on a dataset with a lower amount of samples and features. Therefore, the obtained result could be considered as a non-generalizable model for further application.

4   Conclusions and Future Work

In this work, we made an ACC based exploration of four different unsupervised learning classifiers within the context of volcano LP and VT seismic events classification. According to the experimental setup, only one out of 36 models was selected by the first selection criteria. Afterward, the BFR classifier with $k = 2$ was chosen as the best model statistically ($p < 0.05$), reaching a mean of ACC score of 88%. This value represented a satisfactory and competitive classification performance when compared to the state of art methods. There was another model composed by the CURE with $k = 3$ that attained a mean of ACC value of 87%, which performed slightly lower than the selected best model. However, the CURE model was the only one able to detect LP or VT events with over-lapped signals statistically ($p > 0.05$). Therefore, the proposed clustering-based exploration was effective in providing competitive models in the classification of LP and VT seismic events and in the detection of signals with overlapping.

Future work is aimed to increase the number of samples of existent classes and the inclusion of other types of events in the current experimental dataset. Also, to include other clustering-based models to enlarge the exploration of the classifiers space.

Acknowledgment. Authors thank the Applied Signal Processing and Machine Learning Research Group of USFQ for providing the computing infrastructure (NVidia DGX workstation) to implement and execute the developed source code. Publication of this article was funded by the Academic Articles Publication Fund of Universidad San Francisco de Quito USFQ.

References

1. Ackermann, M.R., Blömer, J., Kuntze, D., Sohler, C.: Analysis of agglomerative clustering. Algorithmica **69**(1), 184–215 (2014)
2. Aletti, G., Micheletti, A.: A clustering algorithm for multivariate data streams with correlated components. J. Big Data **4**(1), 1–20 (2017). https://doi.org/10.1186/s40537-017-0109-0
3. Bebbington, M.S.: Identifying volcanic regimes using hidden markov models. Geophys. J. Int. **171**(2), 921–942 (2007)
4. Benitez, M.C.: Continuous HMM-based seismic-event classification at deception island, Antarctica. IEEE Trans. Geosci. Remote Sens. **45**(1), 138–146 (2007). https://doi.org/10.1109/TGRS.2006.882264
5. Berglund, J.: Clustering with BFR (2018). https://github.com/jeppeb91/bfr
6. Curilem, M.: Pattern recognition applied to seismic signals of the llaima volcano (chile): an analysis of the events' features. J. Volcanol. Geoth. Res. **282**, 134–147 (2014)
7. Daoudi, M., Meshoul, S.: Revisiting BFR clustering algorithm for large scale gene regulatory network reconstruction using mapreduce. In: Proceedings of the 2nd International Conference on Big Data, Cloud and Applications, pp. 1–5 (2017)
8. Guha, S., Rastogi, R., Shim, K.: Cure: an efficient clustering algorithm for large databases. ACM Sigmod Rec. **27**(2), 73–84 (1998)
9. Hammer, C., Beyreuther, M., Ohrnberger, M.: A seismic-event spotting system for volcano fast-response systems. Bull. Seismol. Soc. Am. **102**(3), 948–960 (2012)
10. Hollander, M., Wolfe, D.A., Chicken, E.: Nonparametric Statistical Methods, vol. 751. John Wiley & Sons, Hoboken (2013)
11. Jain, Y.K., Bhandare, S.K.: Min max normalization based data perturbation method for privacy protection. Int. J. Comput. Commun. Technol. **2**(8), 45–50 (2011)
12. Köhler, A., Ohrnberger, M., Scherbaum, F.: Unsupervised pattern recognition in continuous seismic wavefield records using self-organizing maps. Geophys. J. Int. **182**(3), 1619–1630 (2010)
13. Krishna, K., Murty, M.N.: Genetic k-means algorithm. IEEE Trans. Syst. Man. Cybern. Part B (Cybern.) **29**(3), 433–439 (1999)

14. Kuyuk, H., Yildirim, E., Dogan, E., Horasan, G.: An unsupervised learning algorithm: application to the discrimination of seismic events and quarry blasts in the vicinity of istanbul. Nat. Hazards Earth Syst. Sci. **11**(1), 93–100 (2011)
15. Lara-Cueva, R., Carrera, E.V., Morejon, J.F., Benítez, D.: Comparative analysis of automated classifiers applied to volcano event identification. In: 2016 IEEE Colombian Conference on Communications and Computing (COLCOM), pp. 1–6, April 2016. https://doi.org/10.1109/ColComCon.2016.7516377
16. Maaten, L.V.D., Hinton, G.: Visualizing data using t-SNE. J. Mach. Learn. Res. **9**(Nov), 2579–2605 (2008)
17. Messina, A., Langer, H.: Pattern recognition of volcanic tremor data on Mt. Etna (Italy) with KKanalysis-a software program for unsupervised classification. Comput. Geosci. **37**(7), 953–961 (2011). https://www.overleaf.com/project/5de17b1735faa10001aceb85
18. Min, Y., Li, Y.: Vehicles recognition based on the size characteristics and the cure clustering algorithm. In: 2015 IEEE International Conference on Signal Processing, Communications and Computing (ICSPCC), pp. 1–5. IEEE (2015)
19. Molina, I., Kumagai, H., García-Aristizábal, A., Nakano, M., Mothes, P.: Source process of very-long-period events accompanying long-period signals at Cotopaxi Volcano, Ecuador. J. Volcanol. Geothermal Res. **176**(1), 119–133 (2008)
20. Müllner, D.: Modern hierarchical, agglomerative clustering algorithms. arXiv preprint arXiv:1109.2378 (2011)
21. Oliveira Martins, L.D., Braz Junior, G., Corrêa Silva, A., Cardoso de Paiva, A., Gattass, M.: Detection of masses in digital mammograms using k-means and support vector machine. ELCVIA: Electron. Lett. Comput. Vis. Image Anal. **8**(2), 39–50 (2009)
22. Pandove, D., Goel, S.: A comprehensive study on clustering approaches for big data mining. In: 2015 2nd International Conference on Electronics and Communication Systems (ICECS), pp. 1333–1338. IEEE (2015)
23. Pedregosa, F., et al.: Scikit-learn: machine learning in python. J. Mach. Learn. Res. **12**, 2825–2830 (2011)
24. Pérez, N., Venegas, P., Benítez, D., Lara-Cueva, R., Ruiz, M.: A new volcanic seismic signal descriptor and its application to a data set from the Cotopaxi Volcano. IEEE Trans. Geosci. Remote Sens. **58**(9), 6493–6503 (2020). https://doi.org/10.1109/TGRS.2020.2976896
25. Pérez, N., Benítez, D., Grijalva, F., Lara-Cueva, R., Ruiz, M., Aguilar, J.: Eseismic: towards an ecuadorian volcano seismic repository. J. Volcanol. Geoth. Res. **396**, 106855 (2020). https://doi.org/10.1016/j.jvolgeores.2020.106855
26. Phillipson, G., Sobradelo, R., Gottsmann, J.: Global volcanic unrest in the 21st century: an analysis of the first decade. J. Volcanol. Geoth. Res. **264**, 183–196 (2013). https://doi.org/10.1016/j.jvolgeores.2013.08.004
27. Python Core Team: Python 3.7.4: A dynamic, open source programming language. Python Software Foundation (2019). https://www.python.org/
28. Reyes, J.A., Mosquera, C.J.J.: Non-supervised classification of volcanic-seismic events for tungurahua-volcano ecuador. In: 2017 IEEE Second Ecuador Technical Chapters Meeting (ETCM), pp. 1–6. IEEE (2017)
29. Rodgers, M., Smith, P., Pyle, D., Mather, T.: Waveform classification and statistical analysis of seismic precursors to the July 2008 vulcanian eruption of Soufrière Hills Volcano, Montserrat. In: EGU General Assembly Conference Abstracts, vol. 18 (2016)

30. Schmincke, H.-U.: Volcanic hazards, volcanic catastrophes, and disaster mitigation. Volcanism, pp. 229–258. Springer, Heidelberg (2004). https://doi.org/10.1007/978-3-642-18952-4_13

31. Sharma, N., Bajpai, A., Litoriya, M.R.: Comparison the various clustering algorithms of weka tools. Facilities 4(7), 78–80 (2012)

32. Siebert, L., Simkin, T., Kimberly, P.: Volcanoes of the World. University of California Press, California (2011)

33. Tamilselvi, R., Sivasakthi, B., Kavitha, R.: A comparison of various clustering methods and algorithms in data mining. Int. J. Multidiscip. Res. Dev. 2(5), 32–98 (2015)

34. Tilling, R.I.: Hazards and climatic impact of subduction-zone volcanism: a global and historical perspective. Wash. DC Am. Geophys. Union Geophys. Monogr. Ser. 96, 331–335 (1996). https://doi.org/10.1029/GM096p0331

35. Unglert, K., Radić, V., Jellinek, A.M.: Principal component analysis vs. self-organizing maps combined with hierarchical clustering for pattern recognition in volcano seismic spectra. J. Volcanol. Geoth. Res. 320, 58–74 (2016)

36. Venegas, P., Pérez, N., Benítez, D., Lara-Cueva, R., Ruiz, M.: Combining filter-based feature selection methods and gaussian mixture model for the classification of seismic events from cotopaxi volcano. IEEE J. Sel. Topics Appl. Earth Observations Remote Sens. 12(6), 1991–2003 (2019). https://doi.org/10.1109/JSTARS.2019.2916045

37. Zheng, Y., Jeon, B., Sun, L., Zhang, J., Zhang, H.: Student's t-hidden markov model for unsupervised learning using localized feature selection. IEEE Trans. Circ. Syst. Video Technol. 28(10), 2586–2598 (2017)

Seismic Event Classification Using Spectrograms and Deep Neural Nets

Aaron Salazar⬚, Rodrigo Arroyo⬚, Noel Pérez⬚, and Diego S. Benítez$^{(\boxtimes)}$⬚

Colegio de Ciencias e Ingenierías "El Politécnico",
Universidad San Francisco de Quito USFQ, Quito 170157, Ecuador
{assalazar,rodrigo.arroyo}@alumni.usfq.edu.ec,
{nperez,dbenitez}@usfq.edu.ec

Abstract. In this work, we proposed a new method to classify long-period and volcano-tectonic spectrogram images using eight different deep learning architectures. The developed method used three deep convolutional neural networks named DCNN1, DCNN2, and DCNN3, three deep convolutional neural networks combined with deep recurrent neural networks named DCNN-RNN1, DCNN-RNN2, and DCNN-RNN3, and two autoencoder neural networks named AE1 and AE2, to maximize the area under the curve of the receiver operating characteristic scores on a dataset of volcano seismic spectrogram images. The three deep recurrent neural network-based models reached the worst results due to the overfitting produced by the small number of samples in the training sets. The DCNN1 overcame the remaining models by obtaining an area under the curve of the receiver operating characteristic and accuracy scores of 0.98 and 95%, respectively. Although these values were not the highest values per metric, they did not represent statistical differences against other results obtained by more algorithmically complex models. The proposed DCNN1 model showed similar or superior performance compared to the majority of the state of the art methods in terms of accuracy. Therefore it can be considered a successful scheme to classify LP and VT seismic events based on their spectrogram images.

Keywords: Volcanic seismic event classification · Deep-learning models · Artificial intelligence · Spectrogram images

1 Introduction

Volcanic activity monitoring systems are essential to detect early signs of volcanic unrest and possible reawakening that can lead to eruptions [31]. Amongst the techniques used by scientists to estimate activity inside a volcano, the seismicity is one of the most effective tools for monitoring and forecasting eruptions [29]. In this regard, a wide variety of approaches have been used in recent years

Work funded by Universidad San Francisco de Quito (USFQ) through the Poli-Grants Program under Grants no. 10100, 12494 and 16916.

ⓒ Springer Nature Switzerland AG 2021
A. D. Orjuela-Cañón et al. (Eds.): IEEE ColCACI 2020, CCIS 1346, pp. 16–30, 2021.
https://doi.org/10.1007/978-3-030-69774-7_2

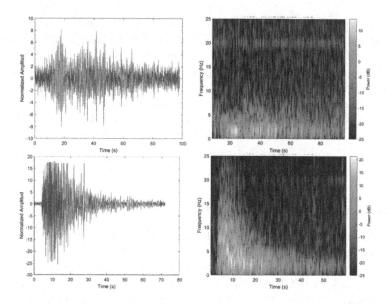

Fig. 1. An LP (top row) and VT (bottom row) seismic signals examples and their respective spectrogram. Taken from [27].

to address the problem of volcano seismic events classification, e.g., long-period (LP) and volcano-tectonic (VT) seismic events, as shown in Fig. 1. Machine learning classifiers (MLC) such as hidden Markov models (HMM) [1], boosting strategies [34], decision trees (DT) [16], random forest (RF) [26,28], Gaussian mixture models (GMM) [33], support vector machine (SVM) methods [7,26], and artificial neural networks (ANN) [2,5] were combined with classical time, frequency and scale domain features and non traditional features such as intensity statistic, shape and texture features extracted from the spectrogram images [26] to differentiate seismic events.

On the other hand, convolutional neural networks (CNN) are particular ANN architectures that are gaining more attention in image analysis contexts [30]. They avoid using intermediate, fully connected layers to employ pooling ones and thus optimizing the information pass-through from layer to layer. Lately, there is evidence of using deep learning techniques to analyze the seismic activity of volcanoes, e.g., deep neural networks to classify feature vectors computed from the time-domain signals [32], deep CNN models to classify spectrogram images [6]. Another well known deep learning architecture is the one based on recurrent neural network (RNN) where information flows sequentially, it is shared between layers and kept as a factor for decision making during the weight calculations [18]. The combination of both the CNN and RNN approach is quite possible, as demonstrated in [36], to classify different objects on individual images. However, the model growing is a must concern aspect. The more internal layers are included in the desired model, the more complex it will be [3].

There are other deep learning-based approaches for object detection [18,36] and classification [37]. But, the use of deep learning techniques in the context of volcano seismic event classification based on their spectrogram images is still limited. Therefore, in this work, we explore the use of eight different deep learning architectures to classify LP and VT spectrogram images to maximize the area under the curve (AUC) of the receiver operating characteristics curve on a dataset of volcano seismic spectrogram images from the Cotopaxi volcano, in Ecuador.

2   Materials and Methods

2.1   Spectrogram Images Dataset

This work considered the use of a public dataset (*MicSigV1*) from the ESeismic[1] repository, which contains several seismic event samples recorded at the Cotopaxi volcano [27]. It has a total of 1187 seismic records from two different seismic stations (VC1 and BREF) installed at the Cotopaxi volcano. This dataset contains samples distributed in five classes: LP, VT, regional (REG), hybrid (HB), and icequakes (ICE). Due to the small number of samples from REG, HB, and ICE events, we considered only the LP and VT events belonging to the same seismic station (BREF) to guarantee the same acquisition protocol and to avoid mixed signals. Therefore, the formed experimental dataset contains 668 spectrogram images (587 of LP and 81 of VT).

2.2   Deep-Learning Networks

Deep learning can enhance computational models by including multiple layers to process large amounts of data and to improve the learning process. Thus, severe problems regarding image classification and recognition in the past are presently easier to tackle. The deep CNN and RNN are two exclusive deep learning models [18,36], which are increasing their popularity on sequential data analysis and image labeling, respectively.

The deep CNN is a multilayered approach of conventional convolutional neural networks that include an input layer, a set of hidden layers (which could vary depending on the network architecture from two to hundreds of layers), and an output layer (fully connected layer). In deep CNN learning, each hidden layer is mainly composed of the CNN architecture core, consisting of at least the convolutional and max-pooling layers. Other configurations extend the basic scheme by adding dropout and flatten layers. This multi-layer structure enables the network to learn different data abstractions while transitioning from layer to layer until reaching the output result [6].

---

[1] ESeismic repository was provided by courtesy of the Instituto Geofísico of Escuela Politécnica Nacional (IGEPN) and collaborators, and it is available at http://www.igepn.edu.ec/eseismic_web_site/index.php. Please note that you must register and complete a disclaimer agreement to obtain the data.

The deep learning RNN is based on the classic feed-forward ANN architecture, but it includes an extra working piece called loops in connections. In contrast to the feed-forward ANN, the RNN architecture processes the inputs in a sequential way considering a recurrent hidden state in which the current activation is dependant on the previous step activation. The main drawback is related to long-term sequential data, where the gradients tend to vanish during the training. However, there is a more sophisticated approach to design recurrent units and to avoid vanishing problems known as long short-term memory [10]. It allows for recurrent units to learn long-term dependencies, which are a vital key when developing deep RNN models [24].

The deep learning autoencoder (AE) architecture is based on a classic AE artificial neural network. It efficiently learns compressed representations (encodings) of the data, typically for dimensionality reduction, by training the network to ignore the noise (signal). This type of architecture utilizes a bottleneck structure reducing the neurons in each layer as well as the volume of information that passes through the entire network reaching the latent space representation. Several variants to the basic AE model have been proven to be effective in learning representations for classification tasks [35], face recognition [9], and to extract the semantic meaning of words [19]. Thus, an adequate AE architecture will be able to recognize the useful features of the input data, while avoiding the redundant ones and the overfitting.

2.3 Proposed Method

We adopted the deep CNN, RNN, and AE neural networks to build the proposed method, which extends these neural networks to eight different deep learning architectures: DCNN1, DCNN2, DCNN3, DCNN-RNN1, DCNN-RNN2, DCNN-RNN3, AE1, and AE2. For a better explanation of the proposed method, we focus our description in the DCNN1, DCNN-RNN1, and AE1 models.

The DCNN1 architecture is composed of several layers, as it is shown in Fig. 2. From this figure, it is possible to read that the spectrogram images are used to feed the first convolutional layer composed of 16 convolutional filters with a 3×3 kernel size each. This layer aims to predict the class probabilities of the input sample by creating a feature map representation computed by the structure of the filters. Subsequently, the feature map enters the pooling layer with a 4×4 kernel size each to reduce irrelevant features (information) while retaining the relevant ones. Then, the reduced feature space is used to feed another convolutional and pooling layer with the same configurations as the previous ones. This second convolutional module concentrated the most relevant (important) features to classify the input sample. Finally, the fully connected layer consists of two dense layers, the flatten to convert the reduced bi-dimensional input feature space into a single feature vector with its corresponding weights and the output layer, which provides the final classification of the feature vector using a sigmoid function.

The DCNN-RNN1 architecture is a mixed model that combines a two convolutional layer based deep CNN architecture with some extra RNN layers, as

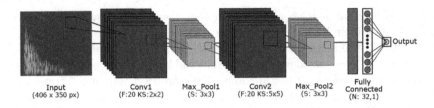

Fig. 2. The DCNN1 architecture of the proposed method; F - number of filters; KS - convolutional kernel size; S - max pool kernel size; N - number of neurons.

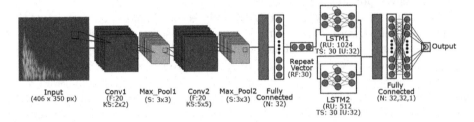

Fig. 3. The DCNN-RNN1 architecture of the proposed method; F - number of filters; KS - convolutional kernel size; S - max pool kernel size; N - number of neurons; RF - repeat factor; RU - recurrent units; TS - time stamp; IU - input units.

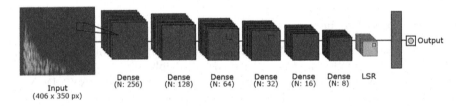

Fig. 4. The AE1 architecture of the proposed method; N - number of neurons; LSR - latent space representation

it is shown in Fig. 3. In such a sense, the first convolutional layer (Conv1.) used 32 convolutional filters with a 2×2 kernel size each and a pooling layer (Max_pool1) with a 3×3 kernel size. The second convolutional unit (Conv2. and Max_pool2 layers) used the same number of filters as in the Conv1., but it increased the convolutional kernel size to 5×5. The Max_pool2 layer remained as equal as the Max_pool1 in terms of configurations. Then, a flatten and dense layer transforms the bidimensional feature space into a single feature vector that is the input to a repeat vector layer. The later transforms the input feature vector into a data stream that is propagated with a repeat factor of 30 as input to the first long-short term memory (LSTM) unit. The LSTM1 unit is composed of 1024 recurrent units (RU) with input shape (IS) size of 30 and input units (IU) number of 32. Then, the LSTM1 layer output feeds the LSTM2 unit that is set to 512 RU and the same input shape size and number of input units as the

LSTM1 layer. After that, a fully connected layer containing a flatten and dense layers with sigmoid function provide the final classification.

On the other hand, the AE1 architecture is composed of multiple dense layers that are gradually reducing the number of neurons per layer, simulating a bottleneck workflow, as shown in Fig. 4. From this figure, it is possible to observe that the input image transits throughout this architecture, starting with a dense layer with 256 neurons. Subsequently, there are five more dense layers, in which the total number of neurons is reduced from layer to layer by a power factor of two until reaching a total of 8 neurons in the fifth layer. After that, it is possible to find the latent space representation (LSR) layer, which holds the compressed data that passed through all the layers and uses them to generate the prediction. Then, a flattened layer that is connected to the final dense layer with one neuron returns the final output. The deep-learning of this architecture is benefited from the data compression for better representation [20].

The remaining architectures, DCNN2, DCNN3, DCNN-RNN2, DCNN-RNN3, and AE2, follow the same base architecture (described here), varying the layers configurations and hyperparameters. The other architectures are summarized next:

The DCNN2 model contains three convolutional layers with 32, 64, and 128 filters with a kernel size of 3×3 each. Three max-pooling layers (one by each convolutional layer) with a pool size of 6×6 each, one flatten layer and a fully connected layer (output) composed of three dense layers (32, 32 and 1 neurons). The DCNN3 model uses two convolutional layers with 20 filters each, and a kernel size of 2×2 and 3×3, respectively. Two max-pooling layers (one by each convolutional layer) with a pool size of 3×3, one flatten layer, and a fully connected layer (output), containing three dense layers (32, 32, and 1 neurons).

The DCNN-RNN2 model employs three convolutional layers with 20 filters each and kernel size of 2×2, 2×2, and 5×5, respectively. Three max-pooling layers (one by each convolutional layer) with a pool size of 3×3, one flatten layer, one dense layer with 32 neurons, one repeat vector layer with a repetition factor of 30 units, two LSTM layers: the first one with 1024 recurrent units and input shape 30×32, and the second one with 512 recurrent units and a fully connected layer (output), composed of three dense layers (32, 32 and 1 neurons). The DCNN-RNN3 model involves three convolutional layers with 32 filters each and with a kernel size of 2×2 each. Three max-pooling layers (one by each convolutional layer) with a pool size of 3×3, one flatten layer, one dense layer with 32 neurons, one repeat vector layer with a repetition factor of 30 units, two LSTM layers with 512 and 256 recurrent units, an input shape of 30×32, and a fully connected layer (output), containing three dense layers (32, 32 and 1 neurons).

The AE2 model used a similar architecture as the AE1 model, but with four dense layers in its composition. In this case, the input image enters the initial dense layer with 32 neurons and transits through three more layers with a reduced number of neurons each (by the power of two of the previous layer), until reaching the last dense layer with four neurons. Then, the LSR and the flatten layers evaluate the final characteristics to obtain the final result in the output layer.

2.4 Experimental Setup

Spectrogram Image Preprocessing: All spectrogram images were down-scaled to 50% from their original size, thus decreasing the volume of information used to feed the learning models. The dataset provides spectrogram images without noise; therefore, the seismic event pattern presented on each image is invariant to the downscaling operation. This operation is use frequently in image analysis context with deep learning [6]. Besides, the pixels values of each spectrogram image were normalized using the min-max method [12] to bring them into the range of 0 to 1, thus, avoiding data dispersion. Besides, we used a data augmentation technique to increase and balance the number of samples per class. Thus, each spectrogram image underwent shearing, scaling, and rotation operations, as defined in [23]. Affinity transformations are widely used [6] and allowed us to reach a total of 1108 spectrogram images, which reinforces the models learning process by training them with more samples per class, helping to avoid overfitting.

Training and Test Partitions: The stratified 10-fold cross-validation method [21] was applied before the classification step to build disjoint training and test partitions and to ensure the sample ratio between both types of events for all folds. Thus, individual deep learning models were trained using different training sets, which enable it to learn from different input space representations. Testing on these different sets promotes trustworthy resulting variability in the classification of individual samples.

Deep Architectures Configurations: For all models, we configured three main hyperparameters to explore the proposed method limits. Thus, the number of iterations (epochs) was set from 50 to 150 with increment step of 50 units; the batch size was tuned to 16, 32 and 64 units, and the learning rate used the *adam* optimizer, which is based on adaptive estimation of lower-order moments [14]. This optimizer was designed to combine the advantages of the well-known optimizers *AdaGrad* and *RMSProp* [15].

Validation Metrics: The classification performance of the proposed method was based on the AUC and accuracy (ACC) metrics. The statistical comparison among all classification schemes was conducted using the Wilcoxon test with a significance decision value of 5% ($\alpha = 0.05$) for a two-tailed test [11]. This test ranks the differences in performances of two MLCs [8] and thus, allowed us to select the best classification model.

Selection Criteria: The best model was selected based on the following criteria: (1) the model with the statistically highest AUC score by architecture, (2) if there was a tie rating performance in the AUC scores, the one that has the lowest algorithm complexity is preferred, and (3) the statistically highest AUC score among all models selected according to the previous two rules. More than one model can be chosen per architecture if there is no significant AUC-based difference between them. This exception is only valid for intra-architectural analysis. Therefore, the proposed method provides only one classification model as a result.

All implementations were done in Python programming language version 3.7.4 using *scikit-learn (SKlearn)* [25], Keras [4] with *ImageDataGenerator* and TensorFlow backend, and sciPy for statistical analysis [13].

3 Results and Discussion

3.1 Performance Evaluation of the Proposed Method

The DCNN1 architecture provided seven out of nine classification models using the first selection criterion. This set of classifiers did not represent statistical differences in terms of AUC performance when compared to each other. The AUC range of variation was above the 0.95, which is an outstanding classification threshold for any classification problem. Although the highest AUC score of 0.99 was reached by the model using a batch size of 32 units and 150 epochs (iterations), the remaining models performed similarly statistically. According to the second selection criterion, the selected classification model in this architecture is the one implementing a batch size of 32 units, 50 epochs, and AUC score of 0.98 (see Table 1, bold line).

Likewise, DCNN2 architecture was able to produce six out of nine classification models that were similar statistically in AUC performances. The range of AUC variation in this set was between 0.71 and 0.79, which are not good enough scores to tackle the problem at hand. The highest AUC score of 0.79 was reached by the model with 16 units of batch size and 100 epochs. But, the model composed of the same batch size and 50 epochs, which obtained an AUC value of 0.71 was selected as the best model from this architecture, taking into consideration the second selection criterion (see Table 1, bold line). Similarly, in the DCNN3 architecture, a total of five out of nine classifiers were highlighted as classification models without statistical difference among them. The AUC scores varied from 0.90 to 0.94, which are considered reasonable scores in the context of spectrogram images classifications. The highest AUC value of 0.94 was obtained by the model composed of a batch size of 64 units and 50 epochs. However, there was another model using the same number of epochs as the highest model, batch size of 16, and AUC score of 0.91, which was selected as the best model inside this architecture according to the second selection criterion (see Table 1, bold line).

The AE1 architecture produced six out of nine models using the first selection criterion. They did not present a statistically significant difference among them

Table 1. Performance results of deep learning models selected by the first selection criterion.

Architecture	AE Dense layer (n).	Conv. layer (f)	Kernel size	Pool size per layer	FC layer (n)	Batch size	Epochs (u)	AUC	Wilcoxon at $\alpha = 0.05$ (p value)	ACC (%)
DCNN1	–	(16, 16)	(3 × 3)	(4 × 4)	(32, 1)	**32**	**50**	**0.98**	**0.19**	95
						64	50	0.99	0.45	97
						16	100	0.99	0.41	96
						32	100	0.98	0.16	98
						64	100	0.99	0.50	99
						32	150	<u>0.99</u>	–	99
						64	150	0.98	0.45	99
DCNN2	–	(32, 64, 128)	(3 × 3)	(6 × 6)	(32, 32, 1)	**16**	**50**	**0.71**	**0.15**	90
						32	50	0.74	0.45	91
						64	50	0.73	0.33	92
						16	100	<u>0.79</u>	–	92
						32	100	0.72	0.23	93
						64	100	0.72	0.33	94
DCNN3	–	(20, 20)	(2 × 2)	(2 × 2) (3 × 3)	(32, 32, 1)	**16**	**50**	**0.91**	**0.26**	94
						64	50	<u>0.94</u>	–	97
						32	100	0.92	0.33	98
						64	100	0.91	0.17	99
						32	150	0.90	0.08	99
AE1	(256, 128, 64, 32, 16, 8)	–	–	–	(1)	**16**	**50**	**0.89**	**0.24**	89
						64	50	<u>0.93</u>	–	92
						32	100	0.89	0.50	89
						64	100	0.89	0.40	91
						32	150	0.87	0.40	87
						64	150	0.90	0.40	90
AE2	(32, 16, 8, 4)	–	–	–	(1)	**16**	**50**	**0.84**	–	88
						32	50	0.80	0.41	92
						64	50	0.73	0.30	95
						16	100	0.70	0.41	92

Conv.- convolutional; f- number of filters per layer; n- number of neurons per layer; FC- fully; connected; u- units; AUC and ACC - mean of AUC and ACC metrics over ten folds; underlined AUC value is the Wilcoxon test pivot value; ACC - mean of accuracy.

in terms of AUC performances. The variation of AUC scores was in the range between 0.87 to 0.93, which is considered as a reasonable performance. Even though the highest score of 0.93 was obtained by the model with a batch size of 64 units and 50 epochs, the selected classification model in this architecture was the one using a batch size of 16 units, 50 epochs, and AUC score of 0.89 (see Table 1, bold line). Similarly, in the AE2 architecture, only four out of nine models did not produce AUC-based statistical differences among them. The AUC scores varied between 0.70 and 0.84. These results evidenced poor performances in the volcano activity context. In this architecture, the highest AUC performance (0.84) and the lowest algorithm complexity (batch size of 16 units and 50 epochs) were reached by the same classification model. Thus, it was selected as the best model on this architecture (see Table 1, bold line).

The combined classification models based on deep CNN and RNN architectures were the worst in terms of AUC performances. The three explored architectures provided AUC scores of 0.50 on all classification models, which means very poor schemes generalization. This effect is extremely linked to the number of samples employed during the models training. Despite using the data augmentation technique and the 10-fold cross-validation method on the experimental

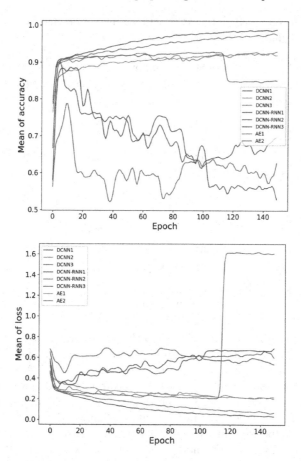

Fig. 5. Performance of proposed deep learning models based on the mean of the accuracy (left) and loss function (right) over ten folds.

dataset before feeding the classifiers, they incur in a poor generalization power (see Fig. 5, top plot) and a week learning (Fig. 5, bottom plot); both causes are symptoms of overfitting. It should be noted that the mean of the loss function never meets the established learning rate on these models, suggesting that more samples are required in the training process.

According to the first two selection criteria, the deep CNN-based classification models provided evidence of successful performance without incurring on overfitting. They performed over the 90% of the mean of ACC in the validation and the loss values converged to the learning rate across the defined epochs (see Fig. 5, top and bottom plots). Despite the good classification performances, the best selection model in the DCNN2 based architecture reached AUC and ACC scores of 0.71 and 90%, respectively. These values are statistically lower ($p < 0.05$) when compared to the best model selection inside the DCNN3 architecture, which achieved AUC and ACC scores of 0.91 and 94%, respectively.

Table 2. Comparison based on the ACC between related previous works and the best selected model produced in this work.

Method	Number of samples	Computed features	Spectrogram images	ACC* (%)
ANN [16]	914	6	No	97
DT [16]	914	3	No	96
ANN [26]	637	17	No	95
RF [26]	637	17	No	93
Linear SVM [17]	914	5	No	97
ANN [5]	1033	8	No	94
HMM [1]	512	39	No	90
GMM [33]	667	2	No	94
CNN [6]	15895		Yes	97
SVM [22]	105000	102	Yes	92
DCNN1 model	**1108**		**Yes**	**95**

ACC - accuracy; *values rounded to the closest integer

The difference in performance is linked to the model complexity inherited from its architecture and the number of samples used to train it. The DCNN2 architecture is the most complex among all the developed deep CNN architectures. Thus, it is very reasonable to assume that this model needs more samples and epochs to learn the feature space properly (see Fig. 5, bottom plot).

Moreover, the selected classification model using the DCNN1 architecture provided the best performances on both validation metrics. It obtained scores of 0.98 and 95% for the AUC and ACC metrics, respectively. It statistically ($p < 0.05$) overcomes the performance of the remaining models (see Table 1). This success is related to the DCNN1 architecture, which employed two convolutional layers with only 16 neurons (filters) per layer (lower than the DCNN3 architecture). Thus, it was able to learn from the provided features space satisfactorily (see Fig. 5, bottom plot). Regarding the third selection criterion, the selected classification model of the DCNN1 architecture constituted the proposed method output and the most appropriate classifier to face the problem of volcano spectrogram image classification.

3.2 State of the Art Based Comparison

Although it is not possible to make a direct statistical comparison against some previously developed state of the art methods such as those developed in [1,5, 6,22], because they used different experimental conditions, we aimed to carry out the comparison based on the ACC scores reported by them, as it is shown in Table 2. The majority of presented machine learning models reached ACC scores ranging from 90 to 97%, being the linear SVM and ANN the models which provided the higher classification performance. The proposed method has similar and superior performance compared to several states of the art methods in terms of ACC scores. That was possible because deep learning-based approaches are able to learn data abstraction from layer to layer, using different mathematical functions. Meanwhile, machine learning methods, except for nonlinear models like ANN, attempt to fit the data with a single mathematical function, which limited the learning ability.

On the other hand, the method developed in [6], used a deep CNN model that achieved an ACC score of 97%. This result was superior when compared to the 95% obtained by the proposed method. However, they classified four types of seismic events instead of two, like in this work. Also, they made the training-test validation using an extensive dataset, which provided a decent number of samples during the model learning.

4   Conclusions and Future Work

We explored the use of eight different deep learning architectures based on deep CNN (DCNN1, DCNN2, and DCNN3), RNN (DCNN-RNN1, DCNN-RNN2, and DCNN-RNN3) and AE (AE1 and AE2) models to classify LP and VT seismic events on a dataset of seismic spectrogram images. The models based on the combination of deep CNN and RNN architectures reached the worst classification performances. The data augmentation operation helped to reinforce the learning of the DCNN1, DCNN2, DCNN3, AE1, and AE2 models. But it was not enough for the deep RNN based models, leading then to the overfitting anyway. The DCNN1 was the best model when compared with the other deep CNN based models, attaining AUC and ACC scores of 0.98 and 95%, respectively. Although these values were not the highest values per metric, they did not represent statistical differences against other results that were obtained by more algorithmically complex models. Furthermore, the proposed DCNN1 model showed similar or superior performance when compared to the majority of the state of the art methods in terms of the ACC metric. Therefore it can be considered as a successful scheme to classify LP and VT seismic events based on their spectrogram images.

As future work, we plan to increase the number of samples per class to experiment with more complex architectures like the deep CNN+RNN models and improve the hyperparameter configurations to explore the limits of the implemented models.

Acknowledgment. We thank the Applied Signal Processing and Machine Learning Research Group of UFSQ for providing the computing infrastructure (NVidia DGX workstation) to implement and execute the developed source code.

References

1. Benitez, M.C., et al.: Continuous HMM-based seismic-event classification at deception island, Antarctica. IEEE Trans. Geosci. Remote Sens. **45**(1), 138–146 (2007). https://doi.org/10.1109/TGRS.2006.882264
2. Bueno, A., Benítez, C., De Angelis, S., Díaz Moreno, A., Ibáñez, J.M.: Volcano-seismic transfer learning and uncertainty quantification with bayesian neural networks. IEEE Trans. Geosci. Remote Sens. **58**(2), 892–902 (2020). https://doi.org/10.1109/TGRS.2019.2941494
3. Canziani, A., Paszke, A., Culurciello, E.: An analysis of deep neural network models for practical applications. arXiv e-prints arXiv:1605.07678, May 2016
4. Chollet, F., et al.: Keras (2015). https://keras.io
5. Curilem, G., Vergara, J., Fuentealba, G., Acuña, G., Chacón, M.: Classification of seismic signals at villarrica volcano (chile) using neural networks and genetic algorithms. J. Volcanol. Geoth. Res. **180**(1), 1–8 (2009)
6. Curilem, M., Canário, J.P., Franco, L., Rios, R.A.: Using cnn to classify spectrograms of seismic events from llaima volcano (chile). In: 2018 International Joint Conference on Neural Networks (IJCNN), pp. 1–8, July 2018. https://doi.org/10.1109/IJCNN.2018.8489285
7. Curilem, M., Vergara, J., San Martin, C., Fuentealba, G., Cardona, C., Huenupan, F., Chacón, M., Khan, M.S., Hussein, W., Yoma, N.B.: Pattern recognition applied to seismic signals of the llaima volcano (chile): an analysis of the events' features. J. Volcanol. Geoth. Res. **282**, 134–147 (2014)
8. Demšar, J.: Statistical comparisons of classifiers over multiple data sets. J. Mach. Learn. Res. **7**(Jan), 1–30 (2006)
9. Hinton, G.E., Krizhevsky, A., Wang, S.D.: Transforming auto-encoders. In: Honkela, T., Duch, W., Girolami, M., Kaski, S. (eds.) ICANN 2011. LNCS, vol. 6791, pp. 44–51. Springer, Heidelberg (2011). https://doi.org/10.1007/978-3-642-21735-7_6
10. Hochreiter, S., Schmidhuber, J.: Long short-term memory. Neural Comput. **9**(8), 1735–1780 (1997)
11. Hollander, M., Wolfe, D.A., Chicken, E.: Nonparametric Statistical Methods, vol. 751. John Wiley & Sons, Hoboken (2013)
12. Jain, Y.K., Bhandare, S.K.: Min max normalization based data perturbation method for privacy protection. Int. J. Comput. Commun. Technol. **2**(8), 45–50 (2011)
13. Jones, E., Oliphant, T., Peterson, P., et al.: SciPy: open source scientific tools for Python (2001). http://www.scipy.org/
14. Kingma, D.P., Ba, J.: Adam: a method for stochastic optimization. arXiv e-prints arXiv:1412.6980, December 2014
15. Kingma, D.P., Ba, J.: Adam: a method for stochastic optimization. arXiv preprint arXiv:1412.6980 (2014)
16. Lara-Cueva, R., Carrera, E.V., Morejon, J.F., Benítez, D.: Comparative analysis of automated classifiers applied to volcano event identification. In: 2016 IEEE Colombian Conference on Communications and Computing (COLCOM), pp. 1–6, April 2016. https://doi.org/10.1109/ColComCon.2016.7516377
17. Lara-Cueva, R.A., Benítez, D.S., Carrera, E.V., Ruiz, M., Rojo-Álvarez, J.L.: Automatic recognition of long period events from volcano tectonic earthquakes at cotopaxi volcano. IEEE Trans. Geosci. Remote Sens. **54**(9), 5247–5257 (2016). https://doi.org/10.1109/TGRS.2016.2559440

18. Lecun, Y., Bengio, Y., Hinton, G.: Deep learning. Nature **521**, 436–444 (2015). https://doi.org/10.1038/nature14539
19. Liou, C.Y., Cheng, W.C., Liou, J.W., Liou, D.R.: Autoencoder for words. Neurocomputing **139**, 84–96 (2014). https://doi.org/10.1016/j.neucom.2013.09.055
20. Liu, G., Yan, S.: Latent low-rank representation for subspace segmentation and feature extraction. In: 2011 International Conference on Computer Vision, pp. 1615–1622 (2011)
21. López, F.G., Torres, M.G., Batista, B.M., Pérez, J.A.M., Moreno-Vega, J.M.: Solving feature subset selection problem by a parallel scatter search. Eur. J. Oper. Res. **169**(2), 477–489 (2006)
22. Malfante, M., Dalla Mura, M., Métaxian, J.P., Mars, J.I., Macedo, O., Inza, A.: Machine learning for volcano-seismic signals: challenges and perspectives. IEEE Signal Process. Mag. **35**(2), 20–30 (2018)
23. Mikołajczyk, A., Grochowski, M.: Data augmentation for improving deep learning in image classification problem. In: 2018 International Interdisciplinary PhD Workshop (IIPhDW), pp. 117–122 (2018)
24. Mou, L., Ghamisi, P., Zhu, X.X.: Deep recurrent neural networks for hyperspectral image classification. IEEE Trans. Geosci. Remote Sens. **55**(7), 3639–3655 (2017)
25. Pedregosa, F., et al.: Scikit-learn: machine learning in Python. J. Mach. Learn. Res. **12**, 2825–2830 (2011)
26. Pérez, N., Venegas, P., Benítez, D., Lara-Cueva, R., Ruiz, M.: A new volcanic seismic signal descriptor and its application to a data set from the cotopaxi volcano. IEEE Trans. Geosci. Remote Sens. **58**(9), 6493–6503 (2020). https://doi.org/10.1109/TGRS.2020.2976896
27. Pérez, N., Benítez, D., Grijalva, F., Lara-Cueva, R., Ruiz, M., Aguilar, J.: Eseismic: towards an ecuadorian volcano seismic repository. J. Volcanol. Geoth. Res. **396**, 106855 (2020). https://doi.org/10.1016/j.jvolgeores.2020.106855
28. Rodgers, M., Smith, P., Pyle, D., Mather, T.: Waveform classification and statistical analysis of seismic precursors to the July 2008 vulcanian eruption of Soufrière Hills Volcano, Uontserrat. In: EGU General Assembly Conference Abstracts, vol. 18 (2016)
29. Schmincke, H.-U.: Volcanic hazards, volcanic catastrophes, and disaster mitigation. Volcanism, pp. 229–258. Springer, Heidelberg (2004). https://doi.org/10.1007/978-3-642-18952-4_13
30. Shin, H.C., et al.: Deep convolutional neural networks for computer-aided detection: cnn architectures, dataset characteristics and transfer learning. IEEE Trans. Med. Imaging **35**(5), 1285–1298 (2016)
31. Tilling, R.I.: Hazards and climatic impact of subduction-zone volcanism: a global and historical perspective. Wash. DC Am. Geophys. Union Geophys. Monogr. Ser. **96**, 331–335 (1996). https://doi.org/10.1029/GM096p0331
32. Titos, M., Bueno, A., García, L., Benítez, C.: A deep neural networks approach to automatic recognition systems for volcano-seismic events. IEEE J. Sel. Topics Appl. Earth Observations Remote Sens. **11**(5), 1533–1544 (2018). https://doi.org/10.1109/JSTARS.2018.2803198
33. Venegas, P., Pérez, N., Benítez, D., Lara-Cueva, R., Ruiz, M.: Combining filter-based feature selection methods and gaussian mixture model for the classification of seismic events from cotopaxi volcano. IEEE J. Sel. Topics Appl. Earth Observations Remote Sens. **12**(6), 1991–2003 (2019). https://doi.org/10.1109/JSTARS.2019.2916045

34. Venegas, P., Pèrez, N., Benítez, D.S., Lara-Cueva, R., Ruiz, M.: Building machine learning models for long-period and volcano-tectonic event classification. In: 2019 IEEE CHILEAN Conference on Electrical, Electronics Engineering, Information and Communication Technologies (CHILECON), pp. 1–6. IEEE (2019)
35. Vincent, P., Larochelle, H., Lajoie, I., Bengio, Y., Manzagol, P.A., Bottou,L.: Stacked denoising autoencoders: learning useful representations in a deepnetwork with a local denoising criterion. J. Mach. Learn. Res. **11**(12) (2010)
36. Wang, J., Yang, Y., Mao, J., Huang, Z., Huang, C., Xu, W.: CNN-RNN: a unified framework for multi-label image classification. arXiv e-prints arXiv:1604.04573, April 2016
37. Yu, Q., Yang, Y., Song, Y.Z., Xiang, T., Hospedales, T.: Sketch-a-net that beats humans. arXiv e-prints arXiv:1501.07873, January 2015

An Android App to Classify *Culicoides Pusillus* and *Obsoletus* Species

Sebastián Gutiérrez[1], Noel Pérez[1], Diego S. Benítez[1(✉)],
Sonia Zapata[2], and Denis Augot[3]

[1] Colegio de Ciencias e Ingenierías "El Politécnico", Universidad San Francisco de Quito USFQ, Quito 170157, Ecuador
msgutierrez@alumni.usfq.edu.ec, {nperez,dbenitez}@usfq.edu.ec
[2] Colegio de Ciencias Biológicas y Ambientales "COCIBA", Universidad San Francisco de Quito USFQ, Quito 170157, Ecuador
szapata@usfq.edu.ec
[3] Usc Vecpar, ANSES LSA, EA7510, Université de Reims Champagne-Ardenne, Reims, France
denis.augot@anses.fr

Abstract. *Culicoides* biting midges are transmission vectors of various diseases affecting humans and animals around the world. An optimal and fast classification method for these and other species have been a challenge and a necessity, especially in areas with limited resources and public health problems. In this work, we developed a mobile application to classify two *Culicoides* species using the morphological pattern analysis of their wings. The app implemented an automatic classification method based on the calculation and reduction of seven morphological features extracted from the wing images, and a naive Bayes classifier to produce the final classification of *C. pusillus* or *C. obsoletus* class. The proposed app was validated on an experimental dataset with 87 samples, reaching an outstanding mean of the area under the curve of the receiver operating characteristic score of 0.973 in the classification stage. Besides, we assessed the app feasibility using the mean of execution time and battery consumption metrics on two different emulators. The obtained values of 5.54 and 4.35 s and 0.0.02 and 0.11 mAh for the tablet Pixel C and phone Pixel 2 emulators are satisfactory when developing mobile applications. The achieved results enable the proposed app as an excellent approximation of a practical tool for those specialists who need to classify *C. pusillus* or *C. obsoletus* species in wildlife settings.

Keywords: *Culicoides* species classification · Android application · Digital image processing · Machine learning classifiers · Feature selection

Work funded by Universidad San Francisco de Quito (USFQ) through the Collaboration Grants (Grant no. 12476) and Chancellor Grants (Grant no. 1114) Programs.

A. D. Orjuela-Cañón et al. (Eds.): IEEE ColCACI 2020, CCIS 1346, pp. 31–44, 2021.
https://doi.org/10.1007/978-3-030-69774-7_3

1   Introduction

Culicoides is a genus of biting midges implicated in the transmission of various human and animal diseases [3]. They are also responsible for insect-transmitted protozoan parasites such as *Haemoproteus, Leucocytozoon* that can attach birds, and *Onchocerca* which can produce blindness in humans. More than 50 arboviruses have also been isolated from *Culicoides* including viruses from *Bunyaviridae, Reoviridae,* and *Rhabdoviridae* families [14]. Thus, it is important to have fast and accurate identification methods to detect the different species of these midges, in order to determine vectors and conduct entomological monitoring programs for evaluating the diversity of species in a specific area and to take defensive actions against such gnats.

Morphological characteristics such as: wing pigmentation pattern, antennal segment length and shape, male genitalia characteristics, antennae sensillae distribution, and the spermathecae number and size in females have been used to identify *Culicoides* species [23]. Adults are remarkable for their wing patterns and pigmentation (distribution and color of spots). These patterns can be used in certain species as the main criteria for identification. Biting midges wing geometric morphometrics is an established, inexpensive, and reliable identification technique of *Culicoides* species [9]. Consequently, the wing appears to be a good character for species discrimination.

In the recent scientific literature, other studies and methods have been applied for mosquito species classification. A convolutional neural network (CNN) model was implemented in [16] to extract features from images and identify species like the genus *Aedes* known for being transmitter of the Zika virus. In [12], the authors implemented ionization time of flight mass spectrometry with protein mass fingerprints as an alternative to identify *Culicoides* species. Furthermore, an artificial neural network (ANN), using ribosomal DNA data, was implemented in [2] for classification of the genus *Anopheles* known for being a malarial transmission vector. Moreover, in [22] the classification of *anopheline* mosquitoes using cluster analysis was carried out based on the characteristics of the habitat were specimens were collected. Finally, the authors in [25] used DNA barcodes to identify the main mosquito specie in China based on morphological characteristics using a Neighborhood-Joining tree.

Despite the recently developed methods for biting midges classification, this problem remains as a challenge. Besides, there is a need for implementing portable tools associated with developed methods. Therefore, in this work, we proposed the development of a mobile application called *MosCla* to classify *Culicoides* species based on the morphological pattern of their wings. The proposed application implements an automatic *Culicoides* species classification method using the Android development environment to produce the final app. An experimental dataset containing wing images from two species: *C. pusillus* (French Guyana), and *C. obsoletus* (France) will be used to benchmark the proposed approach. Also, a feasibility study is carried out to know how practical in terms of classification performance, execution time, and battery consumption, the implemented app could be.

2 Materials and Methods

2.1 Automatic Culicoides Species Classification

We used a set of computer vision functions for image processing to obtain morphological features from the wings images [19] and a set of classifiers to distinguish amongst the species under analysis. Thus, the image pre-processing, wing particles detection and zones segmentation, feature calculation and selection, and machine learning classifiers (MLC) are essential aspects to describe here. It should be pointed out that all the employed functions in this work were carefully selected to maximize performance while minimizing the battery consumption on the target devices.

Image Pre-processing. This module aims to the correctly extraction of a wing binary mask and their corresponding bounding box. Thus, the original RGB (red, green, blue) image was first transformed to a gray-scale (pixels values up to 255) color space. Then, a filtering operation was carried out using a (3×3) median filter to remove possible noises while conserving the contours of the objects of interest in the wing's image [7]. Other mask sizes like (5×5) and (7×7) were tested, but the (3×3) was ideal to carefully clean small objects contours inside the wing, such veins, holes, among others. A morphological erosion operation was then applied to remove all the non-desired objects that were still presenting in the filtered wing, such as isolated pixels or noise. The eroded wing image was followed by a filling operation to obtain the final binary mask of the wing and, subsequently, its bounding box, which was determined by using the Otsu's method [18]. Finally, opening and closing morphological operations were applied to conserve the shape and size of particles inside the wing image without other objects overlapping.

Wing Particles Detection and Zones Segmentation. The Moore-Neighbor tracing algorithm [7] with the Jacob's stopping criteria was applied on the binary wing images to detect the particles inside the wing contour. The presence of particles was verified by tracking whether or not there are changes in the pixel intensity value of the 8-connected pixels in the neighborhood of the current pixel (pixel under analysis), any intensity change was used as the stopping criteria by the algorithm. Moreover, the watershed method [15] was applied to segment the zones inside the wing. This method discovers "basins" and "ridges" in the image surface. The algorithm assumes that light and dark pixels represent elevations and depressions linked to the particles and zones, respectively.

Feature Calculation. A set of seven morphological features [19] (number of particles, number of zones, elongation, solidity, circularity, hydraulic radius, and eccentricity) were computed from the binary images. All the values were normalized using the min-max method [11] to bring them into the range [0,1].

Feature Selection. This technique is efficient when using high-dimensional data to reduce the heavy load of inputs to the MLCs. They are related to avoid overfitting, to improve the model performance, and to provide faster and more cost-effective models [21]. In this work, the feature space is composed of seven numerical variables (features) regarding morphological descriptors of the wing images. Despite the small number of computed features, the feature space is still significant to be explored on equipment with limited resources like mobile devices. Thus, we used a wrapper method with a greedy step-wise search method (to avoid stuck in local minimums) to reduce the feature space. It this way, a minimum set of features was obtained according to their predictive power related to the output class [21].

Classification. The classification of *Culicoides* species is a problem that involves two discrete output classes: *C. pusillus* and *C. obsoletus* species. Hence, it can be modeled as a two-class classification problem. Among the vast number of available MLCs that can be employed, we decided to use the naive Bayes (NB), support vector machine (SVM), and k-nearest neighbors (kNN) classifiers. Since mobile devices have limited resources, it was mandatory to consider a classifier with an acceptable trade-off between successful performance and low battery consumption. A brief description of selected MLCs are next:

NB Classifier. The NB is based on probabilistic models with strong (naive) conditional independence assumptions [6]. It assumes that c is a class variable depending on n input features: $x_1, x_2, \cdots, x_n$ and estimates the probability distribution $p(c)$ of the features. Any test sample will follow the decision rule according to the Bayes' theorem that provides the most probable value of the class as given by:

$$p(c|x_1, x_2, \cdots, x_n) = \frac{1}{z} p(c) \prod_{i=1}^{n} p(x_i|c)$$

where z is a normalization constant.

SVM Classifier. The SVM is based on the definition of an optimal hyperplane, which linearly separates the training data. In comparison with other classification methods, it aims to minimize the empirical risk and maximize the distances (geometric margin) of the data points from the corresponding linear decision boundary [20].

kNN Classifier. The kNN is a non-parametric technique that assigns a test sample to the class of the majority of its k-neighbors (usually by the Euclidean distance). That is, assuming that the number of voting neighbors is $k = k_1 + k_2 + \cdots + k_n$ (where n is the number of samples from class i in the k-sample neighborhood of the test sample), the test sample is assigned to class m if $k_m = max(k_i)$, $i = 1, 2, \ldots, n$ [26].

2.2 Development Environment

Integrated Development Environment (IDE). We used Android Studio version 3.6 for developing the *MosCla* app source code efficiently and neatly. This allowed us to design the Android activities UI's visually together with the XML code. Besides, the java OpenJDK (Java development kit) version 11.0.6 for 64-Bits operating systems was selected as the run-time environment and development tools, respectively. Thus, the developed application will be on the base of the Android mobile operating system with the Android SDK version 9.0 (Pie).

External Libraries. The employed IDEs and development tools do not provide enough support to implement the digital image processing functions needed to fulfill the wing image pre-processing as well as the classification. Thus, we added two third-party's libraries: OpenCV (Open Source Computer Vision Library) release 3.4.8 [17], which will help to store the images as a MAT object, facilitating the heavy image processing operations and transformations on devices with limited resources, and the LIBSVM (Library for Support Vector Machines) version 3.24 [4] for the Android platform. Since both libraries were developed in native C and C++ languages, it was necessary to include the NDK (Native development KIT) version 21.0.6113669 to operate with them. Additionally, the Google API play-services-location version 17.0.0 will be used in the developed app to estimate the latitude and longitude based localization of newly acquired or existing images.

Source Code Optimization. Although using native C, C++ libraries, the performance of some modules like the digital image processing functions, the watershed transform, the particle analysis, and the training-test process of the MLCs are not optimal enough when performing them sequentially. Thus, the Android asynchronous tasks will be exploited to carry out these modules on separate threads, avoiding possible application crashes, and speeding up associated processes.

2.3 Proposed MosCla App

The workflow of the proposed application using the defined development environment to produce an Android application able to classify two *Culicoides* species on limited resources devices is shown in Fig. 1. The application receives as input the wing images. Each entry transits throughout several digital image processing steps to produce a feature vector linked to the entry (wing image). Then, a subset of the computed feature vector is used to feed a MLC, which provides the final classification of *C. pusillus* or *C. obsoletus* class.

Additionally, the initial feature vector together with the final classification of each processed entry is saved in a database file, such files are used for a feature selection process using an external wrapper features selection method.

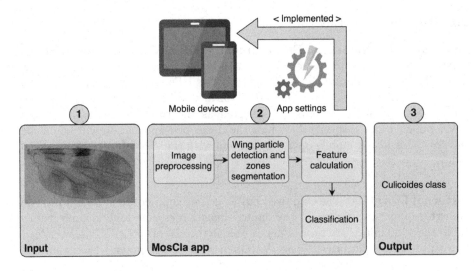

Fig. 1. Workflow of the proposed *MosCla* app implemented on mobile devices.

The wrapper method was implemented outside the app (on the WEKA toolkit version 3.8.3 [8]) and selected three out of seven computed features. Thus, the training - test feature vectors sets were formed with a total of three features and the output class. Besides, these sets are employed for re-training the implemented MLC by the user at any time. The later option of reinforcement learning guarantees the progressive model specialization.

Configuration. For better user experience, the proposed *MosCla* app requires special configurations regarding permissions and initialization. These settings are defined in the *AndroidManifest.xml* file and help to avoid run-time errors. Therefore, the application always checks if the user has granted the following android permissions: INTERNET, CAMERA, READ_EXTERNAL_STORAGE, WRITE_EXTERNAL_STORAGE, ACCESS_COARSE_LOCATION, and ACC-ESS_FINE_LOCATION.

Otherwise, it prompts the user to accept missing permissions. This permission check is done at some control points during the running app because the camera, location, and storage are vital settings to exploit the maximum benefits of the app.

Initialization. There are two actions that the *MosCla* app offers when it starts, either choose an image from the device's photo gallery (*ChooseTakePhoto*) or take a new photo (*TakeNewPhoto*). Choosing a storage image starts an activity through an ACTION.PICK intent, which allows the user to select and load the image into memory. On the other hand, the action of taking a new photo starts an implemented activity that checks the camera's existence before displaying the real-time picture. This activity also defines a real-time region of interest (ROI)

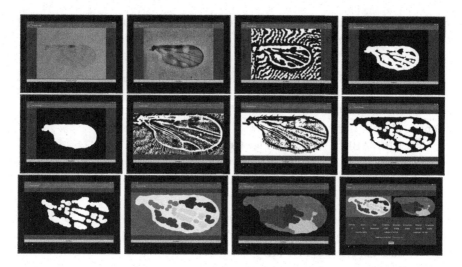

Fig. 2. The proposed *MosCla* app execution on a Pixel C device with Android 9.0 (API 28) based emulator using a *C. pusillus* test sample. From left to right and up to bottom: loading the image from the photo gallery, image enhancement by the CLAHE function, image filtering by a (71×71) median filter, background removing, binary mask creation, bounding box determination, wing region isolation, wing particles determination, particles isolation, wing region coloring, zones segmentation and features calculation with the final classification.

with a rectangle shape to enclose the wing image under analysis. It should be noted that the defined ROI should constitute the maximum area containing the wing image. Enclosing the wing's image inside the ROI is essential for the successful performance of some of the digital image processing functions like the watershed transform, which overflows when desired objects are very close to the image border. An example of execution of the implemented *MosCla* app using a *C. pusillus* test sample is shown in Fig. 2.

2.4   Experimental Setup

***Culicoides* Wing Image Dataset:** *C. pusillus* samples (n = 45) were captured at French Guyana (3°59′56″N, 53°00′00″W) and *C. obsoletus* samples (n = 42) at France (49°59′69″N, 4°01′45″E; 43°58′55″N, 3°42′58″E) by using ultraviolet traps. Samples were stored in 70% ethanol before any morphological analysis. The specimens were separated from other insects according to their wing characteristics using a stereomicroscope [1]. The digital wing images were obtained using an Olympus BX53 microscope equipped with an Olympus SC100 camera magnified at x10 with stream motion software (Olympus). For our study, left and right wings were used indistinctly because of the systematic selection of one side may bias the results in case of differential directional asymmetry between species, the comparison of wings from catalogs and original descriptions with status (left or right) are mostly unknown, and the distribution and color spots on the twice wings are similar [19]. Thus, we formed an experimental dataset with a total of 45 and 42 wing images of *C. pusillus* and *C. obsoletus*, respectively.

Table 1. Summary of experimental mobile device emulators.

Device	Specification	Value
Tablet	Model	Pixel C
	CPU/ABI	Google Play intel Atom (x86)
	API	8 (Android 9.0 Pie)
	Target	google_apis [Google APIs] (API level 28)
	Skin	pixel_c
	Resolution	2560 × 1800 xhdpi
	Camera	Host Camera (Acer Nitro 7 Laptop)
	Internal storage	2048 MB
	RAM	2048 MB
	VM heap	127 MB
Phone	Model	Pixel 2
	CPU/ABI	Googel Play Intel Atom (x86)
	API	29 (Android 10.0 Q)
	Target	google_apis_playstore[Google Play] (API level 29)
	Skin	pixel_2
	Resolution	1080 × 1920 xxhdpi
	Camera	Host Camera (Acer Nitro 7 Laptop)
	Internal storage	6144 MB
	RAM	1536 MB
	VM heap	256 MB

API - application program interface; RAM - random-access memory; VM - virtual machine

Experimental Mobile Devices: Two mobile device emulators were considered for installing and testing the proposed *MosCla* app. They were selected based on the minimum device specifications required to host the proposed app. It should be noted that some digital image processing functions and the classifier itself demand a certain amount of resources to fulfill the assigned tasks. The specifications of the selected devices are summarized in Table 1.

Training and Test Sets: We applied five times the stratified 10-fold cross-validation (CV) method [13] before the classification stage to form separate training and test sets. Therefore, the selected MLCs were trained on different training sets and learned from different input space representations. Testing on these different sets leads to variability in the classification results and allows us to avoid overfitting. Setting the 10-fold CV to be stratified method ensured the observation ratio between both types of *Culicoides* species along all folds. The use of the five times 10-fold CV method provides us a 50-dimensional output vector from each classification model that will serve to perform the statistical comparison according to the selected validation metric.

MLCs Configuration: Except for the NB classifier (a parameterless model), the SVM classifier used a linear kernel to speed up the processing time. The regularization parameter C (cost) was optimized in the range of 10^{-3} to 10^3 (increasing by a factor of 10). The gamma (γ) parameter was tuned to 0, which means an impartial influence on new features. The bounded regularization parameter (μ) was set to 0.5 units, the *cache_size* used was set to 20 (MB) for data exchange size, and the epsilon margin of tolerance (ϵ) was tunned to 10^{-3} units. The kNN classifier involved the estimation of an optimal value of k in determining the size of the neighborhood. The k value was optimized in the range from 1 to 11 with 2 units of increment (the odd values are preferred for helping in the final voting scheme), and the contribution of neighbors always used the weighted Euclidean distance to the instance being classified.

Validation Metrics: The proposed app was validated using a two-step procedure involving (1) the individual assessment of the employed MLCs using the area under the receiver operating characteristic curve (AUC) score, and (2) the feasibility of the implementation using the mean of execution time (mET) and battery consumption (mBC) metrics gathered when running the app. Both validation steps were made on the experimental *Culicoides* wing image dataset. We used the AUC metric over the accuracy because the problem under analysis is a binary classification task. Thus, it allows us to measure how optimal the selected MLCs performance are [24]. Moreover, we used the Wilcoxon statistical test at $\alpha = 0.05$ significant level [10] one time per comparison to assess the importance of the differences between classification models.

Energy Measurement Protocol: The android debug bridge service (adb command line tool) [5] facilitated us a satisfactory way to recover two logs from the emulated mobile devices. The battery stats log, containing important stats regarding the battery consumption of every single process (for our purpose, we took only the information from the process that executed the *MosCla* app) and the process activity log, containing stats about the execution time (in nanoseconds) of the developed app.

Selection Criteria: Since the classification step explored three classifiers with different parameter configurations, the best model to be implemented in the MosCla app was selected based on the following criteria: (1) the model with the highest AUC score statistically per classifier, (2) if there is a tie rating performance between AUC scores, the model with lowest algorithm complexity is preferred, and (3) among the three selected candidates by the two previous rules, the model that performs with the lowest mET and mBC scores, would be considered. Thus, the proposed app implements only one classification model.

3   Results and Discussion

According to the experimental setup section, a total of 87 wing images from both classes were analyzed to produce a three-dimensional feature vectors dataset used to feed the employed MLCs. The classification performance results according to the mean of the AUC metric were outstanding using the five times 10-fold CV method, as shown in Table 2.

Table 2. Summary of the statistical comparison based on the AUC performance of the best model per classifier.

Classifier	Best model	AUC ± SD	Other models	AUC ± SD	Wil ($\alpha = 0.05$)
NB	–	–	–	**0.973 ± 0.07**	–
SVM	$c = 10^2$	0.975 ± 0.05	$c = 10^{-3}$	0.500 ± 0.00	$p < 0.05$
			$c = 10^{-2}$	0.500 ± 0.00	$p < 0.05$
			$c = 10^{-1}$	0.550 ± 0.06	$p < 0.05$
			$c = 10^1$	*0.975 ± 0.05	$p = 1.00$
			$c = 10^3$	*0.967 ± 0.06	$p = 0.41$
kNN	$k = 11$	0.996 ± 0.02	$k = 1$	0.949 ± 0.07	$p < 0.05$
			$k = 3$	*0.977 ± 0.05	$p = 0.05$
			$k = 5$	0.973 ± 0.05	$p < 0.05$
			$k = 7$	*0.981 ± 0.05	$p = 0.17$
			$k = 9$	*0.985 ± 0.04	$p = 0.69$

*similar statistically; c-Cost; k-number of neighbors; SD-standard deviation; bold line means the selected model

3.1   Classification Performance

From Table 2, it is possible to read that the NB classifier was able to obtain an excellent AUC performance. Since this classifier is parameterless, we selected the only model as a candidate to be implemented in the app. The SVM classifier provided six classification models, but only three of them provided significant classification results. The highest performance was obtained by the model using a cost $c = 10^2$, but this AUC score of 0.975 was not statistically superior to the AUC scores of 0.975 and 0.967 obtained by the models with cost $c = 10^1$ and $c = 10^3$, respectively. According to the third selection criteria, we considered the SVM with $c = 10^1$ (less complex among all) as the candidate model inside this classifier.

On the other hand, the kNN classifier provided six successful classification models. All of them obtained AUC scores above a 0.94 value, which means this classifier performed excellently on the experimental feature space. The model with $k = 11$ obtained the best AUC score of 0.996. However, this result was not statistically superior to the AUC scores of $0.977, 0.981$, and 0.985 obtained by the models with $k = 3, 7$, and 9, respectively. In this case, we selected the model with $k = 3$ as the best candidate, which represented the less computationally cost model inside this classifier.

Overall, these results evidence that the majority of the evaluated classification schemes provided successful performances. This situation could be related to the feature space used to feed these models. As it was demonstrated, the three features determined by the external wrapper method provided enough discrimination power to distinguish between classes. The separation of both *Culicoides* species on the whole experimental dataset using the three-dimensional feature space could be seen in Fig. 3. From this figure, it is possible to notice that these features provided a positive environment to find out the class's decision boundary (see Fig. 3).

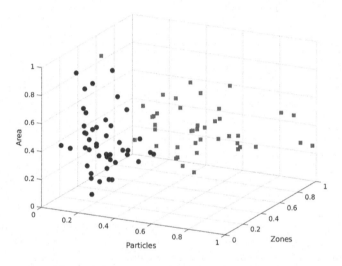

Fig. 3. Separation of both the *C. pusillus* (blue circles) and *C. obsoletus* (red squares) samples according to the reduced feature space. (Color figure online)

3.2   MosCla App Feasibility

Regarding the maximization of resources on mobile devices, we have not yet implemented the proposed app on real tablets or phone devices, and this is the practical limitation of this work. Instead of that, we implemented each of the selected classification models (see Table 2, bold lines), and approximated the time and battery consumption by using the established energy measurement protocol. This evaluation was carried out by implementing the proposed app on two device emulators (see Table 1). Then, the experimental *Culicoides* wing images dataset was processed by the app.

Results in terms of mET and mBC metrics for the three implemented classification models on both emulators are shown in Fig. 4 and 5, respectively. As can be seen from Fig. 4, the NB and kNN based classification models performed faster in the phone Pixel 2 (right plot) emulator than the tablet Pixel C (left plot) emulator. The obtained mET scores of 4.35 s (NB) and 4.43 s (kNN) versus 5.54 s (NB) and 5.99 s (kNN) corroborated the excellent performance in the phone Pixel 2 emulator. However, it should be noted that the difference in the mET scores was insignificant. Only the SVM-based model was faster in the tablet Pixel C (left plot) emulator than the phone Pixel 2 (right plot) emulator, reaching mET scores of 6.12 s against 11.09 s, respectively. This result represented a notable difference in terms of mET scores between both emulators.

From Fig. 5, it is possible to observe that the three implemented classification models consumed less battery in the tablet Pixel C emulator than the phone Pixel 2 emulator, reaching mBC scores of 0.02 (NB), 0.03 (SVM), and 0.02 (kNN) mAh versus 0.11 (NB), 0.13 (SVM) and 0.13 (SVM) mAh, respectively. These results depicted a successfully performance, since the worst case (SVM) consumed less than 0.15 mAh (see Fig. 5, right plot).

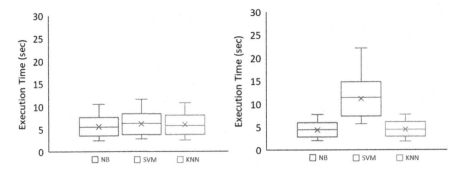

Fig. 4. *MosCla* app performance according to the mean of execution time on a Pixel C (left) and phone Pixel 2 (right) emulators, using the NB (red box), SVM (blue box), and kNN (green box) classifiers. (Color figure online)

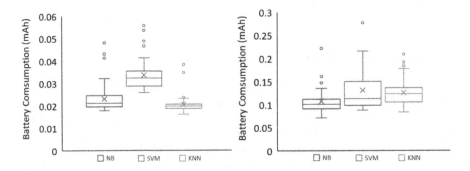

Fig. 5. *MosCla* app performance according to the battery consumption on a Pixel C (left) and phone Pixel 2 (right) emulators, using the NB (red box), SVM (blue box), and kNN (green box) classifiers. (Color figure online)

According to the selection criteria, the NB classifier was selected as the best model to be implemented in the proposed MosCla app. This model performed excellently in terms of the mean of AUC, mET, and mBC metrics on both emulators, beating the remaining classification models.

4   Conclusions and Future Work

In this work, we developed an Android-based mobile application called *MosCla* to classify two *Culicoides* species. The proposed app implemented an automatic classification method based on the calculation of morphological features extracted from wing's images and a NB classifier to produce the final classification between *C. pusillus* or *C. obsoletus* species. The application of an external wrapper method to reduce the features space from seven to three features guaranteed the successful AUC-based classification performance of the NB classifier (0.973) on the experimental wing's images dataset. The *MosCla* app reached satisfactory mean execution time values of 5.54 and 4.35 s and a mean battery consumption values of 0.02 and 0.11 mAh for the tablet Pixel C and phone Pixel 2 emulators, respectively. These results are generalizable, thus, the proposed app could be considered as a valuable tool for those specialists that need a practical tool to classify *Culicoides* species in the wildlife environment. As future work, we plan to include other *Culicoides* species like as cryptic species (*C. foxi* and *C. insignis*) or others species to the experimental dataset. We also plan to implement the app on real mobile devices.

Acknowledgment. Authors thank the Applied Signal Processing and Machine Learning Research Group of USFQ for providing the computing infrastructure (NVidia DGX workstation) to implement and execute the developed source code.

References

1. Augot, D., et al.: Discrimination of *Culicoides obsoletus* and *Culicoides scoticus*, potential bluetongue vectors, by morphometrical and mitochondrial cytochrome oxidase subunit I analysis. Infect. Genet. Evol. **10**(5), 629–637 (2010)
2. Banerjee, A.K., Kiran, K., Murty, U., Venkateswarlu, C.: Classification and identification of mosquito species using artificial neural networks. Comput. Biol. Chem. **32**(6), 442–447 (2008)
3. Borkent, A.: The subgeneric classification of species of *Culicoides* (2014)
4. Chang, C.C., Lin, C.J.: LIBSVM: a library for support vector machines. ACM Trans. Intell. Syst. Technol. (TIST) **2**(3), 1–27 (2011)
5. Developers Android: Android Debug Bridge (ADB). https://developer.android.com/studio/command-line/adb.html. Accessed 25 Mar 2020
6. Duda, R.O., Hart, P.E., et al.: Pattern Classification and Scene Analysis. Wiley, New York (2000)
7. Gonzalez, R.C., Woods, R.E., Eddins, S.L.: Digital Image Processing Using MATLAB. Pearson Education India (2004)
8. Hall, M., Frank, E., Holmes, G., Pfahringer, B., Reutemann, P., Witten, I.H.: The WEKA data mining software: an update. SIGKDD Explor. **11**(1), 10–18 (2009)

9. Henni, L.H., Sauvage, F., Ninio, C., Depaquit, J., Augot, D.: Wing geometry as a tool for discrimination of Obsoletus group (Diptera: Ceratopogonidae: *Culicoides*) in France. Infect. Genet. Evol. **21**, 110–117 (2014)

10. Hollander, M., Wolfe, D.A., Chicken, E.: Nonparametric Statistical Methods. Wiley, Hoboken (1999)

11. Jain, Y.K., Bhandare, S.K.: Min max normalization based data perturbation method for privacy protection. Int. J. Comput. Commun. Technol. **2**(8), 45–50 (2011)

12. Kaufmann, C., Schaffner, F., Ziegler, D., Pflueger, V., Mathis, A.: Identification of field-caught *Culicoides* biting midges using matrix-assisted laser desorption/ionization time of flight mass spectrometry. Parasitology **139**(2), 248–258 (2012)

13. López, F.G., Torres, M.G., Batista, B.M., Pérez, J.A.M., Moreno-Vega, J.M.: Solving feature subset selection problem by a parallel scatter search. Eur. J. Oper. Res. **169**(2), 477–489 (2006)

14. Meiswinkel, R., Baldet, T., De Deken, R., Takken, W., Delécolle, J.C., Mellor, P.S.: The 2006 outbreak of bluetongue in northern Europe–the entomological perspective. Prev. Vet. Med. **87**(1–2), 55–63 (2008)

15. Meyer, F.: Topographic distance and watershed lines. Signal Process. **38**(1), 113–125 (1994)

16. Motta, D., et al.: Application of convolutional neural networks for classification of adult mosquitoes in the field. PLoS ONE **14**(1), (2019)

17. OpenCV Team: Open Source Computer Vision Documentation. https://docs.opencv.org/3.4.8/d1/dfb/intro.html. Accessed 08 Apr 2020

18. Otsu, N.: A threshold selection method from gray-level histograms. IEEE Trans. Syst. Man Cybern. **9**(1), 62–66 (1979)

19. Venegas, P., Pérez, N., Zapata, S., Mosquera, J.D., Augot, D., Rojo-Álvarez, J.L., Benítez, D.: An approach to automatic classification of Culicoides species by learning the wing morphology. PLoS ONE **15**(11), e0241798 (2020)

20. Papadopoulos, A., Fotiadis, D.I., Likas, A.: Characterization of clustered microcalcifications in digitized mammograms using neural networks and support vector machines. Artif. Intell. Med. **34**(2), 141–150 (2005)

21. Pérez, N.P., López, M.A.G., Silva, A., Ramos, I.: Improving the Mann-Whitney statistical test for feature selection: an approach in breast cancer diagnosis on mammography. Artif. Intell. Med. **63**(1), 19–31 (2015)

22. Ramirez, P.G., Stein, M., Etchepare, E.G., Almiron, W.R.: Diversity of anopheline mosquitoes (Diptera: Culicidae) and classification based on the characteristics of the habitats where they were collected in Puerto Iguazú, Misiones, Argentina. J. Vector Ecol. **41**(2), 215–223 (2016)

23. Rawlings, P.: A key, based on wing patterns of biting midges (genus *Culicoides Latreille*-Diptera: Ceratopogonidae) in the Iberian Peninsula, for use in epidemiological studies. Graellsia **52**(11), 57–71 (1996)

24. Rosset, S.: Model selection via the AUC. In: Proceedings of the Twenty-First International Conference on Machine Learning, p. 89 (2004). https://doi.org/10.1145/1015330.1015400

25. Wang, G., et al.: Identifying the main mosquito species in China based on DNA barcoding. PLoS ONE **7**(10) (2012)

26. Wang, S., Summers, R.M.: Machine learning and radiology. Med. Image Anal. **16**(5), 933–951 (2012)

Hammerhead Shark Species Monitoring with Deep Learning

Alvaro Peña[1]🆔, Noel Pérez[1]🆔, Diego S. Benítez[1][✉]🆔, and Alex Hearn[2]🆔

[1] Colegio de Ciencias e Ingenierías "El Politécnico",
Universidad San Francisco de Quito USFQ, Quito 170157, Ecuador
`apenas@alumni.usfq.edu.ec`, {`nperez,dbenitez`}`@usfq.edu.ec`
[2] Colegio de Ciencias Biológicas y Ambientales "COCIBA", Universidad San
Francisco de Quito USFQ, Quito 170157, Ecuador
`ahearn@usfq.edu.ec`

Abstract. In this paper, we propose a new automated method based on deep convolutional neural networks to detect and track critically endangered hammerhead sharks in video sequences. The proposed method improved the standard YOLOv3 deep architecture by adding 18 more layers (16 convolutional and 2 Yolo layers), which increased the model performance in detecting the species under analysis at different scales. According to the frame analysis based validation, the proposed method outperformed the standard YOLOv3 model and was similar to the mask R-CNN model in terms of accuracy scores for the majority of inspected frames. Also, the mean of precision and recall on an experimental frames dataset formed using the 10-fold cross-validation method highlighted that the proposed method outperformed the remaining architectures, reaching scores of 0.99 and 0.93, respectively. Furthermore, the methods were able to avoid introducing false positive detection. However, they were unable to handle the problem of species occlusion. Our results indicate that the proposed method is a feasible alternative tool that could help to monitor relative abundance of hammerhead sharks in the wild.

Keywords: Hammerhead shark detection and tracking · Real-time detector · Deep convolutional neural networks · YOLOv3 architecture · Mask R-CNN architecture

1 Introduction

Object detection and tracking play an important role in real world applications such as: surveillance [22], aiding people with physical disabilities [4], microscopic examination [35] and marine species analysis [36]. The monitoring of marine species has been carried out widely during the past decade. However, the associated analytical tasks still rely heavily on the biologists, which could introduce

---

Supported by Universidad San Francisco de Quito USFQ.

A. D. Orjuela-Cañón et al. (Eds.): IEEE ColCACI 2020, CCIS 1346, pp. 45–59, 2021.
https://doi.org/10.1007/978-3-030-69774-7_4

errors by the manual process. Implementing automated detection and tracking systems can mitigate these errors by reducing human interaction with the environment and providing a second opinion tool for biologists on a range of applications.

Advances in machine learning topics and especially deep learning using convolutional neural networks (CNN) are significant in object detection [16,25,26,33], where they have proven to outperform traditional machine learning methods in accuracy and speed metrics. These improvements make such algorithms favorable for use in real-world applications.

Automated marine species detection and tracking constitute a vital area of application due to the need to track the population status of threatened and endangered species in the aquatic ecosystem. In [13], a method based on region segmentation was proposed, which included deep CNN to improve the recall and precision metrics in detecting marine mammals. The method was tested using a dataset of aerial images retrieved from wildlife surveys. In [36], a study using more complex computer vision techniques in conjunction with deep CNN models was proposed to detect and classify different species of fish. In [32], the YOLO method was implemented to detect and track marine organisms, including sharks. The method obtained satisfactory results when it was tested in deep-sea videos. In [23], an improved version of the YOLOv3 method was proposed for detecting fish and sharks, which overcame the standard YOLOv3 method in the mean of precision score performance. Furthermore, in [6], the Mask R-CNN architecture was used to successfully locate fish in static images using instance segmentation, obtaining high accuracy scores when there is a single fish: 0.994 and when there are overlapping fish 0.984. Also, overlapping fish was tackled since a new evaluation metric that penalizes a single fish's detection when two are present was developed. Additionally, in [31] Mask R-CNN was used to count and identify various species of harvested fish (including sharks) in videos recorded at fishing vessels. Specifically, for the shark class, 400 images were used to train the model, and in the identification task, the model obtained precision and recall scores of 70.96 and 84.61, respectively.

One shark in particular, lends itself to the development of species recognition techniques due to its unique body shape. The scalloped hammerhead shark (*Sphyrna lewini*) is a medium sized coastal-pelagic shark that can attain a size of over 4 m (but usually not more than 2–3 m) [29], which is under considerable threat from fishing activity, and is the main source of hammerhead shark fins in Hong Kong markets [5]. Hammerhead sharks, along with all other shark species, are not officially targeted in countries such as Costa Rica and Ecuador, yet a legal loophole allowing for the sale of sharks caught as "by-catch" has resulted in at least 200,000 sharks landed each year in Ecuador alone [9,14].

Both Ecuador and Costa Rica have made efforts to protect their marine biodiversity, notably the creation of marine protected areas (MPAs) around their oceanic islands of Galapagos and Cocos, respectively. However, scientists have found that hammerheads migrate between the reserves, becoming vulnerable to fishing pressure once they leave protected waters [10]. In late 2019, the red listing status for the species as a whole was amended from "Endangered" to "Critically Endangered" [29]. As yet, neither reserve has a formal process for evaluating the population trends for sharks, but diver observations over a >20 year period at Cocos Island suggested severe declines in numbers, while a study of dive guide perceptions in the Galapagos Islands obtained similar results [19]. There is a need to develop low cost, standardized tools to evaluate their trends in reserves where fishing is not permitted, and thus landings data not an option. In recent years, several tools have been developed which involve the use of video footage, either operated by SCUBA divers or remotely [1]. However, the analysis of the resulting footage can be labor-intensive and would benefit greatly from automation.

Thus, in this study, we propose a new automated method based on a deep CNN architecture to detect and track hammerhead sharks in video sequences recorded at the Galapagos and Cocos Islands. The proposed method improved the standard YOLOv3 deep architecture [26] by including 18 more layers, which increased the model performance in detection and tracking of the species under analysis. With this approach, the biology research community could have a viable tool to help them analyze this shark species.

2 Materials and Methods

2.1 YOLOv3 Framework

This method is a recent deep neural network used for object detection and real-time tracking [26]. Its core consists of a backbone network named Darknet-53 for feature extraction, and YOLO layers for predicting the bounding box of desired objects at three different scales. That means, it is possible to detect little and large objects at the same time, becoming a powerful architecture in the context of object detection.

The Darknet-53 network is composed of residual blocks, containing convolutional layers inside. These blocks serve mainly as feature extractors and since this network needs to explore the whole feature space from block to block, it does not involve any max-pooling layer in its configuration. On the other hand, the YOLO layers are composed of 7 convolutional layers, and 3 upsampling layers between the convolutional ones, to scale up the input RGB (red, green, blue) images with dimensions of $(416 \times 416 \times 3)$ at each time. A brief schematic description of the YOLOv3 architecture is shown in Fig. 1.

This architecture has demonstrated to be competitive in object recognition against other developed methods. Even though it is considered a heavy architecture that consumes significant resources, it is more efficient than ResNet-101 or ResNet-152 [26]; it is three times faster than the SSD (Single Shot Detector neural network) and its variants. Additionally, it is similar in performance to the RetinaNet on the COCO dataset and is optimized for speed as it runs at 51 ms per image.

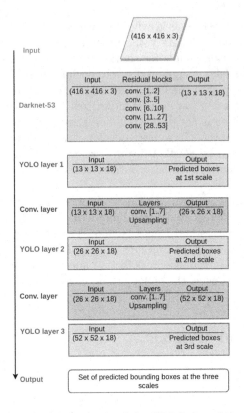

Fig. 1. A brief description of the YOLOv3 architecture.

2.2   Mask-RCNN Framework

This framework is a simple and general state of the art approach for object detection. It has been developed as an extension of the Faster R-CNN framework [27], which is aimed for object detection too. Mask R-CNN is based on two main stages: the region proposal network (RPN) that performs the bounding boxes proposing, and the step of classification and bounding box regression, which provided the segmented mask outputs. The last step highlights the region of interest (ROI) to make the detected objects more evident.

The mask R-CNN model structure comprises a feature extractor backbone architecture (modifiable part) and a network's head to perform the recognition tasks. This model's flexibility allows us to use different backbone architectures such as ResNet, ResNeXt, and ResNet-50-FPN, being the later our selection, and a network's head similar to the employed in [11]. The selected configuration was made based on the development of a successful detector. This model has demonstrated to outperform several variations of the Faster R-CNN framework and the standard YOLOv3 in detecting small and medium objects [26,27]. But,

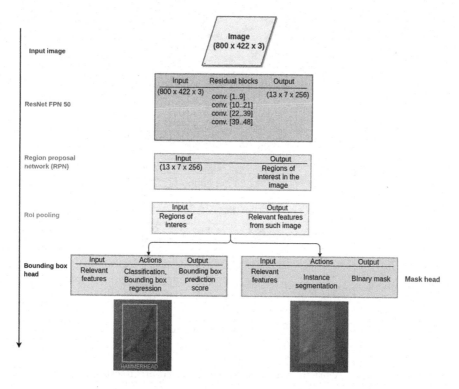

Fig. 2. A brief description of the Mask R-CNN architecture.

its execution time is compromised due to the lack of model optimization. A brief description of the mask R-CNN architecture is shown in Fig. 2.

2.3   Proposed Method

Detecting and tracking marine species, such as hammerhead sharks, is considered to be a challenge. Although the shark silhouette is easy to recognize, there are uncontrolled environmental conditions such as poor lighting, occlusions by other non-desired fish species, and projection against the sunlight, making the task difficult. We proposed a new method to overcome this, which improved the YOLOv3 standard architecture by including 18 more layers. This improvement aims to detect and track the hammerhead sharks species accurately.

Figure 3 shows an overall perspective of our developed method, which combined the standard YOLOv3 architecture plus some specific layers designed to tackle the problem under analysis. The major improvement over the standard YOLOv3 architecture was scaling up the input images, which passed from $(416 \times 416 \times 3)$ to $(608 \times 608 \times 3)$ dimensions. This operation previously demonstrated a successful increase in the model's overall performance [35]. The remainder of the method consists of attaching some layers at the end of the standard

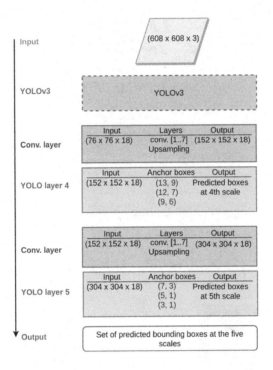

Fig. 3. A brief description of the proposed architectures.

YOLOv3 architecture distributed in the following order: 7 convolutional layers as feature extractors, and 1 upsampling layer to scale up the input image size, both inclusions with similar configurations to the standard YOLOv3 architecture, 1 YOLO layer for predicting a set of bounding boxes at the new scale. This structure was repeated one more time to complete the designed architecture, which accomplished a total of 18 added layers.

It should be noted that the YOLO layers in the proposed method were set to perform at the $4th$ and $5th$ scales, respectively. Also, the anchor box size on both layers was tuned to be smaller than the one employed by the standard YOLOv3 architecture (see Fig. 3). This property represents the ideal size and location of predicted objects in the image, in this case, hammerhead sharks. Thus, the better the property adjustment, the better bounding box prediction, independently of the object size. In contrast, this property in the standard YOLOv3 architecture is pre-determined for the COCO dataset [12]. Since the standard YOLOv3 architecture is configured to detect medium-large objects, adding these improvements enabled the proposed method to detect smaller objects, increase the model's learning rate, and improve real-time detection.

2.4 Shark Database

We used three footage sources as our main shark database. These sources were filmed at the Galapagos [0° 39′ 59.99″ N−90° 32′ 59.99″ W] and Cocos [5° 31′ 4.79″ N−87° 04′ 10.80″ W] Islands. Both sets of islands are surrounded by marine reserves and are UNESCO World Heritage Sites due to their outstanding biodiversity, including large aggregations of several shark species.

The video footage used in this study is mostly of scalloped hammerhead sharks, but other marine species, including other sharks, also feature in the same video samples. The duration of each sample varied between 30 to 50 s, the recording format was *file.mp4* at 24 fps (frames per second) and they were taken by biologists in uncontrolled environments. That means, the sharks are far from the camera lens, the illumination is poor and the projection view is against the sunlight most of the time, thus we used footage that might be considered of typical quality from non-professional film crew with underwater cameras.

2.5 Experimental Setup

This section describes the experimental setup created to validate the proposed deep learning architecture.

Video Pre-processing and Dataset Creation: We applied a decoding operation for all video data sources to extract all the frames contained by the video source by using the *ffmpeg* framework [7]. Each video sequence of 50 s of duration at 24 fps provided 1200 frames. However, we discarded around 50% of frames by removing those who are too blurry or contain species occlusions. After processing the videos, we gathered a total number of 1012 valid frames.

Since the number of collected frames does not fulfill the need to have enough samples for training deep learning models without incurring on overfitting, a data augmentation technique [3] was applied to increase the number of frames containing hammerhead sharks. Thus, each frame was rotated by 30, 45, and 210 degrees to form an experimental dataset containing a total number of 2000 frames with dimensions of (800×422). Besides, a labeling operation was carried out on the frames to mark the regions that belong or not to the hammerhead shark class. This operation provided an annotation file, in which each row contains information about the bounding box and output class label of each marked region within the frame. The experimental dataset of frames and its corresponding annotation file are mandatory to train the standard YOLOv3 model and, thus, the proposed method.

Training and Test Partitions: We applied the stratified 10-fold cross-validation method [20] to build disjoint training and test partitions. In this way, the proposed method is trained using different training sets, which enable it to learn from other input space representations. Testing on these different sets encourages the resulting variability in the classification of individual samples. The use of this method helps to avoid overfitting.

Anchor Box Values: These values were determined experimentally by observing the smallest hammerhead sharks' dimensions (in pixels) across all experimental dataset images (frames). With this information, the objectness score parameter was computed and set to the proposed architecture's YOLO layers. The objectness score manages whether or not found hammerhead shark objects are presented in the frame under analysis [28].

Validation Metrics: A video source that was not considered during the model's training step was used to test the proposed method in real-time. The performance of the method was based on the accuracy (ACC) of hammerhead sharks detection and tracking across a set of retrieved frames of the test video. A variation of this validation protocol was previously used in [30] to assess fish detection in real-time. Thus, we established a three-step procedure for conducting the evaluation as follow: (1) selecting nine frames (empirical selection) in the test video starting at time 0 to the video duration (vd) with an increment factor determined by the splitting time $sp = truncate(\frac{vd}{9})$; (2) counting the number of correct hammerhead shark detections out of the total presented in the current frame under analysis and (3) tracking the hammerhead sharks by counting how many of them were correctly detected across all the inspected frames.

Additionally, for the performance comparison among the standard YOLOv3, mask R-CNN, and the proposed method, we computed the mean value of the precision, recall, and loss function, using the 10-fold cross-validation method in the training-test steps.

All implementations were done in Python language version 3.5 [21] with the *scikit-learn (SKlearn)* [18], *Pytorch* version 0.4 [17], *OpenCV* version 4.0.2.32 [2], *Numpy* [15] and *scikit-image (SKimage)* [34] libraries, and using Darknet [24] as backend. We trained the model using a NVidia DGX workstation with 4 T GPUs but did not use multi-GPU training mode. The elapsed time to train was around 26 h.

3   Results and Discussion

According to the experimental setup section, we validated the detection performance of the proposed method in a real-time scenario by analyzing nine frames recovered from the employed test video. The performance comparison against the standard YOLOv3 and mask R-CNN architectures was made using the 10-fold cross-validation method applied to the frames of the experimental dataset. The obtained ACC, mean of precision, recall, and loss function scores revealed interesting results in detecting hammerhead sharks.

3.1   Performance of Proposed Method

Regarding the detection performance of hammerhead sharks using the frames analysis, the proposed method was able to detect the target species with ACC scores above the 50% for most inspected frames, as shown in Table 1.

Table 1. Comparison based on the ACC per frame among implemented deep-learning models.

Frame (ID)	Time (s)	Sharks per frame (u)	Correct detection			ACC-based detection (%)		
			YOLOv3	Mask R-CNN	Our method	YOLOv3	Mask R-CNN	Our method
1	2	11	0	6	7	0	55	64
2	4	9	0	4	6	0	44	67
3	6	10	0	4	6	0	40	60
4	8	10	2	5	2	20	50	20
5	10	7	2	6	3	29	86	43
6	12	6	3	5	4	50	83	66
7	14	4	1	4	1	25	100	25
8	16	4	2	4	2	50	100	50
9	18	0	0	0	0	100	100	100

ACC - accuracy; *values rounded to the closest integer

From this table, it is possible to read that only the frames with ID 4, 5, and 7 provided a low ACC score of detection. These results could be explained by the filming conditions associated with the marine environment, where camera movements and projections against the sunlight are common issues. In all the database videos, the hammerhead sharks performed random trajectories by approaching and moving away from the camera lens. This behavior provoked either the distortion or blurring of the targets and, consequently, detection failure.

Two additional factors contributed to the non-detection of sharks: the partial shape of the shark in the frame, and the target occlusion by other marine species (see Fig. 4). For example, at the top of the frames with ID 1 and 3 (Fig. 4, top row), there was one hammerhead shark showing half of its silhouette. Although it was close to the camera lens like other sharks captured in the frame, this one was not considered by the proposed method. In terms of occlusions, the proposed method failed to detect several hammerhead sharks in the range of frames with ID from 4 to 8 because fishes occluded them. However, in the frame with ID 3, one hammerhead shark was identified without taking into consideration the other closest fish (see Fig. 4), frame ID 3, (middle-right target). This situation occurs when sharks look bigger than fishes. In opposite, when fishes look similar in size than the sharks, the detector was not activated like in the frame with ID 6 (see Fig. 4, at the center), which is a good sign of performance.

Similarly, the fishes in the frames with ID 7 and 8 are in between the camera lens and the hammerhead sharks, but the detector focused only on the sharks while ignoring the fishes (see Fig. 4). Finally, in the last frame with ID 9, there was only the presence of a fish. As it was expected, the proposed method did not record any detections. Thus, it did not introduce false-positive detection on any inspected frames, which is an excellent detection performance.

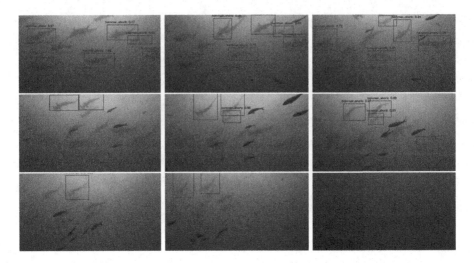

Fig. 4. Performance of the proposed method across the frames under analysis: successfully (green box) hammer shark detection in a test video. (Color figure online)

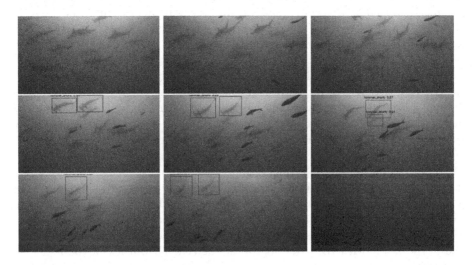

Fig. 5. Performance of the YOLOv3 method [26] across the frames under analysis: successfully (green box) hammer shark detection in a test video. (Color figure online)

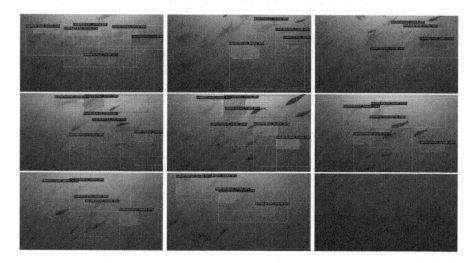

Fig. 6. Performance of the Mask R-CNN method [8] across the frames under analysis: successfully hammer shark detection in a test video.

3.2 Deep-Learning Models Comparison

From Table 1, it is possible to observe that the proposed method outperformed the standard YOLOv3 architecture. But, it performed very similarly to the mask R-CNN architecture. These results could be related to the internal configuration of each method. The proposed method added 18 more layers, including convolutional units (convolutional and upsampling layers), and two Yolo layers for predicting bounding boxes at scales fourth and fifth, which are missing in the standard YOLOv3 architecture. The inclusion of these layers enabled the proposed method to detect hammerhead sharks of different sizes. For example, by analyzing the first three frames, the proposed method could detect 19 versus 0 (by the YOLOv3 architecture) out of 30 hammerhead sharks presented on those frames. On the other hand, the mask R-CNN model incorporated a two-step validation block (bounding box prediction and mask head) as a refinement layer to the relevant features (possible ROIs with hammerhead sharks) determined in the previous layer. That could explain why this model performed similarly to the proposed method. For example, this model correctly detected 14 versus 19 out of 30 shark samples on the first three frames. However, the three models were unable to overcome the problem of occlusions by other subaquatic species. Figures 4, 5, and 6 show a visual comparison among them on the nine recovered frames of the test video.

We also compared these models by analyzing the mean of precision and recall metrics using the 10-fold cross-validation method on the experimental frames dataset. The precision measured the model's ability to predict the shark bounding boxes correctly. Meanwhile, the recall provided the model's importance to detect the sharks in the frames appropriately. Thus, the higher the precision and recall scores, the better performance of the model. The obtained results, according to both metrics, are shown in Fig. 7, left plot. From this figure, we can state that the precision and recall values of 0.99 and 0.93 obtained by the proposed method were superior to the 0.95 and 0.89 reached by standard YOLOv3 architecture, and the 0.98 and 0.91 obtained by the mask R-CNN architecture. Further, neither model incurred in overfitting during the training processes. The mean of the loss function of both methods decreased across the epochs to meet the learning rate value, as can be seen in Fig. 7, right plot.

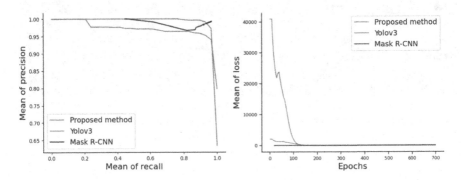

Fig. 7. Performance of the proposed method and the standard YOLOv3 architecture in terms of the mean of precision and recall (left) and mean of the loss function (right) over ten folds.

4   Conclusions and Future Work

In this study, we developed a new automated method based on deep CNN architecture to detect and track hammerhead sharks in video sequences recorded at the Galapagos and Cocos Islands. The proposed method improved the standard YOLOv3 deep architecture by including 18 more layers (convolutional and Yolo layers), which increased the model performance in detecting the species under analysis at different scales. According to the frame-based validation analysis, the proposed method outperformed the standard YOLOv3 model and performed similarly to the mask R-CNN model in terms of ACC scores for most inspected frames. Concerning the mean of precision and recall on an experimental dataset of frames constructed using the 10-fold cross-validation method, the proposed method was better than the standard YOLOv3 and mask R-CNN architectures, reaching scores of 0.99 and 0.93 versus 0.95 and 0.89 (for YOLOv3), and 0.98 and 0.91 (for mask R-CNN), respectively. It should be stated that the three methods were able to avoid introducing false positive detection. However, they were unable to handle the problem of species occlusion. These results provided clear evidence that the proposed method is a feasible alternative tool to help analyze this shark species in the wild. Future work includes a comparison with other methods.

Acknowledgment. The authors thank the Applied Signal Processing and Machine Learning Research Group USFQ for providing the computing infrastructure (NVidia DGX workstation) to implement and execute the developed source code. The hammerhead shark videos used in this study were provided by Jonathan R. Green, Chris Rohner, and Alex Hearn. The publication of this article was funded by the Academic Articles Publication Fund of Universidad San Francisco de Quito USFQ.

References

1. Bouchet, P.J., Meeuwig, J.J.: Drifting baited stereo-videography: a novel sampling tool for surveying pelagic wildlife in offshore marine reserves. Ecosphere **6**(8), art137 (2015). https://doi.org/10.1890/ES14-00380.1. https://esajournals.onlinelibrary.wiley.com/doi/abs/10.1890/ES14-00380.1
2. Bradski, G.: The OpenCV library. Dr. Dobb's J. Softw. Tools **120**, 122–125 (2000)
3. Curilem, M., Canário, J.P., Franco, L., Rios, R.A.: Using CNN to classify spectrograms of seismic events from Llaima Volcano (Chile). In: 2018 International Joint Conference on Neural Networks (IJCNN), pp. 1–8 (2018). https://doi.org/10.1109/IJCNN.2018.8489285
4. Dionisi, A., Sardini, E., Serpelloni, M.: Wearable object detection system for the blind. In: 2012 IEEE International Instrumentation and Measurement Technology Conference Proceedings, pp. 1255–1258. IEEE (2012)
5. Fields, A.T., Fischer, G.A., Shea, S.K.H., Zhang, H., Feldheim, K.A., Chapman, D.D.: DNA zip-coding: identifying the source populations supplying the international trade of a critically endangered coastal shark. Anim. Conserv. https://doi.org/10.1111/acv.12585. https://zslpublications.onlinelibrary.wiley.com/doi/abs/10.1111/acv.12585
6. Garcia, R., et al.: Automatic segmentation of fish using deep learning with application to fish size measurement. ICES J. Mar. Sci. **77**(4), 1354–1366 (2020)
7. GNU Lesser General Public License (LGPL) version 2.1: Ffmpeg tools. https://www.ffmpeg.org/. Accessed 23 Mar 2020
8. He, K., Gkioxari, G., Dollár, P., Girshick, R.: Mask R-CNN. In: Proceedings of the IEEE International Conference on Computer Vision, pp. 2961–2969 (2017)
9. Hearn, A.R., Bucaram, S.J.: Ecuador's sharks face threats from within. Science **358**(6366), 1009 (2017)
10. Hearn, A.R., et al.: Elasmobranchs of the Galapagos Marine Reserve. In: Denkinger, J., Vinueza, L. (eds.) The Galapagos Marine Reserve. SEIGI, pp. 23–59. Springer, Cham (2014). https://doi.org/10.1007/978-3-319-02769-2_2
11. Lin, T.Y., Dollár, P., Girshick, R., He, K., Hariharan, B., Belongie, S.: Feature pyramid networks for object detection. In: Proceedings of the IEEE Conference on Computer Vision and Pattern Recognition, pp. 2117–2125 (2017)
12. Lin, T.-Y., et al.: Microsoft COCO: common objects in context. In: Fleet, D., Pajdla, T., Schiele, B., Tuytelaars, T. (eds.) ECCV 2014. LNCS, vol. 8693, pp. 740–755. Springer, Cham (2014). https://doi.org/10.1007/978-3-319-10602-1_48
13. Maire, F., Alvarez, L.M., Hodgson, A.: Automating marine mammal detection in aerial images captured during wildlife surveys: a deep learning approach. In: Pfahringer, B., Renz, J. (eds.) AI 2015. LNCS (LNAI), vol. 9457, pp. 379–385. Springer, Cham (2015). https://doi.org/10.1007/978-3-319-26350-2_33
14. Martinez-Ortiz, J., Aires-da Silva, A.M., Lennert-Cody, C.E., Maunder, M.N.: The Ecuadorian artisanal fishery for large pelagics: species composition and spatio-temporal dynamics. PLOS ONE **10** (2015)

15. Oliphant, T.: NumPy: A guide to NumPy. Trelgol Publishing, USA (2006). http://www.numpy.org/. Accessed <today>

16. O'Mahony, N., et al.: Deep learning vs. traditional computer vision. In: Arai, K., Kapoor, S. (eds.) CVC 2019. AISC, vol. 943, pp. 128–144. Springer, Cham (2020). https://doi.org/10.1007/978-3-030-17795-9_10

17. Paszke, A., et al.: Pytorch: an imperative style, high-performance deep learning library. In: Advances in Neural Information Processing Systems, pp. 8026–8037 (2019)

18. Pedregosa, F., et al.: Scikit-learn: machine learning in Python. J. Mach. Learn. Res. **12**, 2825–2830 (2011)

19. Peñaherrera-Palma, C., et al.: Evaluating abundance trends of iconic species using local ecological knowledge. Biol. Conserv. **225**, 197–207 (2018)

20. Purushotham, S., Tripathy, B.K.: Evaluation of classifier models using stratified tenfold cross validation techniques. In: Krishna, P.V., Babu, M.R., Ariwa, E. (eds.) ObCom 2011. CCIS, vol. 270, pp. 680–690. Springer, Heidelberg (2012). https://doi.org/10.1007/978-3-642-29216-3_74

21. Python Core Team: Python 3.6.9: A dynamic, open source programming language. Python Software Foundation (2019). https://www.python.org/

22. Raghunandan, A., Raghav, P., Aradhya, H.R., et al.: Object detection algorithms for video surveillance applications. In: 2018 International Conference on Communication and Signal Processing (ICCSP), pp. 0563–0568. IEEE (2018)

23. Raza, K., Hong, S.: Fast and accurate fish detection design with improved YOLO-v3 model and transfer learning. Int. J. Adv. Comput. Sci. Appl. **11**, 7–16 (2020)

24. Redmon, J.: Darknet: open source neural networks in C (2013–2016). http://pjreddie.com/darknet/

25. Redmon, J., Divvala, S., Girshick, R., Farhadi, A.: You only look once: unified, real-time object detection. In: Proceedings of the IEEE Conference on Computer Vision and Pattern Recognition, pp. 779–788 (2016)

26. Redmon, J., Farhadi, A.: YOLOv3: an incremental improvement. arXiv preprint arXiv:1804.02767 (2018)

27. Ren, S., He, K., Girshick, R., Sun, J.: Faster R-CNN: towards real-time object detection with region proposal networks. In: Advances in Neural Information Processing Systems, pp. 91–99 (2015)

28. Ren, S., He, K., Girshick, R., Sun, J.: Faster R-CNN: towards real-time object detection with region proposal networks. In: Cortes, C., Lawrence, N.D., Lee, D.D., Sugiyama, M., Garnett, R. (eds.) Advances in Neural Information Processing Systems, vol. 28, pp. 91–99. Curran Associates, Inc. (2015)

29. Rigby, C., et al.: Sphyrna Lewini. The IUCN red list of threatened species 2019: e. t39385a2918526 (2019)

30. Sung, M., Yu, S., Girdhar, Y.: Vision based real-time fish detection using convolutional neural network. In: OCEANS 2017, Aberdeen. pp. 1–6 (2017)

31. Tseng, C.H., Kuo, Y.F.: Detecting and counting harvested fish and identifying fish types in electronic monitoring system videos using deep convolutional neural networks. ICES J. Mar. Sci. **77**, 1367–1378 (2020)

32. Uemura, T., Lu, H., Kim, H.: Marine organisms tracking and recognizing using YOLO. In: Lu, H., Yujie, L. (eds.) 2nd EAI International Conference on Robotic Sensor Networks. EICC, pp. 53–58. Springer, Cham (2020). https://doi.org/10.1007/978-3-030-17763-8_6

33. Voulodimos, A., Doulamis, N., Doulamis, A., Protopapadakis, E.: Deep learning for computer vision: a brief review. Comput. Intell. Neurosci. **2018** (2018)

34. van der Walt, S., et al.: The Scikit-image contributors: Scikit-image: image processing in Python. PeerJ **2**, e453 (2014). https://doi.org/10.7717/peerj.453
35. Wang, Q., Bi, S., Sun, M., Wang, Y., Wang, D., Yang, S.: Deep learning approach to peripheral leukocyte recognition. PLoS ONE **14**(6) (2019)
36. Xu, L., Bennamoun, M., An, S., Sohel, F., Boussaid, F.: Deep learning for marine species recognition. In: Balas, V.E., Roy, S.S., Sharma, D., Samui, P. (eds.) Handbook of Deep Learning Applications. SIST, vol. 136, pp. 129–145. Springer, Cham (2019). https://doi.org/10.1007/978-3-030-11479-4_7

Towards Automatic Comparison of Online Campaign Versus Electoral Manifestos

Daniel Riofrío[1]([✉])(iD), Pamela Almeida[1], José Dávalos[1],
Ricardo Flores Moyano[1](iD), Noel Pérez[1](iD), Diego S. Benítez[1](iD),
and Pablo Medina-Pérez[2](iD)

[1] Colegio de Ciencias e Ingenierías, Universidad San Francisco de Quito USFQ,
Quito 170157, Ecuador
{pealmeida,jdavalosm}@alumni.usfq.edu.ec
{driofrioa,rflores,nperez,dbenitez}@usfq.edu.ec
[2] Departamento de Estudios Políticos, FLACSO, Quito 170201, Ecuador
mppablofl@flacso.edu.ec

Abstract. Social media is an important information outlet and a new political landscape for politicians. In fact, politicians use social media to promote their candidacies while running for office. In this paper, we discuss about an application prototype built to measure the closeness of a candidate electoral manifesto to hers/his online campaign. We use four different similarity measures on the resulting frequency arrays obtained by processing manifestos and timelines. We show our results tracking the 2019 Ecuadorian Sectional Elections based on data collected from candidates' timelines on Twitter during the campaign and their official campaign manifestos.

We configured our application to gather information from Major candidates in the city of Quito during the 2019 Ecuadorian Sectional Elections. This prototype collected Tweets into a relational database based on each candidate's Twitter account. For this campaign, 18 candidates run for office. From these, we gathered 17 electoral manifestos and fed them to our application. Both, tweets and manifestos were preprocessed in order to produce a high dimensional word vector describing the collected timelines of each candidate and his/her manifesto. Later, each similarity measure, i.e., L1-norm, L2-norm, distance correlation and the cosine similarity were used to compare a candidate political plan against hers or his digital campaign. Our results show agreement from three measures (L2-norm, distance correlation and the cosine similarity) and suggest that candidates drift from their electoral manifestos during social media campaigns. We introduce a small experiment using a designed word query to enhance the discussion of possible reasons for our results and pave the path for future research.

Keywords: Text mining · Elections · Political campaign · Natural language processing

Publication of this article was funded by the Academic Articles Publication Fund of Universidad San Francisco de Quito USFQ.

A. D. Orjuela-Cañón et al. (Eds.): IEEE ColCACI 2020, CCIS 1346, pp. 60–73, 2021.
https://doi.org/10.1007/978-3-030-69774-7_5

1   Introduction

The modern concept of democracy has had many attributes included in its definition, depending on the author or the time in which democracy has been studied. However, one attribute present in every single definition of democracy is the nature of the government appointment. This appointment must be originated, directly or indirectly, in the will of the people [3]. To reach that people's support in an election, at least since the 1800 United States presidential elections, in modern democracies, politicians have depended on campaigning. These campaigns, until the emergence of mass and social media depended on a well-organized group of people able to feed and then transform the candidate's political proposal into a clear message that can be internalized and supported by voters. Once in office, the social function of the government (that is to formulate and carry out policies) could be understood as a by-product of their private motive which was to be elected [5]. So, to ensure that these policies are those that are in the interest of the electorate, democracy counts on its vertical accountability in which, theoretically, voters can reward or punish with their vote the party that has or has not complied with its campaign offerings. In order to keep track of what was promised, the democratic system counts on the electoral manifestos.

However, this basic notion of how democracies work has been challenged by theorist and politicians who state that with our current technology (social networks included), citizens should be able to participate directly and in real time in policy decisions [2]. This emerging idea of democracy, as well as the current technology available, shows us how crucial is to develop new approaches of data analysis that allows political scientist, politicians and the society as a whole to understand how the government is being elected and even more importantly, how it is making its decisions.

Electoral manifestos, as it has been stated, are an important part of any political campaign and serve a twofold purpose vis-à-vis voters: to help them make an informed decision and to hold politicians accountable for their work once elected [14]. Moreover, electoral manifestos also play a role within the party itself by coherently grouping the public policy proposal based on the party's ideology and by strengthening accountability among its members and decreasing the probability that the elite of the political party or a particular leader will disconnect from their base or from the voters who brought them to the democratic elected government.

Now, to fulfill all these purposes, it is not only necessary that the electoral manifesto be constructed with the objective of presenting the electoral proposal of a political party, but the political system of a country must promote strong, well-organized political parties as the principal actor in electoral politics. When this is not the case, we attend personalized electoral scenarios where the important thing is the personal recognition that the candidates have and not the public policy offer that is associated with them. In the latter case, the role of the electoral manifestos loses relevance and the offer of the candidates is focused on marketing the candidate and not the public policy offer that the political party proposes.

In general, if the country's political system has allowed the strengthening of political parties, and thus of democracy, politicians during elections will promote and detail their work plans (electoral pledges or manifestos) through media, and if this is not the case, they will promote the image and personal opinions of the candidate. Nonetheless, voters not necessarily cast their votes based on election pledge fulfilment (in a reelection) or party-voter and party-goals congruence [14,21,25]. In fact, previous research has shown that several other factors such as economic performance and even internal security matters can influence voter preferences which are specially critical in the rise of populist parties that challenge democratic structures [14].

The previous depicted panorama is studied by political scientists that seek ways to strengthen democracy through vertical and horizontal accountability. In fact, the manifesto project provides open digital access to multilingual annotated text corpus of electoral programs around the world since 2009. This project offers 1,800 machine readable documents of 40 different countries [16]. In fact, this project includes a large set of papers using their data and, in the past 5 years, there are no evidence of studies tracking elections based on online campaigning and electoral pledges. Our intention with this research is to start filling this gap by offering tools that allow political scientists to study the effects of online campaigning and electoral manifestos.

In the past decades, Internet has become an utter important means for politicians to communicate with citizens and encourage a political discussion. According to Vergeer et al. [24], at first politicians displayed in their websites specific content and functionality on the political party. Later on, many politicians adopted this form of communication under the standard of informing features, but soon they realized that it was a one-sided thing, this caused to be a disappointing effort for those who expected the main feature of the Internet, interactivity.

Years later, with the development of new web applications that used technology to enable content sharing, collaboration and socializing (social media), politicians were provided with a new way of interaction with the community. For example, web applications like weblogs, social networks (Facebook, Twitter, MySpace, YouTube, etc.) let users to give status updates, upload images and build social networks. These applications meant an improvement compared to static sites and provided politicians with a new set of marketing strategies. For instance, politicians use social media to create social networks and share content. Thereupon, improve the dissemination of information and benefit from the general network effect [24].

With the introduction of the Web 2.0 era, parties, politicians and candidates started to actively use all of the tools available through social media platforms. Thus, politicians were able to customize their campaign style in a more direct and personal communication level. Interestingly, the results of the paper written by Vergeer and Hermans, entitled "Campaigning on Twitter: Micro blogging and Online Social Networking as Campaign Tools in the 2010 General Elections in the Netherlands", showed that the overall adoption of Twitter among candidates was fast and that these online networks were likely to grow instead of declining. Thus, ensuring larger audiences over time [24].

For these reasons, it is essential to better understand the use of social networks in electoral campaigns, as mechanisms for socializing the proposals of the candidates and their parties, but also as mechanisms for the production of voters in the information age and the communications. This knowledge will contribute to a better understanding of the characteristics of a political context in which political parties (as we know them) are in decline, in which political commitments (previously established in party manifests) are less and less observed, especially in presidential systems, and where it is increasingly complex to identify the ideological, regional cleavage, etc., to which a party responds. A region characterized by this decline in political parties and their commitments, as well as by political instability resulting from this decline is the Andes in Latin America [10,12], and especially Ecuador, where the characteristics of the political system have weakened political parties, favoring the emergence of individual political figures [6], for which reason it has been decided to choose this country for this case study.

Hence, in the context of this paper, we use Twitter as a tool that allows us to conduct an electoral analysis regarding candidates who are socially active within this network. In fact, Twitter is one of the most popular micro-blogging platforms that enables users to send and read short text messages, known as Tweets. The platform provides an easy way of communication that enables users to share their personal activities, opinions and status [9]. This social platform has been used to analyze user behavior applied in areas of marketing such as user similarities [7] and sentiment analysis [8] and predictions such as presidential elections [11] and new trends [4].

This research proposes a simple application prototype based on natural language processing techniques (NLP), using common text-mining similarity metrics, that tracks political digital campaigns and provides a direct comparison against candidate's manifestos. We tested our application during the 2019 Ecuadorian sectional elections in Quito and tracked 16 candidate Twitter accounts during the campaign and compared them to their electoral manifestos.

The goal of this preliminary research is to understand how social media is used by politicians during elections. For this, we use a popular set of similarity functions approach, i.e. L1-norm, L2-norm, distance correlation, and the cosine similarity, in order to compare each candidate manifesto against all timeline tweets collected during the campaign. In addition, we use these same NLP techniques to measure how each candidate engaged social media in common critical issues of the city using a designed query based on a set of selected words.

The remainder of the paper is structured as follows. In Sect. 2, the materials and methods used for the development of the research are described. In Sect. 3, the results obtained from the experiments as well as the corresponding discussion are presented. Finally, Sect. 4 reports our conclusions and presents future work paths.

2   Materials and Methods

The following Section describes the application architecture and the case study. In terms of the text mining functions used, we provide a further description to facilitate the discussion of our results.

2.1   Architecture

The application built for this study consists of three mayor components. A social media collector (currently specialized in Twitter), a manifesto collector (a file system interlocutor to save and load manifestos in *pdf* format) and the Text Miner core which pre-process the data sources (Twitter timelines associated with a candidate and his/her manifesto), applies different similarity functions and produces a comparative result. In fact, Fig. 1 shows the components of this application. The arrows show how Tweets travel from Twitter as well as from Manifestos data sources into our collectors. These collectors store incoming data either on a *PostgreSQL* database (for tweets) or the local file system (for manifestos). Our text miner cleans data and transforms tweets and documents into vectorized versions of each. Finally, a set of similarity functions (i.e. L1-Norm, L2-Norm, distance correlation and the cosine similarity) are applied to provide a comparison. This comparison in general terms provides an idea whether both manifestos and Twitter timelines are close to each other (similar) or far from each other (different).

The idea behind this architecture is that one can add specialized collectors to different online data sources to gather campaign related information from candidates. And, this data can be processed as either a unique document or different documents and compared to each candidate's manifesto. In particular, in our case study we used Twitter as our social media main source. We also gathered the official publicly available manifestos from each candidate in *pdf* format. And, we produced meaningful quantitative results to enrich the social and political discussion. Further detail about the implemented process is discussed in Sect. 2.2.

Collector and Database

In particular, for this initial prototype we implemented a specialized Twitter collector. For this collector we decided to collect Twitter data in a relational database manager: *PostgreSQL*. Figure 2 shows the entity relationship diagram used to store specific candidate timelines and the reactions chained to their tweets. We decided to unwrap some fields from the *json* object provided by the Twitter API to facilitate and accelerate data analysis. Nonetheless, we reserve a field *tweet_json* to store tweet copies as provided by the API.

This relational database allowed us to implement fast and accurate queries based on configuring candidate's known *twitter screen name*. Together, the Twitter free API (application programming interface) and a list of candidates' twitter screen names were used to download candidate's twitter user information and create a process to listen to activity related to each account. Notice that we did not only collect the timeline of each candidate but also the reactions by others related to tweets from any candidate.

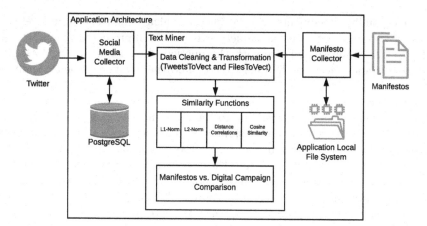

Fig. 1. Application architecture: data travels through the application and produces a comparison output between online campaign and electoral manifestos.

In addition, we realized that the entity relationship diagram summarizes the most important information for most online data sources. In fact, if we remove the prefix *tweet*, we will generally rely on an *id*, a *date*, a *parent id* (if circular or hierarchical relationships are allowed in that social media, otherwise it is not used), a *text*, an *account name or id*, *raw data from the source* (this can even been used for storing images from Instagram), and a *candidate id* related to the study. This allow us to re-use most of our implementation to create new specialized collectors.

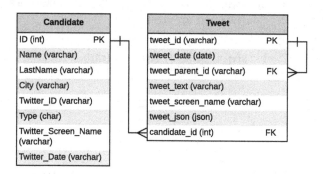

Fig. 2. Entity relationship diagram

Text Mining Similarity Functions

With the aim of finding similarities between documents or text files, Russell and Klassen [20] mention the convenience of modeling a document using a vector space model. The foundation of this model consists of having a large multidimensional space that contains one vector for each document. The similarity of the corresponding documents is determined by calculating the distance between any two vectors. Furthermore, a query can also be represented as a vector in order to determine similarities with the queried documents. In this case, the shortest distance between the query vector and the documents being analyzed is found.

The concept of similarity is subjective and affine to content-based image retrieval systems that gives meaning to the relationship among a set of feature vectors [26]. By using an abstract similarity function between a query (feature vector) and a database (set of feature vectors), it is possible to measure the similarity score between vectors, and thus, to determine how similar or dissimilar they are. Depending on the application environment, the similarity function could represent different semantic contents [22], e.g., in image retrieval, the images are ranked according to the similarity score, where close images (lower score) are similar regarding use and purpose.

In this work, we focused on viewing each document of the candidate's manifesto as a unit vector ($\mathbf{q}$), and each candidate's Twitter timeline as a unit vector ($\mathbf{t}$) with components corresponding to each term in the global "bag of words", along with a weight (frequency) for each component given. If a word does not occur in a particular document, the corresponding weight is zero. By representing the data in a vectored model, we are able to compute the similarity score $s(\mathbf{q}, \mathbf{t})$ of each vector in the feature space $V(\cdot)$.

We implemented four different similarity functions. Three of them based on distances such as the L_1−norm (Manhattan distance) defined by (1) in [26], L_2−norm (Euclidean distance) defined by (2) in [15] and the distance correlation defined by (3), which is an improvement of the Pearson's correlation to measure nonlinear association between two random vectors as well [23]. The other was the traditional cosine similarity defined by (4) in [13]. All the metrics were suited to the problem under analysis and are defined as:

$$s(\mathbf{q}, \mathbf{t}) = \sum_{i=1}^{m} \left| V(\mathbf{q})_i - V(\mathbf{t})_i \right| \tag{1}$$

$$s(\mathbf{q}, \mathbf{t}) = \sqrt{\sum_{i=1}^{m} (V(\mathbf{q})_i - V(\mathbf{t})_i)^2} \tag{2}$$

We modified both the original distance correlation and the cosine similarity equations by analyzing the complement of the obtained scores. This modification only changes the interpretability of the results. In this sense, a higher value means a lower correlation between features vectors or a larger angle between the vectors, respectively. Thus, the employed distance correlation equation is given by:

$$s(\mathbf{q}, \mathbf{t}) = 1 - \frac{\mathrm{dcov}(\mathbf{q}, \mathbf{t})}{\sqrt{\mathrm{dvar}(\mathbf{q}) \, \mathrm{dvar}(\mathbf{t})}} \tag{3}$$

subject to:

$$dcov(\mathbf{q}, \mathbf{t}) = \sum_{i=1}^{m} \left(V(\mathbf{q})_i - \overline{V(\mathbf{q})} \right) \left(V(\mathbf{t})_i - \overline{V(\mathbf{t})} \right)$$

$$dvar(\mathbf{x}) = \sum_{i=1}^{m} \left(V(\mathbf{x})_i - \overline{V(\mathbf{x})} \right)^2$$

And, the modified cosine similarity equation:

$$s(\mathbf{q}, \mathbf{t}) = 1 - \frac{V(\mathbf{q}) \cdot V(\mathbf{t})}{|V(\mathbf{q})||V(\mathbf{t})|} \tag{4}$$

2.2 Case Study

The 2019 Ecuadorian Sectional Elections took place on March 24th and the campaign period lasted from February 5th until March 20th, 2019. We focused on the Quito's Major election, since together with the Major of Guayaquil's election, it is probably the second most important electoral process for the election of an executive authority in the country, after the election of the president. In this election, 18 individuals registered their candidacies.

We searched for all candidates' twitter accounts but only 16 had a twitter account and engaged on political campaign in that social media. For each candidate *twitter_id*, *twitter_screen_name* and *twitter_date* (account's date of creation) were gathered into our Twitter collector database. In addition, manifestos related to these 16 candidates were collected by our manifesto collector in *pdf* format.

Data gathering (tweet collection) started a few days after the beginning of campaign period on February 17th and spanned for 84 days until May 12th, 2019. During that period of time, a permanent process collected data using the Twitter API following all API terms of use described in their developer policies. The data were stored on a local server running *PostgreSQL* 10 on Ubuntu 18.04 LTS. At the end of this period, a total of 964,440 tweets were collected. Out of this number 58.4% were directly related to our candidates timelines (562,940 tweets). The complement, 41.6%, are reactions to tweets that mention or are in response to candidate's *screen names*.

As Sect. 2.1 explains, a document or text file can be modeled and manipulated as vectors. This method follows a document-centric or "bag of words" approach. According to Russell and Klassen [20], although a document-centric approach performs well most of the time, the context and semantic of the words are not really appreciated. In this light, a context-driven approach that analyzes in detail the semantics of human language data is more appropriate. Nonetheless, as a first approach we follow a document-centric approach combined with a set of natural language processing (NLP) techniques prior to the application of the similarity functions. Next, we provide a detailed explanation of the NLP and text mining pipelines defined for this study case.

The text mining process was divided in several problems that needed to be tackled in a sequential order to accomplish our research goals. First, tweets and electoral manifestos were collected as described above. Second, the data extraction process initiated. This process consisted of reading, formatting and problem solving any issue that may occur from the *tweets* and *pdf* files, for instance, a few manifestos were not standard text-based documents and required to remove images and then it was possible to extract text. Third, the data processing phase consisted of removing *stop words*, i.e., words that are irrelevant to the analysis or that do not contribute with meaning such as articles and prepositions which are commonly used in Spanish.

Furthermore, a text frequency counter was implemented in order to obtain the number of times a word repeats in a document and a tweet. This was an iterative process done for each candidate. Table 1 depicts the outcome of this process.

Table 1. Words and text frequency by candidate: (from left to right) the highest frequency words are displayed first followed by the lowest frequency words.

Candidate's last name	First frequency term	Second frequency term	. . .	Hundredth frequency term
benavides	('plan', 266)	('ciudad', 261)	. . .	('discapacidad', 18)
buendia	('quito', 94)	('ciudad', 69)	. . .	('diferentes', 9)
corral	('transporte', 188)	('quito', 152)	. . .	('destino', 17)
davalos	('metropolitano', 161)	('distrito', 153)	. . .	('av', 17)
erazo	('ciudad', 16)	('quito', 12)	. . .	('taxis', 1)
guayaquil	('metropolitano', 53)	('concejo', 47)	. . .	('cultura', 6)
holguin	('quito', 320)	('ciudad', 210)	. . .	('vanguardia', 19)
jacome	('ciudad', 55)	('quito', 39)	. . .	('mascotas', 9)
maldonado	('desarrollo', 92)	('quito', 79)	. . .	('verdes', 4)
moncayo	('dmq', 504)	('quito', 155)	. . .	('mejorar', 23)
montufar	('ciudad', 206)	('quito', 102)	. . .	('centros', 13)
pasquel	('metropolitano', 129)	('gobierno', 104)	. . .	('coordinación', 10)
sarsoza	('políticas', 24)	('quito', 21)	. . .	('llegar', 2)
vazquez	('eje', 320)	('garantizar', 192)	. . .	('toda', 10)
vintimilla	('quito', 18)	('provincial', 16)	. . .	('constitucionales', 3)
yunda	('quito', 149)	('ciudad', 135)	. . .	('mayor', 14)
sevilla	('quito', 7)	('mayor', 5)	...	('talento', 1)

Afterwards, following the methodology discussed in Manning's book [13], we made a data transformation into a vector space model using a min-max normalization. It is important to note that each candidate's timeline as well as his/hers manifesto are considered as individual vectors. These vectors are the ones used for comparison by the similarity functions discussed in Sect. 2.1.

3   Results and Discussion

Four different criteria were used to compare candidate's timelines versus their own manifestos: L1-Norm, L2-Norm, distance correlation, and cosine similarity.

Figure 3 shows these results in a heat map, where lighter blue tones mean a greater concordance between timelines and manifestos, and darker blue tones the opposite. In addition, this figure shows the ranking in ascending order (lower rank means higher concordance as well) in parenthesis and the value of the similarity function calculated by equations in Sect. 2.1.

In general terms, Fig. 3 shows coherence among three similarity functions while comparing how all candidate's timelines and manifestos behaved; hence, L2-Norm, distance correlation, and the cosine similarity rank candidate's timelines and manifestos relative closeness exactly the same while L1-Norm differs significantly. For instance, for candidate 'Sevilla' L1-Norm ranks him first while the others rank him thirteenth. This disagreement is the result of the nature of the metric that is influenced by the higher dimensionality of the vector space $V(\cdot)$ (please refer to Sect. 2.1 for more information) and the fact that timelines and manifestos with very few text will generate sparse vectors in $V(\cdot)$ and therefore will give an idea of "closeness" or agreement, which is misleading. L1-Norm seems more suitable to describe manifestos and timelines that were more rich in terms of its content.

According to Fig. 3, candidate 'Montúfar' has the highest online campaign and electoral manifesto concordance. This means that candidate 'Montúfar' wrote tweets using similar language and addressing topics related to his electoral manifesto than any of the remaining candidates. On the other hand, the candidate 'Guayaquil' has the lowest online campaign and electoral manifesto concordance, which means that he did not refer or use language related to his electoral manifesto while addressing the public during his online campaign.

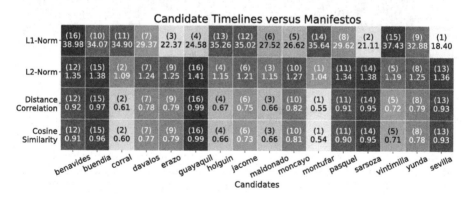

Fig. 3. Candidate's similarity based on comparing timeline tweets and own manifesto. Lighter blue means higher concordance between the timeline and manifesto. The first value is the overall ranking, and the second is the similarity function result.

Even though the similarity score for candidate 'Montúfar' is the lowest, this value is still relative high (0.55 for distance correlation, 0.54 for the cosine similarity, and a relative 74% for the L2-Norm with respect to the maximum) showing that social media interactions of any candidate tend to significantly drift from each correspondent electoral manifesto. Although these results are consistent with the political science literature that indicates that in a weak party system, such as the Ecuadorian, the probability of the existence of political personalities increases to the detriment of political parties. Nonetheless, this could have several other meanings, for instance, that social media is not necessarily used as a mean to share electoral pledges or that language used in social media tend to target a different audience.

In order to enrich our discussion and provide a different perspective to analyze our results, we designed a query based on a set of words relevant to the election and compare it against all tweets collected per candidate using the same similarity functions. An example of these words are: 'development: desarrollo', 'transportation: transporte', 'employment: empleo', among others of citizens' interest. Figure 4 shows results obtained from this analysis. As we mentioned in our first set of comparisons, there is a strong relationship among L2-Norm, distance correlation and the cosine similarity results, but in this case the lower dimensionality of the designed query reduces the impact of the L1-Norm. In fact, for candidates 'Corral', 'Benavides', and 'Buendia' this metric produces the same overall ranking. It can also be observed that candidate 'Corral' has the lowest score, meaning that this candidate uses Twitter to informally address common issues of interest for citizens.

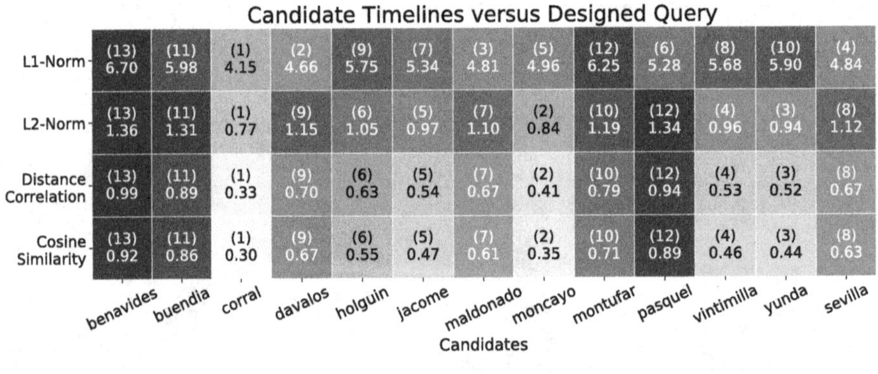

Candidate Timelines versus Designed Query

	benavides	buendia	corral	davalos	holguin	jacome	maldonado	moncayo	montufar	pasquel	vintimilla	yunda	sevilla
L1-Norm	(13) 6.70	(11) 5.98	(1) 4.15	(2) 4.66	(9) 5.75	(7) 5.34	(3) 4.81	(5) 4.96	(12) 6.25	(6) 5.28	(8) 5.68	(10) 5.90	(4) 4.84
L2-Norm	(13) 1.36	(11) 1.31	(1) 0.77	(9) 1.15	(6) 1.05	(5) 0.97	(7) 1.10	(2) 0.84	(10) 1.19	(12) 1.34	(4) 0.96	(3) 0.94	(8) 1.12
Distance Correlation	(13) 0.99	(11) 0.89	(1) 0.33	(9) 0.70	(6) 0.63	(5) 0.54	(7) 0.67	(2) 0.41	(10) 0.79	(12) 0.94	(4) 0.53	(3) 0.52	(8) 0.67
Cosine Similarity	(13) 0.92	(11) 0.86	(1) 0.30	(9) 0.67	(6) 0.55	(5) 0.47	(7) 0.61	(2) 0.35	(10) 0.71	(12) 0.89	(4) 0.46	(3) 0.44	(8) 0.63

Candidates

Fig. 4. Candidate's similarity based on comparing timeline tweets to designed query. Lighter blue means higher concordance between the timeline and designed query. The first value is the overall ranking, and the second is the similarity function result.

Both charts show important and interesting information about each candidate and the use of their social media account. However, since any similarity function achieves low relative values (less than 50%), it can be said that candidates use their Twitter account for other purposes. This interpretation of data may require the understanding of a sentiment breakdown in conjunction of a emoji contextualization since this may be key elements in order to a clearer understanding of the use of the candidate's Twitter Account. In terms of the importance of this data in the field of political science, one might wonder if the information of the electoral manifestos is published through other channels or if it is simply not published at all.

Last but not least, regarding the data collection and text processing, data was collected almost two weeks after the campaign period started. Therefore, some data relevant to the study may have not been collected. Also, because tweets and *pdf* files were written in Spanish, some accent marks may cause duplicates. As the study does not consider roots of words due to the lack of context, some words that have the same meaning, are included, modifying the vector size and the metric score between documents. Additionally, *pdf* files reading is format dependent. As each candidate developed their electoral pledges using their own design and structure, further cleaning techniques must be added to our collectors to avoid truncating words.

4   Conclusions and Future Work

Our study presents a path for building applications that allow political scientist and political analysts compare candidates' social media interactions to their electoral manifestos. Our case study results show how a vector based analysis of candidate's timeline tweets and hers/his electoral manifesto provide interesting insights about how a candidate engage citizens during an electoral campaign. In particular, we show how L2-Norm, distance correlations and the cosine similarity are well suited to compare these documents. We also show that L1-Norm disagrees with the other similarity functions when the vector space $V(\cdot)$ has a higher dimensionality. We understand that our results demand further research to provide stronger conclusions. As one future work path, we plan to continue this research using neural networks to convert documents or words into a vector space (*doc2vec* or *word2vec* [17]) and review the metrics used by political scientists from the R package "quanteda" [1] as well as trying to compare or correlate the election results with the implemented similarity functions in future elections.

Also, it was possible to determine the similarity between a candidate's timeline and a designed query composed by words selected by the researchers about known problems and solutions that were mainstream during the election. According to the results, no candidate's electoral manifesto has a close relation to hers or his timeline tweets. Based on the designed query of relevant words, 'Corral' is the candidate that has a closest concordance. These results are consistent with the political science literature that indicates that in political systems that do not strengthen the structure of political parties, as the personalization of politics increases, the accountability of elected authorities decreases [18,19]. The Ecuadorian political system, since the return to democracy in 1979, has generated norms that have systematically weakened the structure of political parties and have led to the personalization of politics [6]. As a result, we can understand that the electoral manifestos, a fundamental tool of accountability, are not widely disseminated.

Apart from a sentiment and emoji analysis. As future work, the feature space of words could be reduced using synonyms or special characters elimination.

This promises to eliminate potential language ambiguities and reduce language specific usages from an electoral pledge to social media micro blogging. In addition, we plan on reverse engineer our results to get samples of relevant tweets that contributed the most to either high score similarity or low score similarity in order to provide further empirical evidence of our findings.

Finally, from a political point of view, this type of analysis could be used as a real-time tool to help voters and analysts detect populist engagement in social media by candidates, which is of great importance to maintain healthy democratic structures targeted by populist parties. It could also be used as a tool to measure what other candidates are doing during a political campaign, to understand the political landscape and to adjust strategies accordingly. In this context, our research could contribute and dialogue with different fields of political science such as the democracy theory and democracy quality studies, political parties' studies, electoral and political accountability (vertical and horizontal accountability), public policy and political marketing.

References

1. Benoit, K., et al.: quanteda: an R package for the quantitative analysis of textual data. J. Open Source Softw. **3**(30), 774 (2018). https://doi.org/10.21105/joss.00774
2. Brill, M.: Interactive democracy. In: Proceedings of the 17th International Conference on Autonomous Agents and MultiAgent Systems, AAMAS 2018, International Foundation for Autonomous Agents and Multiagent Systems, Richland, SC, Stockholm, Sweden, pp. 1183–1187 (2018)
3. Dahl, R.A., Shapiro, I., Cheibub, J.A. (eds.): The Democracy Sourcebook. MIT Press, Cambridge (2003)
4. Doshi, Z., Nadkarni, S., Ajmera, K., Shah, N.: TweerAnalyzer: Twitter trend detection and visualization. In: 2017 International Conference on Computing, Communication, Control and Automation (ICCUBEA) (2017). https://doi.org/10.1109/iccubea.2017.8463951
5. Downs, A.: An economic theory of political action in a democracy. J. Polit. Econ. **65**(2), 135–150 (1957). https://doi.org/10.1086/257897
6. Freidenberg, F., Pachano, S.: El sistema político ecuatoriano. Serie Atrio, FLACSO Ecuador, Quito, Ecuador (2016). oCLC: ocn953235373
7. Goel, A., Sharma, A., Wang, D., Yin, Z.: Discovering similar users on Twitter. In: 11th Workshop on Mining and Learning with Graphs (2013)
8. Jansen, B.J., Zhang, M., Sobel, K., Chowdury, A.: Twitter power: tweets as electronic word of mouth. J. Am. Soc. Inform. Sci. Technol. **60**(11), 2169–2188 (2009)
9. Java, A., Song, X., Finin, T., Tseng, B.: Why we Twitter. In: Proceedings of the 9th WebKDD and 1st SNA-KDD 2007 Workshop on Web Mining and Social Network Analysis - WebKDD/SNA-KDD 07 (2007). https://doi.org/10.1145/1348549.1348556
10. Kornblith, M., Ágora Democrática (Organization), International Institute for Democracy and Electoral Assistance: Partidos políticos en la región Andina: entre la crisis y el cambio. International IDEA, Stockholm (2004). http://www.idea.int/publications/upload/pp_andean.pdf. oCLC: 226864128
11. Lassen, D.S., Brown, A.R.: Twitter. Soc. Sci. Comput. Rev. **29**(4), 419–436 (2010). https://doi.org/10.1177/0894439310382749

12. Mainwaring, S., Bejarano, A.M., Pizarro Leongómez, E. (eds.): The Crisis of Democratic Representation in the Andes. Stanford University Press, Stanford (2006). oCLC: ocm64098483

13. Manning, C., Raghavan, P., Schuetze, H.: Introduction to Information Retrieval, p. 581 (2009). https://nlp.stanford.edu/IR-book/html/htmledition/irbook.html

14. MATTHIEß, T.: Retrospective pledge voting: A comparative study of the electoral consequences of government parties' pledge fulfilment. Eur. J. Polit. Res. n/a(n/a). https://doi.org/10.1111/1475-6765.12377

15. Merigó, J.M., Casanovas, M.: A new Minkowski distance based on induced aggregation operators. Int. J. Comput. Intell. Syst. 4(2), 123–133 (2011). https://doi.org/10.1080/18756891.2011.9727769

16. Merz, N., Regel, S., Lewandowski, J.: The manifesto corpus: a new resource for research on political parties and quantitative text analysis. Res. Polit. 3(2), 2053168016643346 (2016). https://doi.org/10.1177/2053168016643346

17. Mikolov, T., Chen, K., Corrado, G., Dean, J.: Efficient estimation of word representations in vector space (2013)

18. O'Donnell, G.A.: Horizontal accountability in new democracies. J. Democracy 9(3), 112–126 (1998)

19. Pachano, S.: Partidos y clientelismo en ecuador. Quórum: revista de pensamiento iberoamericano (2), 21–39 (2001)

20. Russell, M.A., Klassen, M.: Mining the Social Web: Data Mining Facebook, Twitter, LinkedIn, Instagram, GitHub, and More. O'Reilly Media, Sebastopol (2018)

21. Schwarzbözl, T., Fatke, M., Hutter, S.: How party-issue linkages vary between election manifestos and media debates. West Eur. Polit. 43(4), 795–818 (2020). https://doi.org/10.1080/01402382.2019.1609292

22. Smeulders, A.W., Worring, M., Santini, S., Gupta, A., Jain, R.: Content-based image retrieval at the end of the early years. IEEE Trans. Pattern Anal. Mach. Intell. 22(12), 1349–1380 (2000). https://doi.org/10.1109/34.895972

23. Székely, G.J., Rizzo, M.L.: Brownian distance covariance. Ann. Appl. Stat. 3(4), 1236–1265 (2009). https://doi.org/10.1214/09-AOAS312

24. Vergeer, M., Hermans, L., Sams, S.: Online social networks and micro-blogging in political campaigning: the exploration of a new campaign tool and a new campaign style. Party Polit. 19(3), 477–501 (2013). https://doi.org/10.1177/1354068811407580

25. Werner, A.: Representation in Western Europe: connecting party-voter congruence and party goals. Br. J. Polit. Int. Relat. 22(1), 122–142 (2020). https://doi.org/10.1177/1369148119873102

26. Zhou, W., Li, H., Tian, Q.: Recent advance in content-based image retrieval: a literature survey. CoRR abs/1706.06064 (2017). http://arxiv.org/abs/1706.06064

Biomedical and Power Applications

Time and Frequency Domain Features Extraction Comparison for Motor Imagery Detection

Alvaro D. Orjuela-Cañón[1]([⊠]) [iD] and Juan Sebastian Ramírez Archila[1,2]

[1] School of Medicine and Health Sciences, Universidad del Rosario, Bogotá, D.C, Colombia
alvaro.orjuela@urosario.edu.co
[2] Escuela Colombiana de Ingeniería Julio Garavito, Bogotá, D.C, Colombia

Abstract. The brain computer interface area has increased the number of applications in the last years, searching to improve the quality of life in injured people. In spite of the progress in the field, different strategies are analyzed in order to contribute in specific problems related to the main applications. Present proposal shows a comparison between the use of time or frequency domain for feature extraction in upper limbs motor imagery. Four machine learning techniques as K-Nearest Neighbor, Support Vector Machine, Neural Networks and Random Forest were trained to detect motor imagery from EEG signals. Comparison for feature extraction and the employed detection models were analyzed to find the best election in an application for close-open fist in hands for two scenarios, according to two or three classes classification. The results achieved more than 90% in accuracy for both domain approaches in the two classes case. For the three classes detection, the results dropped out to 87% in accuracy. In general, the frequency domain is preferable for feature extraction and the KNN classifier was the best strategy for the present study.

Keywords: Brain computer interfaces · Feature extraction · Motor imagery · Machine learning · Time domain · Frequency domain

1 Introduction

According to the World Health Organization (WHO), around 500.000 people in the world suffer some type of spinal cord injury. A complete lesion is considered when the sensitive and motor function below the injury level is lost, representing the 45% of all spinal cord injury cases [1]. This condition prevents the movement of lower and upper limbs, reducing the mobility of people under this physical state. For this, the independence to develop any activity is the primary objective of rehabilitation processes, involving people with quadriplegia mainly. In this case, the improvement of the functional scale reaches a probability of 10% [1]. In addition, due to the motion impossibility in upper and lower limbs, mobility alternatives are usually associated with wheelchairs controlled by lingual, facial, shoulder or other devices to regulate these artificial movements.

© Springer Nature Switzerland AG 2021
A. D. Orjuela-Cañón et al. (Eds.): IEEE ColCACI 2020, CCIS 1346, pp. 77–87, 2021.
https://doi.org/10.1007/978-3-030-69774-7_6

From the beginning of this millennium, technologies as brain computer interface (BCI) have been increased in an exponential mode [2, 3]. This is due to the analysis of the electroencephalographic (EEG) signals, which allow obtain information from different mind tasks in a decoding process. One of most important action to identify in BCI is related to the motor imagery [4–6]. For this purpose, it is necessary to acquire a registration close to the primary motor cortex from the brain while a subject is performing the imagination task. Then, it is possible to extract important information from the recorded signal related to the planning or performing movements in upper limbs, mainly.

BCI in the motor imagery (MI) context is composed by four stages mainly: acquisition, preprocessing, processing and interface device [7]. Therefore, one of the areas of study is related to processing stage, where the feature extraction and classification represent two challenges to treat. For this, different techniques and models have been employed to find the best performance in terms of detection rate. The first one problem associated to the feature extraction has been analyzed in different studies. For example, Resalat and Saba employed autoregressive models and other computations strategies in time domain, using a classification stage based on linear discriminant analysis [8].Taking advantage of the time domain, other proposals include kernel methods as support vector machines (SVM), neural networks (NN), and principal component analysis (PCA), and in this way, to analyze performance behavior for discriminating the mentioned mental exercises [9–11].

In addition to the time domain, frequency domain has been used for this cerebral tasks, comparing different techniques as frequency distribution, fast Fourier transform, and eigenvectors, mainly [12]. Strategies based on the short time Fourier transform has been employing with the use of the Hjorth parameters, too [13]. Combining two mentioned domains simultaneously, the time-frequency domain exploits these two information sources, studying the use of Wavelet transform broadly [14–16]. A more current technique known as common spatial pattern (CSF) filters has been employed due the relevance in the feature extraction process for BCI applications [17, 18]. However, the results reached by this strategy, especially in motor imagery applications is extremely susceptible to artifacts and non-stationarities [19]. Furthermore, CSP has been proven mostly for feature extraction in applications related to two classes in EEG, evincing problems for more classes [19, 20]. A final aspect is associated to high number of channels necessary to its implementation due to the technique is based on a complete EEG acquisition, which has between 32 to 64 channels in most of cases.

Other important aspect in the processing stage corresponds to the classification task, where models from machine learning (ML) area are mainly used. Making use of these techniques as support vector machines (SVM), reported results reached accuracy values upper than 76% and 82% in performance. This, employing features extracted from time and frequency domains and relative power relation in alpha and beta bands [21–23]. The non-parametric supervised learning algorithms as the k nearest neighbors (KNN), achieved a performance of 82% with the use of eleven neighbors and a Minkowski distance measurement [24, 25]. Models based on classification trees also have been employed to determine motor imagery actions, obtaining accuracies upper than 94% in specific cases [26]. As it is common, frequency domain features were employed to determine the class of a new sample that would corresponds to right or fist imaginary movement, and foot movement imaginary movement. More recently, some complex models from the deep learning have been used lastly [27, 28]. However, these models have the disadvantage of a high number of samples for training and more computational resources than ML approaches due to the parameters that have to be adjusted [29]. Finally, neural networks (NN) have presented different architectures driven to classify different scenarios and domains [5, 30, 31].

In relation to the exhibited aspects for BCI in MI applications, where the number of channels and participants is reduced, more analyses are important to contribute to this field. In order to improve the number of studies in the feature extraction stage, the present work deals with a comparison of features computed from two domains: time and frequency. The objective is the MI detection for upper limbs, employing four different models from the machine learning techniques.

2 Methodology

This section resumes information about the employed database, feature extraction and classification stages. As the feature extraction comparison is the main objective of this work, two different groups of features are explained: time and frequency domains. Finally, three machine learning techniques aspects are described in terms of the parameters for training and validation.

2.1 Database

Database consists of signal registration from five subjects in a similar way to described in [31], having as a main difference the number of subjects employed in relation to the present study. For every subject, ten different EEG acquisitions were stored in a registration called *run*. Each run is composed by 12 *trials*, where the subject developed the experiment of motor imagery. This trial had three different actions to guide the volunteer in the performing (see Fig. 1).

The first type of action consisted on being on a rest state for three seconds, where it is necessary to pay attention to develop the motor imagery. Then, the subject imagines over three seconds the opening and closing the right or left fist (depending on row indication), and finally, the subject had to be relaxed three more seconds (see Fig. 1). The motor imagery indication for left and right hands was equivalent and sorted randomly throughout each one, completing six events for each hand out the 12 total trials.

Signals from the relaxed state (last three seconds) were removed because in this segment of the trial the subject could move, blink and relaxing, generating artifacts and noise in the signals without relevant information for MI application.

The employed device for signals recording was the g.Nautilus from g.Tec company, which offers a sampling rate at 250 Hz. This acquisition system holds thirty-two active electrodes over the cortex connected wirelessly, employing the 10–20 reference system. It was decided to work only with C3, Cz, and C4 electrodes due to their proximity with the primary motor cortex. For each signal was applied a Butterworth bandpass filter with cutoff frequencies at 0.5 Hz and 35 Hz, according to the EEG spectrum bandwidth. At the same way, the signal trend was removed by overriding the DC component.

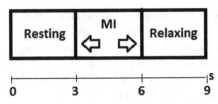

Fig. 1. Two types of trials implemented to acquire data from right and left open fist motor imagery.

2.2 Feature Extraction

The signals were divided into segments of 500 ms and an overlapping of 50%, due to the promising results in other studies using this approach [23, 25, 31], obtaining six segments for every state (rest and motor imagery).For each segment of the signals were extracted different time and frequency features, according to the previous studies [9, 23].

Time domain features. Statistical measures were obtained from each segment: mean (1), variance (2), skewness (3), kurtosis (4), Hjorth mobility (5), and Hjorth complexity (6). These last parameters are indicators of statistical properties used to represent a signal in time domain. Hjorth activity was not used due to similarity with the variance (2) value.

$$mean = \frac{1}{N} \sum_{m=1}^{N} x_m \tag{1}$$

$$variance = \frac{1}{N} \sum_{m=1}^{N} (x_m - \bar{x})^2 \tag{2}$$

$$skewness = \frac{\sum_{m=1}^{N} (x_m - \bar{x})^3}{\sigma^3} \tag{3}$$

$$kurtosis = \frac{1}{N} \frac{\sum_{m=1}^{N} (x_m - \bar{x})^4}{\sigma^4} \tag{4}$$

$$Hjorth\ mobility = \sqrt{\frac{\sigma^2(\dot{x})}{\sigma^2(x)}} \tag{5}$$

$$Hjorth\ complexity = \sqrt{\frac{Hjorth\ mobility\ (\dot{x})}{Hjorth\ mobility\ (x)}} \tag{6}$$

where x_m represents each value of the signal segment with N samples, $\bar{x}$ is the mean of the segment, $\dot{x}$ is the derivative computed on x, σ is the standard deviation, and σ^2 is the variance.

Frequency Domain Features. A computation was developed after the employment of Fourier transform. For this, the root mean square (RMS) value (7) was used and the relative power bands for δ, θ, α, β and γ. Table 1 shows the features computed for each domain.

$$RMS = \sqrt{\frac{1}{N} \sum_{m=1}^{N} x_m^2} \tag{7}$$

Table 1. Features extracted to partitioned EEG signals.

Domain	Features
Time	Mean, Variance, Skewness, Kurtosis, Hjorth mobility, Hjorth complexity
Frequency	Root mean square (RMS), and relative power for δ, θ, α, β and γ bands

For both approaches, the mentioned features were obtained for each one of the three channels, obtaining a vector with 18 attributes or features to represent the input to the ML technique.

2.3 Machine Learning Techniques

Three ML techniques were applied: Fine KNN, Bagged Trees, and SVM. The specifications for these models were found in a heuristically way, searching for the best result according to the features described in the previous subsection.

Fine K-Nearest Neighbors. This is a technique which find a predefined number of samples closest in distance to a new point to be classified. The Euclidean distance with eleven neighbors were the parameters with better results.

Support Vector Machine. It is a supervised method from the ML where support vectors are obtained from training data. In the beginning, the SVM were developed for a classification based on a lineal function [3, 32]. However, a solution for this problem is to employ a kernel function, which is based on a polynomial kernel with a third order for the present case. At the same time, the SVM is trained to classify dichotomy problems [33]. This was solved through the strategy known as one vs. All, adjusting N classifiers when it is demanded, for example the three classes classification.

Bagged Trees. This method, based on ensemble of several decision trees, where the variance of the decision tree is reduced with the employment of a bootstrap aggregation. For this, thirty learners and a maximum number of 2880 splits of data were parameters to determine the best configuration with thirty epochs in the training.

Neural Networks. This model takes advantage of the capacity to extract hidden linear and non-linear relationships between the data through an association between input and output mapping [34]. From the different architectures that can be employed, the multilayer perceptron was chosen for this work. One hidden layer was implemented, modifying the neurons from two to ten and finding the best architecture. The resilient backpropagation was the algorithm preferred to train the model, according to the speed and performance related to the local minima [35].

ML models were trained under the same validation specifications. For this, a five-fold cross validation folds was carried out. A natural way to develop a BCI application is implemented by subject. For this, the fold division was performed for each subject, according to the acquisition. This means that each run was divided into five subsets to validate the models. The strategy was applied to all models in the same way to have an equally comparison.

Two scenarios were implemented: *i)* Two class classification was driven, where the ML techniques were trained to discriminate between rest and some motor imagery (right or left). For this, the features from left and right hand were joined in a one class. *ii)* This scenario was given by three classes, training the ML models to discriminate the specific side of the movement: right, left and rest. This implies more complexity in the models, according to the number of classes that the model has to learn. For example, in the SVM case, it was necessary to develop a multiclass where three models are combined from the three class vs. no class possibilities. All experiments were developed using Matlab © software and toolboxes related to machine learnings and classification learners.

3   Results

Accuracy and the variance due to the cross validation strategy for the four models, employing the time domain feature extraction is shown in Table 2 for the two classes scenario and Table 3 for the three classes scenario.

Table 2. Results for features extracted from the time domain and two classes classification.

Subject	Accuracy			
	Fine NN	SVM	Bagged trees	MLP
1	94.66%	90.25%	75.89%	88.33%
2	93.50%	93.63%	74.55%	86.67%
3	92.09%	91.26%	74.14%	75.83%
4	93.96%	85.97%	77.28%	74.17%
5	92.13%	91.25%	78.87%	71.67%
Mean	**93.26%**	**90.47%**	**76.14%**	**79.33%**
Variance	**0.010%**	**0.063%**	**0.030%**	**0.076%**

Table 4 and 5 show the results for the feature extracted from the frequency domain and two and three classes scenarios. Differences can be visualized in terms of classification rates. Table 2 and 4 show that the use of frequency domain features increased the performance in a 6% approximately.

For the three classes scenario, the increment was less than for two classes case, improving the performance in around 3%.

For the NN models, employing the time domain feature extraction, the number of units in hidden layer for the MLP with the better results were obtained with two, ten, six, ten and nine for the subjects one to five in Table 2. For Table 3, models had three, four, ten, four and ten neurons in the hidden layer for the five subjects, respectively. For frequency domain, the NN models with better results had five, ten, nine, nine and ten

Table 3. Results for features extracted from the time domain and three classes classification.

Subject	Accuracy			
	Fine NN	SVM	Bagged trees	MLP
1	85.24%	76.00%	70.24%	71.67%
2	87.91%	84.54%	73.85%	67.50%
3	90.97%	85.00%	66.59%	66.39%
4	84.75%	73.78%	70.62%	61.67%
5	86.49%	76.94%	74.51%	66.67%
Mean	**87.07%**	**79.25%**	**71.16%**	**66.78%**
Variance	**0.049%**	**0.21%**	**0.08%**	**0.035%**

Table 4. Results for features extracted from frequency domain and two classes classification.

Subject	Accuracy			
	Fine NN	SVM	Bagged trees	MLP
1	98.68%	94.35%	84.31%	98.33%
2	97.08%	92.92%	80.80%	97.92%
3	98.89%	92.22%	77.82%	96.39%
4	97.60%	88.65%	82.08%	91.88%
5	98.33%	96.94%	84.29%	89.00%
Mean	**98.11%**	**93.01%**	**81.86%**	**94.70%**
Variance	**0.0045%**	**0.073%**	**0.058%**	**0.04%**

Table 5. Results for features extracted from frequency domain and three classes classification.

Subject	Accuracy			
	Fine NN	SVM	Bagged trees	MLP
1	89.24%	84.24%	74.24%	75.83%
2	91.25%	88.30%	73.74%	76.67%
3	93.13%	86.91%	68.54%	80.83%
4	88.37%	79.97%	71.91%	80.83%
5	89.55%	89.13%	76.87%	72.50%
Mean	**90.31%**	**85.71%**	**73.06%**	**77.33%**
Variance	**0.02%**	**0.10%**	**0.076%**	**0.035%**

neurons in the hidden layer in the two classes scenario. In the three classes problem, these numbers of units were eight, three, six, seven and seven for the five subjects.

4 Discussion

Results exhibited how the simplest model obtained the best results for all scenarios and feature extraction domains. In second place in terms of accuracy, the SVM achieved comparative results for almost four cases, having the NN better results for the three classes with features in the frequency domain.

Analyzing the SVM models, the necessity of using a multiclass classification for determine three classes in the second scenario, indicate that the one vs. All strategy is more demanding, worsening the results for this application. The mechanism used to compute every response of each SVM depends of this recategorization of the classes. Therefore, the final accuracy value is directly affected by the performance of every single class vs. no class SVM classifier.

For the frequency domain, other aspect to analyze is the employment of the relative powers bands computed from alpha and beta for detecting motor imagery (right, left and rest states). The technique used was a multilayer perceptron NN applying a back-propagation algorithm, obtaining accuracies around 75%. It is important to note, that the database employed for that study was also used in the present work [26]. This suggest that the number the subjects contributes to improve the results. In addition, it may be due to the selected features, because in the created models five more training samples can imply a substantial improve, because the model has more samples to recreate the output, obtaining better generalization for the classification.

Continuing with the analysis of the results for the frequency domain, it is possible to see that are comparable to the reported in the literature. Accuracies around 82% have been exhibited in relative power for the five EEG signals bands [21–23]. In the present work, the accuracy value reached 90% for the scenario with three classes, showing an increment in relation to the reported results. This does not implies that the methodology employed here is better than the previously exhibited, the context of the experimentation as acquisition and preprocessing can represent significant differences, making difficult to compare the result values in a similar mode. In terms of the present proposal, the objective is to visualize more alternatives for motor imagery classification, evaluating two approaches: frequency and time domains.

Related to this last aspect, the use of time domain features reached results compared to the described in previous works with accuracies around 87% measures [24, 25]. It is evident that the fine KNN technique shows better performances than SVM, Badged Tree and NN, improving the classification from 3% to 17% approximately between the analyzed models. In addition, the percentage of the variance between the results for this technique shows that a good generalization is done, maintaining the minimum variance between subjects for the KNN model.

As limitations of present study, there are the number of subjects employed in the experimentation and the chosen ML models used, mainly. For this, future work includes the acquisition more participants in the study. Furthermore, more techniques for the feature extraction and more ML models also are considered to extend the analyses.

Furthermore, deeper analysis in relation to identification of left or right hand is necessary. In the present case, the left hand discrimination holds the worst results, exhibiting more complexity. This phenomenon happened to all the analyzed classifications, requiring more analyses to determine the causes out of the scope in this work.

5 Conclusions

A comparison between time and frequency domains methods for feature extraction related to the motor imagery detection was developed for upper limbs. The results show that a proposal based on features obtained from frequency domain represents a better option.

At the same time, from the implemented experiments it was possible to see that the motor imagery detection for the left hand it was more difficult to discriminate. This work took as classification three machine learning techniques, evincing the fine KNN as the best.

Future work considerations as the increment of the number of participants, explore the combination of the time and frequency domains and to train more models from the ML must be taken into account. Classification techniques as deep learning can be other alternative to analyze for the problem studied here.

Acknowledgements. Authors thank the Universidad del Rosario for the support in this work and the *Semillero en Inteligencia Artificial en Salud – Semill-IAS*. Also, the Universidad Antonio Nariño developed an important role for the signals acquisition which can be devised this work.

References

1. Jazayeri, S.B., Beygi, S., Shokraneh, F., Hagen, E.M., Rahimi-Movaghar, V.: Incidence of traumatic spinal cord injury worldwide: a systematic review. Eur. Spine J. **24**(5), 905–918 (2014). https://doi.org/10.1007/s00586-014-3424-6
2. Nicolas-Alonso, L.F., Gomez-Gil, J.: Brain computer interfaces, a review. Sensors (Basel). **12**, 1211–1279 (2012)
3. Iacoviello, D., Petracca, A., Spezialetti, M., Placidi, G.: A real-time classification algorithm for EEG-based BCI driven by self-induced emotions. Comput. Methods Programs Biomed. **122**, 293–303 (2015)
4. Fakhruzzaman, M.N., Riksakomara, E., Suryotrisongko, H.: EEG wave identification in human brain with Emotiv EPOC for motor imagery. Procedia Comput. Sci. **72**, 269–276 (2015)
5. Hamedi, M., Salleh, S.-H., Noor, A.M., Mohammad-Rezazadeh, I.: Neural network-based three-class motor imagery classification using time-domain features for BCI applications. In: 2014 IEEE Region 10 Symposium, pp. 204–207 (2014)
6. Wang, L., Xu, G., Yang, S., Wang, J., Guo, M., Yan, W.: Motor imagery BCI research based on sample entropy and SVM. In: 2012 Sixth International Conference on Electromagnetic Field Problems and Applications, pp. 1–4 (2012)
7. Bamdad, M., Zarshenas, H., Auais, M.A.: Application of BCI systems in neurorehabilitation: a scoping review. Disabil. Rehabil. Assist. Technol. **10**, 355–364 (2015)

8. Resalat, S.N., Saba, V.: A study of various feature extraction methods on a motor imagery based brain computer interface system. Basic Clin. Neurosci. **7**, 13 (2016)
9. Vega, R., et al.: Assessment of feature selection and classification methods for recognizing motor imagery tasks from electroencephalographic signals. Artif. Intell. Res. **6**, 37 (2017)
10. Uktveris, T., Jusas, V.: Application of convolutional neural networks to four-class motor imagery classification problem. Inf. Technol. Control. **46**, 260–273 (2017)
11. Yuksel, A., Olmez, T.: A neural network-based optimal spatial filter design method for motor imagery classification. PLoS One **10** (2015)
12. Al-Fahoum, A.S., Al-Fraihat, A.A.: Methods of EEG signal features extraction using linear analysis in frequency and time-frequency domains. ISRN Neurosci. (2014)
13. Oh, S.-H., Lee, Y.-R., Kim, H.-N.: A novel EEG feature extraction method using Hjorth parameter. Int. J. Electron. Electr. Eng. **2**, 106–110 (2014)
14. Hettiarachchi, I.T., Nguyen, T.T., Nahavandi, S.: Motor imagery data classification for BCI application using wavelet packet feature extraction. In: Loo, C.K., Yap, K.S., Wong, K.W., Beng Jin, A.T., Huang, K. (eds.) ICONIP 2014. LNCS, vol. 8836, pp. 519–526. Springer, Cham (2014). https://doi.org/10.1007/978-3-319-12643-2_63
15. Aydemir, Ö., Kayikcioglu, T.: Investigation of the most appropriate mother wavelet for characterizing imaginary EEG signals used in BCI systems. Turkish J. Electr. Eng. Comput. Sci. **24**, 38–49 (2016)
16. Ravelo-Garcia, G., Navarro-Mesa, J.L., Murillo-Diaz, M.J., Julia-Serda, J.G.: Application of RR series and oximetry to a statistical classifier for the detection of sleep apnoea/hypopnoea. In: Computers in Cardiology, pp. 305–308 (2004)
17. Xygonakis, I., Athanasiou, A., Pandria, N., Kugiumtzis, D., Bamidis, P.D.: Decoding motor imagery through common spatial pattern filters at the EEG source space. Comput. Intell. Neurosci. (2018)
18. Álvarez-Meza, A.M., Velásquez-Mart\'\inez, L.F., Castellanos-Dominguez, G.: Time-series discrimination using feature relevance analysis in motor imagery classification. Neurocomputing. **151**, 122–129 (2015)
19. Jafarifarmand, A., Badamchizadeh, M.A.: Real-time multiclass motor imagery brain-computer interface by modified common spatial patterns and adaptive neuro-fuzzy classifier. Biomed. Sig. Process. Control. **57**, 101749 (2020)
20. Khan, J., Bhatti, M.H., Khan, U.G., Iqbal, R.: Multiclass EEG motor-imagery classification with sub-band common spatial patterns. EURASIP J. Wirel. Commun. Networking **2019**(1), 1–9 (2019). https://doi.org/10.1186/s13638-019-1497-y
21. Alomari, M.H., Awada, E.A., Samaha, A., Alkamha, K.: Wavelet-based feature extraction for the analysis of EEG signals associated with imagined fists and feet movements. Comput. Inf. Sci. **7**, 17 (2014)
22. Bonnet, L., Lotte, F., Lécuyer, A.: Two brains, one game: design and evaluation of a multiuser BCI video game based on motor imagery. IEEE Trans. Comput. Intell. AI games. **5**, 185–198 (2013)
23. Boelts, J., Cerquera, A., Ruiz-Olaya, A.F.: Decoding of imaginary motor movements of fists applying spatial filtering in a BCI simulated application. In: Ferrández Vicente, J.M., Álvarez-Sánchez, J.R., de la Paz López, F., Toledo-Moreo, F.J., Adeli, H. (eds.) IWINAC 2015. LNCS, vol. 9107, pp. 153–162. Springer, Cham (2015). https://doi.org/10.1007/978-3-319-18914-7_16
24. Isa, N.E.M., Amir, A., Ilyas, M.Z., Razalli, M.S.: The performance analysis of K-nearest neighbors (K-NN) algorithm for motor imagery classification based on EEG signal. In: MATEC Web of Conferences, p. 1024 (2017)

25. Orjuela-Cañón, A.D., Renteria-Meza, O., Hernández, L.G., Ruíz-Olaya, A.F., Cerquera, A., Antelis, J.M.: Self-organizing maps for motor tasks recognition from electrical brain signals. In: Mendoza, M., Velastín, S. (eds.) CIARP 2017. LNCS, vol. 10657, pp. 458–465. Springer, Cham (2018). https://doi.org/10.1007/978-3-319-75193-1_55
26. Miah, M.O., Rahman, M.M., Muhammod, R., Farid, D.M.: Prediction of Motor Imagery Tasks from Multi-Channel EEG Data for Brain-Computer Interface Applications. bioRxiv (2020)
27. Walker, I., Deisenroth, M., Faisal, A.: Deep convolutional neural networks for brain computer interface using motor imagery. Imp. Coll. Sci. Technol. Med. Dep. Comput. (2015)
28. Chiarelli, A.M., Croce, P., Merla, A., Zappasodi, F.: Deep learning for hybrid EEG-fNIRS brain–computer interface: application to motor imagery classification. J. Neural Eng. **15**, 36028 (2018)
29. Zhang, L., Tan, J., Han, D., Zhu, H.: From machine learning to deep learning: progress in machine intelligence for rational drug discovery. Drug Discov. Today. **22**, 1680–1685 (2017)
30. Orjuela-Cañón, A.D., Renteria-Meza, O., Hernández, L.G., Ruíz-Olaya, A.F., Cerquera, A., Antelis, J.M.: Self-organizing maps for motor tasks recognition from electrical brain signals (2018)
31. Triana Guzmán, N., Orjuela-Cañón, Á.D., Jutinico Alarcon, A.L.: Incremental training of neural network for motor tasks recognition based on brain-computer interface. In: Nyström, I., Hernández Heredia, Y., Milián Núñez, V. (eds.) CIARP 2019. LNCS, vol. 11896, pp. 610–619. Springer, Cham (2019). https://doi.org/10.1007/978-3-030-33904-3_57
32. Abe, S.: Support vector machines for pattern classification. Springer, New York (2005). https://doi.org/10.1007/1-84628-219-5
33. Prajapati, G.L., Patle, A.: On performing classification using SVM with radial basis and polynomial kernel functions. In: 2010 3rd International Conference on Emerging Trends in Engineering and Technology, pp. 512–515 (2010)
34. Haykin, S.: Neural Networks and Learning Machines. Prentice Hall, Upper Saddle River (2009)
35. Naoum, R.S., Abid, N.A., Al-Sultani, Z.N.: An enhanced resilient backpropagation artificial neural network for intrusion detection system. Int. J. Comput. Sci. Netw. Secur. **12**, 11 (2012)

Automatic Classification of Diagnosis-Related Groups Using ANN and XGBoost Models

Angelower Santana-Velásquez[1]([⊠])(iD), John Freddy Duitama M.[1,2](iD),
and Julián D. Arias-Londoño[1,2](iD)

[1] Intelligent Information Systems Lab, Universidad de Antioquia, Medellín, Colombia
{angelower.santana,john.duitama,julian.ariasl}@udea.edu.co
[2] Department of Systems Engineering, Universidad de Antioquia, Medellín, Colombia

Abstract. The optimization of the resources used in hospitals is a key problem in hospital management. In this sense, the development of tools that can help health care providers to ensure that inpatients can be discharged at the times indicated by international standards according to their pathological condition is of great interest for the optimization of resources, especially in developing countries. There are different standards for grouping patients according to their diagnoses and procedures information, this work focuses on the Diagnosis-Related Groups (DRG) patient classification system. Typically, DRG are obtained after hospital discharge, only for billing and payment purposes, which reduce the ability of health providers to take corrective actions when the health care attention deviates from the standard attention of specific patient conditions. This work focuses on the use of ML techniques as an alternative to DRG regular classification methods. The main aim is to evaluate whether ML methods can classify patients according to the DRG standard, using the information available at the hospital discharge. This result would be the base line for further analysis focused on the prediction of DRG in early stages of the inpatient. The results shown that DRG classification using ANN and Ensemble methods can achieve up to 96% of accuracy in a real database of more than 57.032 health records.

Keywords: Diagnosis-related groups · DRG · Patient costs · Case mix · Machine learning · Patients classification

1 Introduction

Healthcare systems in developing countries face many challenges to provide appropriate attention to patients from very limited resources. Commonly, two kinds of entities are involved in patients' attention: Healthcare Providers Institutes (HPIs) and Health Promoting Entities (HPEs) (i.e. insurance companies). As their name stand for, HPIs are the organisations that actually provide healthcare services to patients, including medical consultation, laboratory analysis,

© Springer Nature Switzerland AG 2021
A. D. Orjuela-Cañón et al. (Eds.): IEEE ColCACI 2020, CCIS 1346, pp. 88–102, 2021.
https://doi.org/10.1007/978-3-030-69774-7_7

surgeries, etc. Consequently, HPIs face high pressures from HPEs in order to optimize services costs without lowering the quality of the healthcare services. Moreover, users and government claim to HPI for improving the quality of service and expand the portfolio of services provided to the general public. Under this context, clinics and hospitals are adopting techniques that allow the standardization and optimization of the costs of patients admitted to hospital and thus meet the needs of health care systems. In this sense, Diagnosis-Related Groups (DRG) is one of the most used methods for standardizing the grouping of patients. DRGs are based on demographic information, significant characteristics of diagnoses and procedures performed throughout hospital stay, and allow to determine the level of resources that should have been consumed by a patient according to his/her primary diagnosis and to the treatments applied until discharge [1,2]. DRGs are required by HPEs, mainly for billing and payment purposes, as a way to control the increment of costs associated with health care procedures that do not have a clear support according to the diagnoses and also to explain the variability of clinical practices in apparently similar patients [3]. In a GRD-based patient classification system, typically called DRG-grouper, patients are classified according to their clinical characteristics and similarities in the resources used for their treatment during the hospital stay. Such a classification is carried out deterministically after patient discharge, when the diagnosis, comorbidities and medical procedures applied to the patient are known. All this information is what insurance companies use to fix payments for each patient. The problem with this approach is that HPIs do not have any monitoring tool that allow them to control expenses (or at least monitoring them) according to the corresponding DRG, since it is unknown during the patient's stay, which can yield to financial problems if the final payment does not recognise some of the procedures performed on the patient. One of the alternatives to tackle this problem, is to make available a system able to predict the most likely DRG of a patient from partial information (preventing the use of DRG-groupers), which could be used by HPIs to monitor the expenses and budget consumption from the HPEs' point of view.

Bearing this in mind, the present work addresses the problem of classification of inpatients according to DRG using Machine Learning (ML) techniques, as an alternative to DRG traditional classification method. The first aim is to evaluate whether ML techniques are able to classify patients according to the DRG standard, using the information available at the patient discharge, as a first step in the search of a system capable of predicting DRGs using partial an incomplete information[1]. The second aim raised in this work is to determine if ML techniques need to use the same number of attributes as traditional groupers or if they can exclude some variables that do not contribute or that contribute little to the classification process.

---

[1] Note that in this case we differentiate between classification and prediction, depending on the moment (and therefore on the available information) at which the estimation of the DRG is made.

The remainder of the paper is structured as follows. Section 2 provides a survey of relevant literature. Section 3 includes an analysis about the ML techniques used in this study. Section 4 describes the dataset along with the set of features included. Experiments and results are summarized in Sect. 5. Finally in Sect. 6 some conclusions derived from the results are discussed.

2   Related Works

This section is divided into three parts; the first part deals with the basic concepts behind DRGs, their creation and use in hospital management. The second part is aimed at describing the traditional classification method based on a well-known flowchart and the last part deals with recent DRG classification methods supported by computational intelligence techniques.

2.1   Diagnosis-Related Groups - DRG

A DRG-based system is a patient classification system that has four main characteristics: (1) the data routinely collected during the hospital stay (mostly related to the patient, the treatment and the characteristics provided) are used to classify the patients; (2) a manageable number of groups (i.e., DRG), which claim to be (3) clinically significant and (4) economically homogeneous [4]. The DRGs consolidate the large number of different (individual) patients treated in hospitals in a considerable number of clinically significant and economically homogeneous groups, thus providing a concise measure of hospital activity or, in other words, defining hospital products. As a result, the implementation of DRGs facilitates comparisons of costs, quality and efficiency of hospitals, and contributes to greater transparency [4]. Another use of DRG is to standardize the estimate of expenses in the treatments performed on patients. The HPEs and the National Health Systems take them as a basis to make their payments to the HPIs; for this, fixed costs are established for patients grouped in the same DRG. This reimbursement system has in turn a weight associated with the DRG that are the result of the common routines that are carried out in the different treatments of the majority of the patients, this is where the utility of the weights assigned to the DRG of the patients is seen, since they have a variety of uses among which are the comparative standards, the execution of payments and the elaboration of budgets, among others [2].

2.2   Traditional Method of DRG Classification

There are several software used for the classification of patients according to DRG standards, some of these computer tools are free to use and others are commercial. In general all those tools are called DRG-Groupers and are based on a hierarchical classification algorithm described in Fig. 1.

The traditional algorithm implemented in the DRG-groupers has three phases. In the first stage (section A of the diagram in Fig. 1), it determines

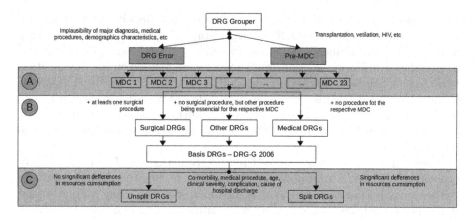

Fig. 1. Flow chart of the traditional algorithm for classifying patients in DRG. Image taken from [5]

1 of 23 Major Diagnostic Categories (MDC), which are defined by the primary diagnosis. In case of the primary diagnosis is not available, the algorithm provides an *Error-DRG* label [6]. There are different variants of DRG according to the number of MDC considered. The variant described in Fig. 1 corresponds to the International Refined DRG (IR-DRG) which, like the G-DRG variant (from Germany), contains 23 MDC. There are other variants such as AP-DRG, APR-DRG and HCFA-DRG that uses 25 MDC and the GHM-DRG variant that contains 26 MDC, among others [7]. The dataset used in this work uses the LAT-GRC grouper variant that contains 21 MDC, which according to their authors, is the only DRG grouper adapted to the epidemiology and information systems in Latin America [8]. After determining the MDC, in the second phase of the algorithm clinical procedures and comorbidities enable the classification of a patient into a DRG that can be surgical, procedural or other types. Finally in section C, the algorithm classify the patient into different DRG subtypes. At this point, the age of the patient or his/her weight in the case of newborns, are taken into account to establish the potential level of resources consumption. These characteristics can be used to determine the stage of the pathology, which leads to a different consumption of resources and finally to a specific DRG [6].

Note that, in early stages of hospitalization, DRG cannot be identified clearly, due to incomplete information and non-standardized input parameters such as the patient review using free text [9]. For this reason the traditional algorithm conceives the classification of patients in DRG after they are discharged, when the information about the hospital stay of patient has been consolidated.

2.3   Classification of Patients in DRG Using ML

Computational intelligence methods have recently been used in various applications in the area of health [10]. Thus, the automatic classification of DRG using ML techniques have been recently addressed as a way to overcome the problems of traditional groupers. Moreover, ML techniques can also be used to provide classifications about potential DRG in early stage of the inpatient's stay, which could yield to improvements in patient monitoring, health-care procedures and lastly in the optimization of resources. The first work focused on the classification of DRG using ML techniques was published in [11], and reports the comparison of models for the determination of medical costs of Spinal Fusion in Diagnosis-Related Groups by using ML algorithms. The authors concluded that methods of this type can also be used to address related problems, such as predicting the costs of other DRGs.

Other studies have been proposed to classify patients in DRG, at an early stage of the patient's stay and after discharge. In [9], the authors evaluate whether an early classification and after discharge of a DRG using computational intelligence techniques, can improve both contribution margins and the allocation of resources such as operating rooms and beds. This study focused on the accuracy of the classification at the time the patient seeks admission, and after it, i.e., since admission to discharge. This work used a dataset with 16.601 patients who were admitted during the year 2011 in a hospital near Munich, Germany. Every patient was described using 47 features and assigned to 680 different DRG. The ML techniques compared were Naïve-Bayes, Bayesian Networks, Classification Trees, Voting-Based Combined Classification, among others. The results showed that computational intelligence techniques can significantly increase the accuracy in the early classification of patients in DRG and obtain results very similar to the classification after discharge. Additionally, it was shown that ML techniques combined with mathematical programming can increase contribution margins and improve the allocation of scarce resources. According to the authors, the best result obtained using ML techniques achieved an accuracy of 99.4% using all the information available after patient's discharge.

The work published in [12] addresses the problem of predicting the inpatient's mean stay. Although that work does not classify a patient according to a DRG category, it tries to determine whether the patient will stay more than five days (long stay) or less than or equal to five days (short stay), which is strongly related to the DRG classification problem, since the DRGs are directly linked to the days of hospital stay, i.e., each DRG has a maximum patient stay associated with it. In [12] the authors used a vanilla neural network with two hidden layers for the classification of short or long stay using samples from the MIMIC database [13]. The variables used included: diagnoses, procedures, demographic information, among others. The authors reported a prediction accuracy between 75.3% and 82.3%.

To the best of our knowledge, no work has addressed the problem of DRG prediction in the sense that we treat this concept here, i.e., even though there are some approaches with good results regarding the classification of patients in DRG using ML, this classification was made after the patient discharge. Furthermore, it is also noteworthy that each work uses a variant of DRG adapted to the epidemiology of each country or at least, from a very similar context. This work uses a database labeled according to the a Latin American epidemiology standard developed by [8] that has not been tested before for DRG prediction nor classification purposes using ML techniques.

3   Methods

In this work, the classification of DRG is performed using two extensively used ML techniques: Artificial Neural Network (ANN) and eXtreme Gradient Boosting (XGBoost). ANNs are well-known for their flexibility and adaptation capacity to many different problems. On the other hand, ensemble methods such as XGBoost have shown high performance in many health-related task, and they are equipped with a natural way to evaluate the importance of the features in the addressed ML task; according to [14], the features importance depends on whether the prediction performance changes significantly when that feature is replaced with random noise. XGBoost is also scalable, that is a desirable characteristic when the problem involves the processing of dozens of thousand of samples. Furthermore, both models are part of the most popular ML techniques today, e.g., in 11 out 29 kaggle competitions during 2017, the winner solution was based on ANN, and in many of those cases, ANNs were combined with a XGBoost model [15].

4   Dataset

For the development of this work, a database of clinical discharge composed of 57.032 health records grouped into 47 DRG was used. The database includes information of patients hospitalized during the years 2016, 2017 and 2018 at the *IPS Universitaria Clínica León XIII*, a complexity third-level Hospital in Medellín-Colombia which, according to the management indicators of 2018, had 626 beds distributed in: Adult hospitalization 531, Pediatric hospitalization 21 and Intensive Care Unit - Especial Care Unit (ICU-ECU) 74.

The dataset was labeled using a DRG-grouper which uses a total of 168 variables as input. The 168 variables can be split into three groups: *1) Administrative Information* as insurer, hospital code, type of income; *2) Patient Information* such as gender, age, date of birth, age group and *3) Medical Information* such as primary diagnosis and other diagnoses all coded according to ICD-10 (International Statistical Classification of Diseases and Related Health Problems 10th Revision) standard, and Unique Classification of Health Procedures (in Spanish *Clasificación Única de Procedimientos en Salud* - CUPS) coded procedures. However, based on the scientific literature, the opinion of expert physicians and after a simple analysis it is clear that many of those features corresponds to unique identifiers no related with neither the patients diagnoses nor health care procedures. Some of those features include information about the insurance company, hospital code, etc., so all of those features were removed from the dataset. In this sense, the features that according to medical criteria could contribute the most to the ML models were selected. The final set of features is listed in

Table 1. The ICD-10 standard is a code assigned by the treating physician and represents the primary diagnosis, is the reason for the patient admission.

Additionally to the features described above, Table 1 also includes a couple of additional variables related to ICD-10 primary diagnoses. 1) *ICD-10 - MDC*: the Major Diagnostic Categories is the first character of any particular ICD-10 code. This corresponds to a single organ system or etiology and in general, it associates the diagnosis with a particular medical specialty. In this work, 20 different MDCs were present in database; 2) *ICD-10 - category*: corresponds to the three-character block in every ICD-10 code, which points to specific categories of diseases that have characteristics in common [16]. The database contains 1057 different *ICD-10 - categories*.

Table 1. Features description in the dataset.

No	Feature	Data type	Features numbers
1	Month of admission	Nominal	12
2	Age in years	Continue	1
3	Gender	Nominal	2
4	Type of admission	Nominal	2
5	Age group	Nominal	5
6	ICD-10 - MDC	Nominal	20
7	ICD-10 - category	Nominal	1057
8	ICD-10	Nominal	1692
9	ICD-9 Proc.	Nominal	1592

Regarding the procedures, DRGs are separated into two groups: medical and surgical, the latter referring to the procedures that were performed to the patients during their length of stay. For this work, 14.566 patients were underwent at least to one procedure during stay and were classified as surgical DRG. The rest, that is, 42.466 patients were labeled as medical DRG. The patients classified into surgical DRG have information about the procedures performed with the CUPS code. Additionally, this information is organized in chronological order so it is possible to know what procedures were performed day by day. This information is going to be helpful for further analysis on DRG prediction using partial or incomplete information.

The number of procedures vary in quantity according to the days of the hospital stay. Unlike the ICD-10 diagnosis codes, where only the primary diagnosis was considered, all the different procedures per patient were taken into account, which could even meant that, in many cases, a procedure was done several times to the same patient. For this reason, the procedures were coded using frequency variables, where each different procedure became a new feature representing the number of times that a specific procedure was applied to the patient. It is clear that not all the available procedures were applied to every patient, so in those cases the corresponding features were marked as "zero".

4.1   Cohort of Study

Several of the DRG groups included in the database contain a small number of samples. Therefore, in this study a cohort of 57.032 health records representing the 70% of whole database was used. This cohort includes the 47 most frequent DRG in the dataset. Figure 2 shows the distribution of the samples in the different DRGs selected. It is possible to observe that, even after the selection of the cohort, there is a strong imbalance among the 47 classes. For example, the class more frequent (C-09-07) has 4.765 records, while the class less frequent (C-10-14 label) has 496 records. After the cohort selection, and by using the feature codification described above, the number of features was finally set to 4.370. Table 2 shows a summary of the number of features per attribute in the dataset.

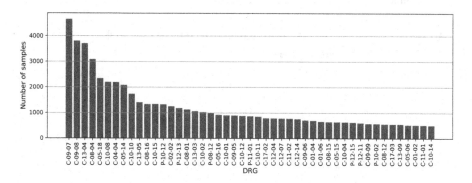

Fig. 2. Samples distribution among the most frequent DRGs in the dataset, which represent 70% of all cases.

Table 2. Total number of features per attribute

Demog. Info.	ICD-10	ICD-10 category	ICD-10 MDC	ICD-9 Proc.	Total features
9	1692	1057	20	1592	4370

5   Experiments and Results

5.1   Experimental Setup

To evaluate the performance of the models, a cross-validation methodology with five folds was used. The hyperparameters of the models and learning algorithms were adjusting following a grid search approach. The grid evaluated for every parameter can be seen in Tables 3 and 4, corresponding to XGBoost and ANN models respectively. During training stage, different seeds were used in each fold in order to evaluate sensitivity to the initial conditions and convergence issues of the models. Additional, the class weight parameter was set following a balanced heuristic rule [17] in order to compensate the imbalance problem in the dataset.

Table 3. Grid search intervals for XGBoost hyperparameters tuning. *Note: Objective: multi:softma*

Parameter	Values grid	Best values
Estimators number	[100, 200, 300, 1000]	300
Max depth	[3, 5, 10, 15]	5
Min child weight	[1, 3, 5]	1
Gamma reg	[0.0, 0.1, 0.2, 0.3, 0.4]	0.2
Subsample	[0.6, 0.7, 0.75, 0.8, 0.85, 0.9]	0.8
Colsample bytree	[0.6, 0.7, 0.75, 0.8, 0.85, 0.9]	0.8
L1 reg	[0, 1e-5, 0.001, 0.005, 0.01, 0.05, 0.1, 1, 100]	0
Booster	gbtree, dart	gbtree
Stratifed	True	True

Table 4. Grid search intervals for ANN hyperparameters tuning

Parameter	Values grid	Best values
Epochs	[20, 50, 100, 500, 1000]	20
Batch size	[256, 512, 1024, 2048]	1024
Optimizer	adam, SGD, RMSprop	adam
Dropout	[0, 0.1, 0.2, 0.5, 0.8]	0.1

The set of experiments for ANN started from a vanilla neural network architecture (M1 model) similar to that in the study [12], that was discussed in Sect. 2. Furthermore, the model architecture was varied to include several hidden layers with different numbers of neurons, in this experiment 12 models were built; Table 5 shows the model architectures evaluated. Moreover, every architecture was evaluated also according to the grid search of the remaining set of considered hyperparameters in Table 4. For the XGBoost technique, 12 model architectures were evaluated (see Table 6) too and like the RNA technique, each architecture of the XGboost was evaluated with the grid search of the remaining set of hyperparameters considered in the Table 3. Lastly, the performance of the models was evaluated in terms of accuracy and F_1 for each of the classes.

In addition to the classification experiments, the gain index extracted from XGBoost which is based on the variance of the impurity in the nodes of the generated trees, was used to find the most relevant features in the classification of DRGs.

Table 5. Specific ANN model configurations evaluated in Fig. 3

Model	Layers	Nodes per Layer
M1	2	5, 3
M2	1	4
M3	1	8
M4	1	16
M5	1	32
M6	1	64
M7	**2**	**256, 128**
M8	1	512
M9	2	1024, 512
M10	5	1024, 512, 256, 128, 64
M11	5	1024, 1024, 1024, 1024, 1024
M12	5	2048, 2048, 2048, 2048, 2048

5.2 Results

Figure 3 shows the behavior of the ANN and XGBoost techniques when the two more important hyperparameters are varied during the tuning process. No major changes in XGBoost performance are observed when the number of estimators and maximum depth were changed. While in the case of ANN, it is observed that the performance of the models improves as the complexity of the network increases, that is, when more layers and more numbers per layer are added, but

Table 6. Specific XGBoost model configurations evaluated in Fig. 3

Model	Estimators	Max. Depth
M1	100	3
M2	100	5
M3	100	10
M4	200	3
M5	200	5
M6	200	10
M7	200	15
M8	300	3
M9	**300**	**5**
M10	300	10
M11	300	15
M12	1000	5

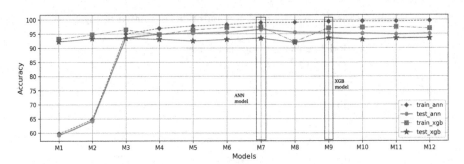

Fig. 3. Performance for different model architectures

this complexity has a limit, from M12 model an overfitting in the results begins to be observed. The best results during this stage were obtained with the M7 and M9 models for ANN and XGBoost respectively.

Table 7 shown the best results obtained for the classification of DRG using both XGBoost and ANN models. Tables 3 and 4 shown in bold the configuration of parameters that yield to the best results in both XGBoost and ANN models, respectively. According to the results in Table 7, the performance of the models is very consistent for training and test stages; that the standard deviation estimated over the different folds and parameters initialization is less than 0.04% in both models, which indicates that regardless of the seed the model is converging to a similar minimum of the cost function. Most importantly, the results show high classification accuracy for both techniques, but specially for ANN, indicating that ML models are able to mimic, in more than 96% of the cases, the class assigned by a conventional DRG grouper. These positive results are also due to the management of class imbalance implemented in both of the evaluated techniques.

It is also worth to highlight that, as expected, most of the relevant information to determine the DRG class is included in the attributes containing patient and medical information, so many of the administrative attributes required by conventional groupers are useless to determine the correct DRG class. In this sense, using only 9 out of the original 168 attributes used by the grouper, the XGBoost can correctly classify 93% and the ANN 96% of the patients at the hospital discharge.

Table 7. Best results obtained for the DRG classification

Model	Train accuracy	Test accuracy
XGBoost	97.04% ± 0.01	93.55% ± 0.02
ANN	99.00% ± 0.02	96.56% ± 0.04

Figure 4 shows F_1 statistic for each of the DRG classes using the ANN model. It is important to highlight that the classes with the lowest F_1 value correspond to DRGs categorized as surgical, which are those where the label begins with the letter P, as in the case of P-12-02 that corresponds to *Procedures for Vertebral Fusion* or P-12-15 (*Other procedures in knee and leg except arthroplasty*). This poor behaviour could be explained because of the variability in the number of different ICD-10 diagnoses in those classes, which prevent the model from finding a clear pattern to classify correctly those DRGs. In order to clarify this argument, lets take a look to the P-12-15 class; in the database it contains 1186 samples, but those samples can take 170 different diagnosis and up to 129 different procedures. This is in contrast to some of the classes with the best F_1, where all the samples take the same primary diagnosis.

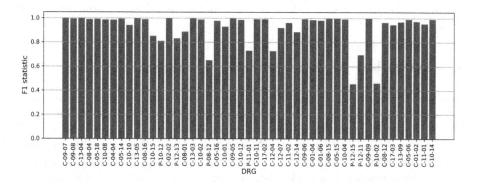

Fig. 4. F_1 obtained using the ANN model for each of the 47 DRG classes

Regarding features importance, Fig. 5 shows the average gain across all splits when every feature is used in the training of XGBoost model. The figure shows only the top 30 most relevant features according to the gain index. The highest gain is obtained for the feature *Z511 - Encounter for antineoplastic chemotherapy and immunotherapy*, that is directly related with the DRG *C-02-02 - Admission for chemotherapy session*. As it can be observed in Fig. 4, the F_1-*score* obtained for C-02-02 was equal to 1, that is, the 100% of the inpatients who were given the ICD-10 diagnosis code Z511 were classified correctly by the ANN model. From a prediction perspective, this kind of behaviour is very promising since only one feature can be the indicator of some the DRGs, and that information could be available in an early stage of the patient's stay. Figure 5 shown the top 30 most important features determined by XGBoost technique. From Fig. 5 it can be seen that 16 out of the 30 features correspond primary diagnoses; 13 of the remaining features correspond to the ICD-10 categories, and only one of 30 selected features is related with the chapters of the MDC, specifically the E chapter which corresponds to Sect. 4 - Endocrine, nutritional and metabolic diseases.

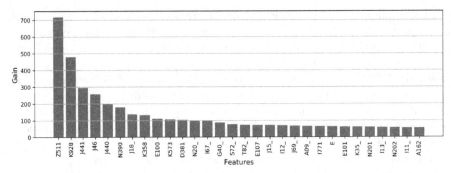

Note: the characteristics related here are primary diagnoses and are coded with the ICD-10 standard

Fig. 5. Top 30 of the most relevant features according to XGBoost feature important index.

6　Conclusions

This work addressed the automatic classification of DRG using ML techniques. The set of selected features includes demographic information, ICD-10 Diagnosis, and ICD-9 Procedures. The best classification accuracy obtained was around 96% for 47 different DRG and was achieved by an ANN with not a quite complex architecture. Although a perfect classification of the DRGs using a DRG-grouper as ground truth was not possible, the performance can be considered high taking into account that only 9 out of the 168 original attributes used by the grouper were included for the ML models, making the follow-up of the attributes involved in the DRG classification more manageable. Moreover, this 9 attributes are more likely to be available in early stages of hospitalization, which is a key element to develop DRG prediction systems.

As observed in the analysis of the features importance, the most important attributes are the primary diagnoses, which are the code assigned by the treating physician to the patient at admission. For the XGBoost to correctly classify the 93% of the patients, it does not require the information of the procedures performed on the inpatient, this conclusion is reached because according to the gains obtained in the analysis of features importance from XGBoost, none of the codes of procedures appears in the top 30 of the most important features. Additionally, regarding the MDC chapters represented by the first letter of the ICD-10 code, only one of them was included in the top 30 of the features that more influence had in the classification of patients according to the DRG. At this point it is worth to highlight that many of the 4.370 variables used as features for the training of the ML models, came from a one-hot-encoding strategy of 9 of the original attributes used by the conventional grouper (see Table 1). Therefore, if the XGBoost gain obtained by the features is grouped (summed) according to the original 9 attributes, the two most important attributes are the ICD-10 diagnosis and the ICD-10 category.

Lastly, the network architecture proposed in [12] was used as a starting point for comparison purposes. This ANN obtained less than 60% of accuracy for the DRG classification. That results is understandable since the problem addressed in [12] was a two class classification problem, whilst in this work the number of different classes rose to 47. Using a similar architecture but by increasing the number of neurons, the performance improved yielding to more than 96%. Notwithstanding, special care must be taken to set regularization parameters in order to avoid overfitting. Further analysis should be performed in order to establish how much discriminative power is lost, when only partial information about the patient's stay is available. Those analyses will be a step forward aiming the development of a DRG prediction system.

References

1. Gómez Montoya, L.F., Duque Roldán, M.I., Carmona López, J.: La información contable y de costos en las entidades de salud: una herramienta para su transformación (2008) (in Spanish)
2. Rivero Cuadrado, A.: Análisis y desarrollo de los gdr en el sistema nacional de salud. Ministerio de Sanidad y Consumo **70** (1999) (in Spanish)
3. Aiello, F.A., Roddy, S.P.: Inpatient coding and the diagnosis-related group. J. Vascular Surg. **66**(5), 1621–1623 (2017)
4. Quentin, W., Geissler, A., Scheller-Kreinsen, D., Busse, R.: Understanding DRGs and DRG-based hospital payment in Europe. In: Diagnosis-Related groups in Europe: Moving Towards Transparency, Efficiency and Quality in Hospitals. Open University Press and McGraw Hill: Berkshire, England, pp. 23–36 (2011)
5. Schreyögg, J., Tiemann, O., Busse, R.: Cost accounting to determine prices: how well do prices reflect costs in the German DRG-system? Health Care Manag. Sci. **9**(3), 269–279 (2006)
6. Gartner, D., Padman, R.: Improving hospital-wide early resource allocation through machine learning. Stud. Health Technol. Informatics **216**, 315–319 (2015)
7. Roeder, N., Rochell, B., Juhra, C., Mueller, M.: Empirical comparison of DRG variants using cardiovascular surgery data: initial results of a project at 18 German hospitals. Aust. Health Rev. **24**(4), 57–80 (2001)
8. AVEDIAN: ¿qué es un agrupador de GRD y cuál es su importancia para los sistemas de salud latinoamericanos? https://avediangrd.com/#!/-que-es-un-agrupador-de-grd-y-cual-es-su-importancia-para-los-sistemas-de-salud-latinoamericanos
9. Gartner, D., Kolisch, R., Neill, D.B., Padman, R.: Machine learning approaches for early DRG classification and resource allocation. INFORMS J. Comput. **27**(4), 718–734 (2015)
10. Tomar, D., Agarwal, S.: A survey on data mining approaches for healthcare. Int. J. Bio-Sci. Bio-Technol. **5**(5), 241–266 (2013)
11. Kuo, C.-Y., Yu, L.-C., Chen, H.-C., Chan, C.-L.: Comparison of models for the prediction of medical costs of spinal fusion in Taiwan diagnosis-related groups by machine learning algorithms. Healthcare Informatics Res. **24**(1), 29–37 (2018)
12. Gentimis, T., Ala'J, A., Durante, A., Cook, K., Steele, R.: Predicting hospital length of stay using neural networks on MIMIC III data. In: IEEE 15th International Conference on Dependable, Autonomic and Secure Computing (DASC/PiCom/DataCom/CyberSciTech) **2017**, 1194–1201. IEEE (2017)

13. Johnson, A., Pollard, T., Shen, L.: MIMIC-III, a freely accessible critical care database. Sci. Data **3** (2016)
14. Zheng, H., Yuan, J., Chen, L.: Short-term load forecasting using EMD-LSTM neural networks with a XGBoost algorithm for feature importance evaluation. Energies **10**(8), 1168 (2017)
15. Ogunleye, A.A., Qing-Guo, W.: XGBoost model for chronic kidney disease diagnosis. IEEE/ACM Trans. Comput. Biol. Bioinformatics (2019)
16. W. H. Organization, International Statistical Classification of Diseases and Related Health Problems, 10th version, Volume 2 - Instruction manual, 10th edn. WHO Library Cataloguing-in-Publication Data (2010)
17. King, G., Zeng, L.: Logistic regression in rare events data. Polit. Anal. **9**(2), 137–163 (2001)

Power Management Strategies for Hybrid Vehicles: A Comparative Study

Fernanda Cristina Corrêa[1]([⊠]) [ID], Jony Javorski Eckert[2] [ID],
Fabio Mazzariol Santiciolli[2] [ID], Marcella Scoczynski Ribeiro Martins[1] [ID],
Cristhiane Gonçalves[1] [ID], Virgínia Helena Varoto Baroncini[1] [ID],
Ludmila Alckmin e Silva[2] [ID], and Franco Giuseppe Dedini[2] [ID]

[1] Federal University of Technology - Paraná, Ponta Grossa, Brazil
fernandacorrea@utfpr.edu.br
[2] University of Campinas - UNICAMP, Campinas, Brazil

Abstract. The hybrid electric vehicle (HEV) is an alternative to reduce
fuel consumption and increase vehicle performance, maintaining the
safety and trustworthiness of conventional vehicles. The power management
strategy (PMS) influences directly the fuel economy and performance
of HEVs. This paper presents two different management
approaches for the power management: rule-based control and fuzzy control.
Through analysis of the engine consumption map, the results of the
simulation show that the fuzzy strategy demonstrates better performance
than a rule-based strategy. Therefore, this study indicates that the fuel
economy can be substantially enhanced with a correct power management
strategy.

Keywords: Hybrid electric vehicle · Power management strategy ·
Rule-based control · Fuzzy logic

1 Introduction

Hybrid electric vehicles (HEVs) are widely rated as one of the most feasible
solutions to the world's necessities for cleaner and more fuel-efficient vehicles.
The adoption of hybrid propulsion technology has contributed to reduce the
emission of particulate materials and gases [1]. Furthermore, HEV maintains the
characteristics attributed to conventional vehicles such as performance, safety
and reliability.

Comparing with a classic vehicle, the hybrid one is more complex. In order to
obtain the maximum efficiency in HEV, the main control strategy seeks to select
the propulsion source, e.g. internal combustion engine (ICE) or electric motor
(EM), depending on the load [2]. The ICE has a low efficiency at low load,
for transient regimes and for idling [3]. However, considering full loads and high
speed, the engine has the maximum efficiency. The HEV control strategy intends
to avoid the low efficiency by using the control algorithms to manage the energy

A. D. Orjuela-Cañón et al. (Eds.): IEEE ColCACI 2020, CCIS 1346, pp. 103–116, 2021.
https://doi.org/10.1007/978-3-030-69774-7_8

sources in order to minimize the fuel consumption and the gas emissions [1,4], sustaining the battery state of charge (SoC).

According to [5] various methods and solutions have been proposed in the literature to HEV management control. The rule based strategies are based on heuristics, intuition, human expertise and even mathematical models without a previous knowledge of a predefined driver cycle [6]. The rules depend on the power demand, the driver's acceleration and the SoC of the battery. Then taking into account the value of such variables a powertrain configuration is adopted. In [7], a rule-based controller is designed and simulated for a two-modes power-split hybrid electric vehicle, whose powertrain is modeled using the bond-graph technique. Moreover, the rule base power split control for HEV is also applied in [2,4], considering rules optimized by genetic algorithm.

A similar approach to rule-based control has been followed using fuzzy logic technique [3,8]. Thermostat strategy, power follower strategy and fuzzy rule-based strategy are the examples and their purpose is load-leveling [9]. On the other hand, optimization-based strategies try to find a global optimum using linear programming, dynamic programming, genetic algorithm etc. However, these strategies show the limit of non-availability in the real-time environment [6].

In this context, this work focuses on the development and the analysis of PMS in a HEV parallel configuration with EM coupled in the rear wheels. For this, two management strategies are developed, the first is rule-based and the second strategy is using fuzzy systems. The results of this study allow to observe when each propulsion system is triggered and to analyze the fuel consumption for each power management strategy.

2   Vehicle Longitudinal Dynamic

The vehicle studied in this paper is a parallel electric hybrid and is shown schematically in Fig. 1. It has a 1.0L gasoline engine coupled to the front axle through a 5-speed transmission. Two EM are directly coupled in each rear wheel and the energy is stored in a battery pack.

The vehicle power demand is a function of the movement resistance torque T_r [Nm] like the aerodynamic drag, rolling resistance, powertrain inertia and the driving behavior [10] as shown in Eq. (1), as a function of the drag coefficient C_D, vehicle frontal area A [m^2], air density ρ [kg/m^3], gravitational acceleration g [m/s^2], vehicle speed V [m/s], mass M [kg] and the tire radius r [m].

$$T_r = \left(\frac{1}{2} \rho V^2 C_D \ A + 0.01 \left(1 + \frac{0.62 \ V}{100} \right) Mg + Ma_{req} \right) r \tag{1}$$

The driving behavior can be simulated by means of standard cycles [11] that define the vehicle required acceleration a_{req} [m/s^2] calculate by Eq. 2 according to the target speed V_t [m/s] (located time step Δ_t [s] ahead the current simulation time), compared to the current vehicle speed V. In this study the FTP-75 standard driving cycle is applied as its speed profile. Once the applied

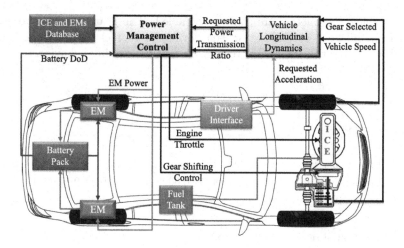

Fig. 1. Parallel HEV power management controller.

drive cycle does not provide any information regarding the track altimetry, the climbing resistance effects are neglected in this study.

$$a_{req}(t) = \frac{V_t(t + \Delta_t) - V(t)}{\Delta_t} \quad (2)$$

This required traction torque is the divided by the HEV PMC, with split the T_r value between the ICE T_r^{ICE} [Nm] and the electric motors T_r^{EMs} [Nm]. The engine required torque T_{ICE} [Nm] in then defined by Eq. 3 as a function of the gearbox N_t and differential N_d gear ratios, inertias of the rotation components I_e [kgm^2] (engine), I_t [kgm^2] (gearbox), I_d [kgm^2] (differential) and I_w [kgm^2] (wheels) and the overall powertrain efficiency η_{td}. On the other hand, the EMs are coupled directly to the vehicle rear wheels (Fig. 1) and it required torque T_{EM} [Nm] is then defined by Eq. 4 by adding the EMs inertia I_{EMs} [kgm^2].

$$T_{ICE} = \frac{T_r^{ICE}}{N_t N_d \eta_{td}} + \left((I_e + I_t)(N_t N_d)^2 + I_d N_d^2 + \frac{I_w}{2} \right) \frac{a_{req}}{r} \quad (3)$$

$$T_{EM} = T_r^{EMs} + \left(\frac{I_w}{2} + I_{EMs} \right) \frac{a_{req}}{r} \quad (4)$$

Bout requested torque values T_e and T_{EM} are the evaluated by its available torque curves. If the requested values exceeds the available one, its value is replaced by the maximum available torque. After these constrains, the current HEV acceleration a_x [m/s^2] is given by Eq. (5). The resulting a_x value is numerically integrated twice by the Simulink^{TM} ODE113 (Adams Solver) that define the HEV speed V displacement.

$$a_x = \frac{T_{ICE} N_t N_d \eta_{td} + T_{EM} - T_r}{r M + (I_e + I_t)(N_t N_d)^2 + I_d N_d^2 + I_w + I_{EMs}} \quad (5)$$

The vehicle parameters are shown by Table 1. The gear shifting strategy is based in standard gear shifting speeds developed to fuel economy previously studied by [2,3] with satisfactory results for a urban driving behavior.

Table 1. Vehicle parameters [3]

Components	Units	Speed				
		1st	2nd	3rd	4th	5th
Engine inertia	kgm^2	0.1367				
Transmission inertia	kgm^2	0.0017	0.0022	0.0029	0.0039	0.0054
Transmission ratio	-	4.27	2.35	1.48	1.05	0.8
Differential inertia	kgm^2	9.22E−04				
Differential ratio	-	4.87				
Wheels inertia	kgm^2	2				
EMs inertia	kgm^2	0.1				
Vehicle frontal area	m^2	1.8				
Drag coefficient	-	0.33				
Tires	-	175/65 R14				
ICE vehicle mass	kg	980				
HEV mass	kg	1120				

2.1 Engine Model

Due to the high complexity of the ICE, in this study it was modeled based on throttle and specific fuel consumption maps. The ICE torque curves (Fig. 2a), present the available torque in function of the its throttle percentage and speed, which is applied as constrain for the T_{ICE} torque as mentioned previously. If the required torque exceeds the 100% throttle available torque, the simulation will use the maximum torque of the curve and there will be a speed decrease and a loss in the vehicle acceleration performance [2].

In the simulations it was used a Otto cycle gasoline ICE model and the fuel consumption was estimated by the specific consumption map shown in Fig. 2b as a function of ICE operation pointy (speed and torque). The volume of fuel consumption (C_l) for each simulation step dt is calculated by (6) as a function of the engine power (P_e), the fuel density (ρ_f) and the fuel specific consumption (C_e) obtained from the consumption map. The total fuel consumption is given by the sum of all the consumption steps.

$$C_l = \frac{C_e P_e dt}{\rho_f} \tag{6}$$

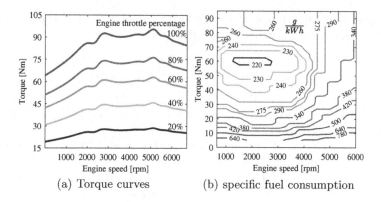

(a) Torque curves   (b) specific fuel consumption

Fig. 2. Engine torque curves and consumption map.

2.2 Electric Motor Model

EM was modeled according to the dynamic equations for a DC electric machine with independent field. The direct relationship between the armature current (I_a) and the electrical torque (T_{el}) developed by the rotor is given by torque constant (K_T):

$$T_{el} = K_T I_a \tag{7}$$

Through of the union of this with (8) that produces the armature current and (9), that produces the angular velocity it is possible to construct a block diagram equivalent for modeling the EM, as represented by Fig. 3.

$$I_a(s) = \frac{(V_t(s) - E_a(s))}{(r_a + sL_a)} \tag{8}$$

where: V_t - motor voltage, E_a - back EMF, r_a - armature resistance, L_a - armature inductance.

$$\omega(s) = \frac{(T_{el}(s) - T_{load}(s))}{(D + sJ)} \tag{9}$$

where: $\omega(s)$ - angular velocity, T_{load} - load torque, D damping constant, J motor inertia.

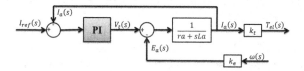

Fig. 3. DC electrical motor block diagram.

It is possible to obtain the angular velocity ($\omega(s)$) of the EM through vehicle velocity using the (10), where r is the wheel radius.

$$\omega(s) = \frac{V_{el}N\eta}{r} \tag{10}$$

Based on the study by [12], and as shown in Fig. 3, a controller uses proportional and integral coefficients (PI) for generating the voltage value of the armature circuit ($V_t(s)$) of (8).

When the vehicle is at braking mode, the EM is able to act as a generator. Therefore, all or a portion of the regenerated energy is used to charge the battery. The recharging process is limited due to maximum battery power charging for each time instant. Another feature of this model is about slight loss coefficient (or drain) by iron and/or copper. In other words, the proposed model shows an ideal case with 100% efficiency for electric machine operating as a motor and also as a generator. The constants used for solving the EM modeling were: K_T - 1.98 V/rad, $r_a = 0.082\,\Omega$, L_a - 0.2 mH.

2.3 Battery Model

The battery used as source of energy for parallel HEV is the lead acid. The model inputs are the battery power demand (P_b) from PMS, the depth of discharge (DoD) and the total charge removed (CR_n). DoD and CR_n are feedback to battery model to control the charging and discharging energy at each instant of the simulation. The main output of this model is the available power from battery (Pot) to the propulsion system.

For appropriate execution of the battery power in study, was chosen a bench composed of two batteries, each one with 10 cells, capacity of 32 Ah and Coefficient of Peukert, (k) equal to 1.2. In the simulations the DoD operates between predetermined values of charging and discharging (DoD_{max} and DoD_{min}), 0.45 and 0.4 respectively, which are considered to extend the battery life lead-acid used in this work. DoD was limited to maintain the battery life, because if the battery is completely discharged, its life cycle is dramatically reduced.

3 Power Management Strategy

The PMS must determine the power necessary to drive the wheels based on the driver inputs, control the charge and discharge of the battery and share the power between ICE and EMs.

Two different approaches of PMS were developed and implemented in the co-simulation program. The first strategy was based on rule-based due to clean implementation. Owing to some inaccurate information and variations in the current plant operating condition, the second approach was the fuzzy logic.

3.1 PMS Rule-Based

In this strategy, the power demand corresponding to vehicle power request will be called P_{dem}, the power requested by the ICE (P_{ICE}), the power requested by the (P_{EM}) and the power requested from the battery will be P_b.

The rules of PMS are determined in accordance with DoD of battery, P_{dem} and also the required torque (T_{req}) which are identified as inputs, and the P_{ICE}, P_{EM}, T_{brake} which are identified as PMS outputs (Table 2).

Table 2. Set of rules used in the PMS

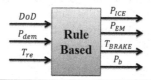

Acceleration Condition	Braking Condition
If $P_{dem} < 7500$ and $DoD \leq DoD_{max}$	If $P_{dem} < -P_{load}$ and $DoD > DoD_{min}$
$P_{EM} = P_{dem}$	$P_{EM} = -P_{load}$
$P_{ICE} = 0$	$P_{ICE} = 0$
$T_{BRAKE} = 0$	$T_{BRAKE} = T_{re}$
$P_B = P_{EM}$	$P_B = P_{EM}$
If $P_{dem} < 7500$ and $DoD > DoD_{min}$	If $P_{dem} < -P_{load}$ and $DoD < DoD_{min}$
$P_{EM} = 0$	$P_{EM} = P_{dem}$
$P_{ICE} = P_{dem} + P_{load}$	$P_{ICE} = 0$
$T_{BRAKE} = 0$	$T_{BRAKE} = T_{re}$
$P_B = -P_{load}$	$P_B = P_{EM}$
If $7500 < P_{dem} < 35000$	If $P_{dem} > -P_{load}$ and $DoD > DoD_{min}$
$P_{EM} = 0$	$P_{EM} = P_{dem}$
$P_{ICE} = P_{dem}$	$P_{ICE} = 0$
$T_{BRAKE} = 0$	$T_{BRAKE} = 0$
$P_B = 0$	$P_B = 0$
If $P_{dem} > 35000$ and $DoD \leq DoD_{max}$	If $P_{dem} > -P_{load}$ and If $DoD < DoD_{min}$
$P_{EM} = P_{dem} - P_{ICE}$	$P_{EM} = P_{dem}$
$P_{ICE} = 25000$	$P_{ICE} = 0$
$T_{BRAKE} = 0$	$T_{BRAKE} = 0$
$P_B = P_{EM}$	$P_B = P_{EM}$
If $P_{dem} > 35000$ and $DoD > DoD_{min}$	-
$P_{EM} = 0$	-
$P_{ICE} = P_{dem} + P_{load}$	-
$T_{BRAKE} = 0$	-
$P_B = -P_{load}$	-

In this PMS, the EM operates by providing the requested power value (P_{dem}) and operates at maximum capacity when it is necessary ($P_{EM_{max}}$) until the maximum DoD (DoD_{max}) be reached. Therefore, when the DoD maximum is reached, the EM acts as a generator, recharging the battery. When P_{dem} exceeds the value of $P_{EM_{max}}$ and DoD is the maximum (DoD_{max}), the ICE become the source responsible for supplying additional power. ICE also acts alone when P_{dem} is greater than $P_{EM_{max}}$ and less than 35 kW, featuring a region of good efficiency about ICE operation. However, if the value of DoD is below the maximum limit (DoD_{max}), the ICE will work together with the EM providing the P_{dem} to HEV.

However, if the value of P_{dem} is negative it denotes that the value of the required torque (T_{req}) is also negative, which indicates a vehicle deceleration. During braking, when the EM acts as a generator transforming kinetic energy into electricity, the energy can be stored in the battery in case of it is below its maximum load limit (DoD_{max}). The amount of power that the battery can absorb in the charging process is limited by the maximum power value of charge (P_{charge}) that can be absorbed, and the excess amount must be discarded (P_{loss}).

3.2   PMS Based Fuzzy

Fuzzy systems are known by approaching the computational decision to human decision. A major feature is the independence of mathematical modeling and the ability to approach complex nonlinear models. The fuzzy systems were quite suitable for the control of HEVs.

The fuzzy system based on PMS was used to control the power supplied by the propulsion systems based on P_{dem} and DoD of the battery.

For adjusting the membership functions, the number of functions used as well as the intervals for which were defined in their respective universes of discourse, preliminary tests were performed using results from rule-based strategy. The purpose of these tests was the reduction of fuel consumption compared with strategies based on rules. In this context, linguistic variables, which represent the fuzzy sets of inputs for PMS in question were determined as follows:

- Demand power (P_{dem}): this input variable was specified in the universe of discourse between -20000 and 60000 W, with set of terms NM (negative medium), LN (low negative), Z (zero), L (low), M (medium) and H (high) represented by their respective sets fuzzy. The limits of the universe of discourse for this variable were obtained from maximum and minimum values assumed by the power demand of the vehicle operating in urban cycle.
- Depth of discharge of the battery (DoD): is specified in the universe of discourse between 0 and 1, with a set of terms VL (very low), L (low), M (medium) and H (high) represented by their respective sets fuzzy. The limits for the universe of discourse are the same for which DoD is defined in the battery model.
- Request braking (T_{req}): This variable was specified in the universe of discourse between -5000 and 0, with sets of terms represented by their respective sets fuzzy. The limit of the universe of discourse defined, in this case, is the limit of braking required by HEVs added the safety margin.

Linguistic variables which represent the outputs fuzzy sets to PMS based on fuzzy are listed below:

- Electric motor power (P_{EM}): This output variable is specified in the universe of discourse between -8000 and 7500 W with set of terms NC (negative constant), N (negative), Z (zero), P (positive) and PC (positive constant) represented by their respective sets fuzzy. Similar to other variables, the limits of the universe of discourse for this variable were obtained from maximum and minimum values that the electric motor can take over its operation. For the validation of the fuzzy inference process is necessary to map the knowledge related to the system studied through fuzzy rules. These rules can be implemented from the expert knowledge of the process being described in linguistic form using the If-Then structure. Therefore, the process of knowledge expressed by the rules is shown in Table 3.

Table 3. Set of rules fuzzy.

P_{EM}				
Pdem \ DoD	VL	L	M	H
NM	Z	P	NC	NC
LN	N	N	N	N
Z	Z	Z	Z	Z
L	P	P	Z	Z
M	P	P	P	Z
H	PC	PC	P	Z

P_{ICE}				
Pdem \ DoD	VL	L	M	H
NM	Z	Z	Z	Z
LN	Z	Z	Z	Z
Z	z	Z	Z	Z
L	Z	Z	ML	ML
M	ML	ML	ML	M
H	H	M	Z	H

P_b				
Pdem \ DoD	VL	L	M	H
NM	Z	Z	Z	NC
LN	Z	Z	N	N
Z	Z	Z	Z	Z
L	P	P	NC	NC
M	P	P	P	Z
H	PC	PC	P	Z

T_{break}				
B_{req} \ DoD	VL	L	M	H
L	M	M	L	L
M	M	M	M	M
H	M	H	H	H

- Engine power (P_{ICE}) was specified in the universe of discourse between 0 and 55000 W by the limit of operation of ICE, with term set Z (zero), L (low), ML (medium low), M (medium) and H (high) represented by their respective sets fuzzy. The fuzzy rules for engine power are presented in Table 3.
- Power Battery (P_b): This output variable is specified in the same way as the electric motor, the universe of discourse between -8000 and 7500 W, since the battery must provide the same power as the required by the electric

motor. In this same way of the EM, the output variable is the set of terms
NC (negative constant), N (negative), Z (zero), P (positive) and PC (positive
constant) represented by their respective sets fuzzy. The rules are given by
Table 3.

– Braking Torque (T_{break}): This output variable corresponding to variable input
braking request (B_{req}), thus the variable output responds in proportion to
the input variable related to it, this case B_{req}. Therefore, this output variable
is specified in the universe of discourse between -5000 and 0 with the set of
terms L (low), M (medium) and H (high) as present in the Table 3. This output variable is enabled only if the demand power (P_{dem}) is on NM (negative
medium).

The rules were drawn up so that the DoD kept the value around its maximum equal to 0.45. This PMS was chosen using the operator Mandani which
is responsible for the relation of inference through minimum values between
input and output of the system. The last step (defuzzification) is required in
the replacement of this region by a single fuzzy value that acts as the controller
output. For this, it was used the maximum area of the first region fuzzy result
and determined the output value of the point at which the degree of relevance
reaches the first maximum value.

4   Simulation Results

The results are conducted by observing the fuel consumption and battery DoD
behavior during the simulated driving cycle. For the HEV simulations, the vehicle mass increases in 140 kg because the addition of EMs and batteries pack. The
simulations start with the battery fully charged ($DoD = 0$), the Table 4 presents
the fuel consumption and the consumption average (km/l) for the analyzed vehicles. Also is important to highlight that all simulated configurations were able
to fulfill the velocity profile of the FTP-75 standard, presenting a satisfactory
performance.

Even with the mass increase, the HEV configuration presents a lower fuel
consumption as compared to the conventional vehicle. Figure 4 show a comparison of the ICE operation points of the conventional and both analyzed HEV
control strategies, regarding the specific and volumetric fuel consumption maps.

Table 4. Fuel consumption (liter) by varying the mass of the vehicle.

Simulated vehicles	Mass [kg]	Fuel consumption [ml]	Average consumption [km/l]
Conventional ICE	980	660.0	18.18
HEV rules	1120	484.9	24.75
HEV fuzzy	1120	443.9	27.09

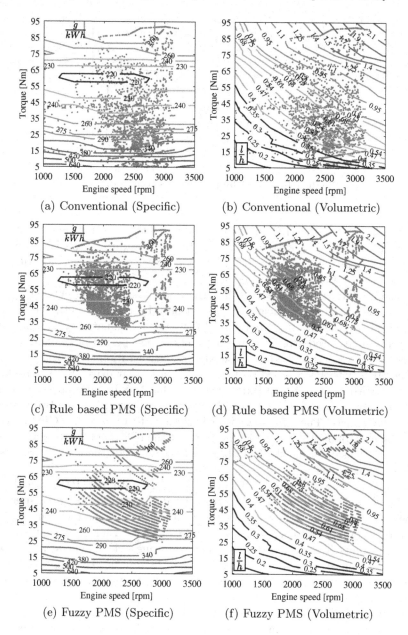

Fig. 4. HEV fuel consumption dispersion

According to the presented results is possible to see that the conventional vehicle ICE operates at lower efficiency regions if compared with the results reached by the HEV. The HEV avoids these low efficiency regions, due to its capacity of single electric propelling at low speed when the power demand is low.

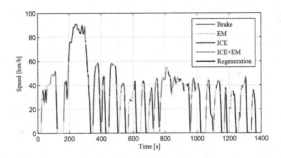

Fig. 5. HEV (PMS by rules) drive system profile.

Figure 5 shows that the HEV operates only when the power demand increases and overcomes the EM system capacity. In that condition, the EMs operate at maximum capacity and the ICE fulfill the power demand, keeping the ICE running in a good consumption region.

When the battery *DoD* reaches 45% the PMS based on rules cuts off the use of EMs (200 s) and the vehicle is propelled only by the ICE until the battery recharges, by regeneration, a minimum charge. In the simulated cycle it happens during the high speed stretch that represents a long period of discharge when the use of the EMs is limited in the next three acceleration stretches.

The HEV with PMS based on fuzzy shows a similar drive system profile as compared with the rule based PMS. However, the PMS based on fuzzy presents a better power management between both drive systems when the two systems propel the vehicle. The PMS based on fuzzy acts to reduce the ICE fuel consumption controlling the power demand so that the ICE operates consuming less fuel and at the same time the PMS based on fuzzy avoids the EMs operation at the maximum capacity to reduce the battery discharges.

Comparing the PMS based fuzzy (Fig. 4e, f) with the PMS rule based (Fig. 4c, d), it is possible to observe that the ICE operation points dispersion, in the case of rule based, is concentrated at the lower specific fuel consumption region of the map. However, the fuzzy PMS presents a large concentration of operation points in a region of lower engine torque, which represents a worst efficiency region as compared to rule based PMS results. Although, the fuzzy PMS presents lower fuel consumption between the simulated vehicle configurations (Table 4).

The fuzzy PMC reaches fuel savings by means of meeting the power demand in a ICE region, with a minimum fuel consumption, however it is not necessarily the best efficiency region of the ICE. These maps show that the fuel consumption increases with the engine torque and speed. The engine speed is defined by the vehicle longitudinal speed and the powertrain transmission ratio, however it is possible to reduce the ICE torque by transferring part of the power demand to the EMs system that will reduce the engine fuel consumption. By this reason, the PMS based fuzzy does not operate at the excellent efficiency region even though operates in a good efficiency with less fuel consumption. Moreover, keep the

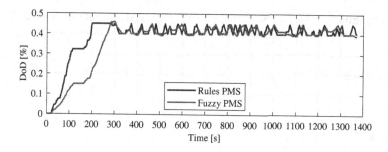

Fig. 6. Behavior battery for PMS using rules and PMS using fuzzy.

engine running at the best efficiency region cloud decrease the battery charge drive range, resulting in the bets combustion performance, while the electric auxiliary driving is available, but limiting the HEV PMC after the maximum *DoD* is reached. Figure 6 shows the *DoD* behavior for the both HEV PMS strategies.

As demonstrated, in the PMS using rules the *DoD* reaches the maximum discharge in 200 s of the driving cycle, and consequently oscillates between maximum and minimum values of charge and discharge because of the EMs breaking regeneration process. Using the PMS based on fuzzy, the battery is discharged until the limit of 300 s and after the battery is between maximum and minimum limits of charge and discharge due to constant request from EMs operation. However, the battery and hence the EM are ordered at a lower frequency when considering PMS using fuzzy, so this PMS performs better management of propulsion sources.

5 Conclusion

In this paper, two PMS were studied and developed. The proposed methods are classified into deterministic: based on rules and fuzzy. Both PMS strategies were developed in order to obtain the lower fuel consumption of the ICE. The presented results, shown that the HEV presented an expressive 30% fuel savings as compared to the conventional vehicle, keeping similar performance in urban driving conditions.

Comparing the performance of the rule-based and the fuzzy logic controllers, the fuzzy PMC was 8% more efficient, regarding fuel consumption, due to its better power split distributions between the ICE and EMs, which decreases the battery discharges, extending its range. Once the battery is not fully discharged in the implemented controllers, the power supply will not be compromised. When the battery reaches the maximum *DoD* value, the regenerative braking enables the its recharge until a minimum charge value that allows a new discharge.

Finally, the fuzzy PMC was selected, due to its robustness and adaptation capabilities, which are superior to the deterministic rule-based method. Consequently, for online implementation, the fuzzy method is an appropriate choice.

Acknowledgment. This work was supported by the Federal University of Technology - UTFPR and the University of Campinas - UNICAMP.

References

1. Holjevac, N., Cheli, F., Gobbi, M.: Multi-objective vehicle optimization: comparison of combustion engine, hybrid and electric powertrains. Proc. Inst. Mech. Eng. Part D J. Autom. Eng. **234**(2–3), 469–487 (2020)
2. Eckert, J.J., Silva, L.C.A., Costa, E.S., Santiciolli, F.M., Corrêa, F.C., Dedini, F.G.: Optimization of electric propulsion system for a hybridized vehicle. Mech. Based Des. Struct. Mach. **47**(2), 175–200 (2019)
3. Eckert, J.J., Santiciolli, F.M., Yamashita, R.Y., Corrêa, F.C., Silva, L.C., Dedini, F.G.: Fuzzy gear shifting control optimisation to improve vehicle performance, fuel consumption and engine emissions. IET Control Theory Appl. **13**(16), 2658–2669 (2019)
4. Eckert, J.J., Santiciolli, F.M., Corrêa, F.C., Dedini, F.G., et al.: Design of an aftermarket hybridization kit: reducing costs and emissions considering a local driving cycle. Vehicles **2**(1), 210–235 (2020)
5. van Reeven, V., Hofman, T.: Multi-level energy management for hybrid electric vehicles—part I. Vehicles **1**(1), 3–40 (2019)
6. Bayindir, K.Ç., Gözüküçük, M.A., Teke, A.: A comprehensive overview of hybrid electric vehicle: powertrain configurations, powertrain control techniques and electronic control units. Energy Convers. Manag. **52**(2), 1305–1313 (2011)
7. Cipek, M., Pavković, D., Petrić, J.: A control-oriented simulation model of a power-split hybrid electric vehicle. Appl. Energy **101**, 121–133 (2013)
8. Schouten, N.J., Salman, M.A., Kheir, N.A.: Fuzzy logic control for parallel hybrid vehicles. IEEE Trans. Control Syst. Technol. **10**(3), 460–468 (2002)
9. Wu, J., Zhang, C.H., Cui, N.X.: Fuzzy energy management strategy for a hybrid electric vehicle based on driving cycle recognition. Int. J. Automot. Technol. **13**(7), 1159–1167 (2012). https://doi.org/10.1007/s12239-012-0119-z
10. Eckert, J.J., de Alkmin Silva, L.C., Dedini, F.G., Corrêa, F.C.: Electric vehicle powertrain and fuzzy control multi-objective optimization, considering dual hybrid energy storage systems. IEEE Trans. Veh. Technol. **69**(4), 3773–3782 (2020)
11. Barbosa, T.P., Eckert, J.J., Silva, L.C.A., da Silva, L.A.R., Gutiérrez, J.C.H., Dedini, F.G.: Gear shifting optimization applied to a flex-fuel vehicle under real driving conditions. Mech. Based Des. Struct. Mach. 1–18 (2020). https://doi.org/10.1080/15397734.2020.1769650
12. Waltermann, P.: Modelling and control of the longitudinal and lateral dynamics of a series hybrid vehicle. In: Proceedings of the 1996 IEEE International Conference on Control Applications, pp. 191–198. IEEE (1996)

Alternative Proposals and Its Applications

FCM Algorithm: Analysis of the Membership Function Influence and Its Consequences for Fuzzy Clustering

Luis Mantilla[1]([✉])[iD] and Yessenia Yari[2]

[1] Universidad Católica de Trujillo Benedicto XVI, Trujillo, Peru
l.mantillas@uct.edu.pe
[2] Universidad Católica San Pablo, Arequipa, Peru
ydyari@ucsp.edu.pe

Abstract. Image segmentation in satellite images is a task widely investigated since we can extract some information of an image and analyze it. We propose to use a weighted factor for each of the distances used to calculate the degree of membership of each element to the cluster. In this way, we seek to reduce the influence of the upper and the lower bounds on the FCM equation. This paper reports preliminary results of the experiments and shows that the proposed algorithm performs accurately on a real dataset. For the evaluation of the algorithm, different cluster validity indexes are employed.

Keywords: Satellite image · Clustering · Segmentation · Fuzzy C-means · Fuzzy clustering

1 Introduction

Image Segmentation is an essential step in image processing because we can divide the image into multiple sub-images. Generally, each sub-image has different kinds of information, or many of them are similar in such a way that we can group or classified them. The information we can obtain could be the color, intensity, or texture. For solving the problem, we should find a technique or algorithm that helps to split the image taking into consideration several aspects such as the type of image, the characteristics that the image has or the characteristics that should be extracted, etc.

Image segmentation of Satellite images is used in many areas such as mining, military, agriculture, etc. Those images contain information to analyze and to process. The problems related to these activities could be solved by identifying the better solution or proposing efficient methods. There are many techniques to help us to split the image such us Fuzzy theory, Partial Differential Equation (PDE), Artificial Neural Network (ANN), threshold based image segmentation, and Region based image segmentation [8].

© Springer Nature Switzerland AG 2021
A. D. Orjuela-Cañón et al. (Eds.): IEEE ColCACI 2020, CCIS 1346, pp. 119–132, 2021.
https://doi.org/10.1007/978-3-030-69774-7_9

The process to classify the patterns in an image is named clustering. There are two main clustering strategies: the hard clustering and the fuzzy clustering [9]. Hard clustering assigns each point of the dataset only to one cluster, and on the other hand, Fuzzy clustering is a soft segmentation method since it employes Fuzzy set theory [13] and introduces the idea of partial membership. The Fuzzy C-means (FCM) algorithm [2] is one of the most used in image segmentation because it has robust characteristics for ambiguity, it captures more information [11] than hard segmentation, and it is robust to noise and to other imaging artifacts [9].

Many authors proposed different algorithms to solve the problem, for example, Krinidis and Chatzis [9] have developed the Fuzzy Logic Information C-Means Clustering (FLICM) algorithm, where the authors incorporate a new factor in the objective function of FCM. This method is independent of the types of noise, incorporates local spatial and the local gray level relationship. The fuzzy local constraints can automatically be determined, and the balance between image details and noise is automatically achieved by the fuzzy local constraints. Likewise, Kannan et al. [7] proposed a Novel Fuzzy Clustering C-Means Algorithm (NFCM) where they presented a center knowledge method to reduce the running time of the algorithm. The advantage of NFCM is that it can be applied at an early phase of automated data analysis, and it deals effectively with image intensity inhomogeneities and noise of the image.

Other authors combine the FCM with space color such as Kalista et al. [6], who created the PFCM (Possibilistic Fuzzy C-Means) where clustering avoids various shortcomings of FCM and PCM (Possibilistic C-Means). The PFCM addresses the noise sensitivity problem of FCM and answers the coincident clusters problem in PCM clustering. Furthermore, the authors incorporate the color based segmentation, i.e. they transformed images from RGB color space into HSL space. Ganesan and Rijini [5] proposed an efficient satellite image segmentation based in YIQ and Modified FCM, where first the satellite image in RGB color space is transformed into YIQ; next the component Y (luminance which is very similar to the grayscale) is equalized using a histogram to increase the contrast on the luminance image; and finally, apply Modified FCM clustering (FCM + spacial information).

Feng et al. [4] created FQABC, in which they combine fuzzy C-means (FCM) and four-chain quantum bee colony optimization (QABC). In the FQABC algorithm, firstly, the four chains quantum encoding method is introduced to the artificial bee colony (ABC) algorithm to propose the QABC algorithm. Then, QABC algorithm is applied to search for the optimal initial clustering centers of FCM. The FQABC algorithm overcomes the drawbacks of FCM, which is sensitive to initial clustering centers and noisy data. It performs better in convergence, segmentation accuracy, time complexity, and robustness.

Singn and Garg [12] proposed a $SCFCW_{mf}$ approach for satellite image segmentation to extract relevant class information, which shows the existing objects, namely, concrete area, healthy trees and vegetation, shadow, and road area. The image segmentation process requires some prior knowledge; therefore, $SCFCW_{mf}$ incorporates it to express the unsupervised FCM algorithm in a better way and hence obtain the most accurate clustering results, so that the $SCFCW_{mf}$ approach has flexible initialization for satellite and added spatial constraints (SCs). The objective function is also modified iteratively by the semi-supervised approaches. However, the well-defined weights correspond to each attribute for comparing and differentiating between the desired class and the classified one, using the proposed approach. Furthermore, this $SCFCW_{mf}$ approach is also used to speed up the clustering process to achieve the finest initial clustering centers close to the actual clustering centers with the adjustment of prior knowledge.

Finally, Mantilla et al. [10] created a novel Fuzzy Probabilistic Clustering Algorithm. The authors added a factor into the objective function, whose estimation needs the probability of occurrence of the intensity values of pixels. Besides, the proposed model computes the parameter of the Gaussian function, which determines the weight of the contribution of the neighbors of a pixel.

In this paper, we present the revision of the variables that compose the FCM equation, especially the degree of membership. In order to evaluate this term, it is necessary to apply mathematical analysis to determine the more relevant terms, and in this way, be able to analyze the upper and lower bounds. Next, we conclude that the sum of the distances between the centroids and each element has a high degree of influence on the FCM equation. Therefore, we propose to employ a Gaussian model, which provides a weighted factor to each of the distances; and as a result, it reduces the influence of the bounds of the FCM equation.

The rest of this paper is organized as follows. In Sect. 2, we present the details about Fuzzy clustering. Thereafter, we analyze the FCM equation in Sect. 3. Our proposed method is described in Sect. 4, and the results are presented in Sect. 5. Finally, the conclusions and some analyses about future works are drawn in Sect. 6.

2   Clustering and Fuzzy Clustering

The elements of a dataset can be quantitative, qualitative or both. In this paper, the dataset used contains quantitative features, which were obtained by discretizing the light spectrum.

Let be X a dataset of n elements, where each element x_j is composed by k features that are stored in a vector, i.e., $x_j = [x_1, x_2, x_3, \ldots, x_k], x_j \in \mathbb{R}^k$. Notice that we use the consensus notation of pattern recognition, i.e., the columns of the X matrix represent patterns or elements, and the rows represent features or attributes. For our case of study, each column represents the values for a range of the light spectrum.

On the other hand, a cluster is a group of elements that are similar to each other compared to the elements of other groups. In this paper, the term similarity must be understood as a mathematical similarity, which is usually defined by norms.

The process of clustering can be approached from two perspectives: one called hard clustering, in which each element of a dataset belongs to one cluster and do not belongs the rest of them; and the other called soft clustering, in which each element can belong to more than one cluster with a certain degree of membership. Under these perspectives, fuzzy clustering is a particular type of soft clustering.

In hard clustering, a set of c clusters is a partition of X, i.e., a set whose elements A_i are subsets of X such that these three constraints are met:

$$\bigcup_{i=1}^{c} A_i = X, \tag{1}$$

$$A_i \cap A_j = \emptyset, i \le i \neq j \le c, \tag{2}$$

$$\emptyset \subset A_i \in X, 1 \le i \le c. \tag{3}$$

The degree of membership μ_{ij} of the j-th element to the i-th cluster can be 0 or 1, i.e., $\mu_{ij} \in \{0, 1\}$.

Generally, a cluster i is represented by its centroid, v_i. On the other hand, in fuzzy clustering, the degree of membership μ_{ij} must meet the following restrictions:

$$\mu_{ij} \in [0, 1], 1 \le i \le c, 1 \le j \le n, \tag{4}$$

$$\sum_{i=1}^{c} \mu_{ij} = 1, 1 \le j \le n, \tag{5}$$

$$0 < \sum_{j=1}^{n} \mu_{ij} < n, 1 \le i \le c. \tag{6}$$

3   Fuzzy C-Means Method

The Fuzzy C-Means algorithm (FCM), introduced by Dunn [3] and developed by Bezdek in 1980 [1] is one of the most well-known fuzzy clustering algorithms. A great number of fuzzy algorithms have been derived from it. FCM algorithm aims to minimize the objective function $J(U, V)$,

$$J(U, V) = \sum_{i=1}^{c} \sum_{j=1}^{n} \mu_{ij}^{m} ||x_j - v_i||^2, \tag{7}$$

where, $||x_j - v_i||$ is the Euclidean distance between j-th element and the centroid of cluster i; m is a parameter that determines the fuzziness of the obtained clusters, and it lies in the interval $[1, \infty)$. Generally, μ_{ij}'s are stored in a matrix, denoted $U \in \mathbb{R}^{c \times n}$, i.e., $U = [\mu_{ij}]$, and v_i's are stored in a vector $V = [v_1, v_2, \ldots, v_c]$. Besides, for sake of simplicity, we denote $||x_j - v_i||$ as d_{ji}.

3.1 Fuzzy C-Means Algorithm

In order to minimize the objective function defined in Eq. (7), the FCM algorithm iterates by alternating between the minimization of $J(U|V^*)$ and $J(V|U^*)$. More precisely, for a specific iteration, the FCM algorithm minimizes the function J for a fixed V^*, by updating U; and subsequently, it minimizes the function J for a fixed U^*, by computing V.

Hence, both the estimation of U, computed via,

$$u_{ij} = \frac{1}{\sum_{k=1}^{c} \left(\frac{||x_j - v_i||}{||x_j - v_k||} \right)^{\frac{2}{m-1}}}, \tag{8}$$

and V, calculated via,

$$v_i = \frac{\sum_{j=1}^{n} (u_{ij})^m x_j}{\sum_{j=1}^{n} (u_{ij})^m}, \tag{9}$$

mainly describe the behavior of the algorithm.

Algorithm 1. Fuzzy C-Means (FCM)

Input: c is the number of clusters, $c > 1$, n is the number of examples of the dataset X, and ϵ is an error, $\epsilon > 0$, defined by the user.

1: Set $t = 0$.
2: Initialize randomly $\mu_{ij}^{(0)}, \forall ij, 1 \leq j \leq n, 1 \leq i \leq c$
         ▷ The superindex in $\mu_{ij}^{(0)}$ indicates the value of μ_{ij} computed in time $t = 0$.
3: Initialize randomly $V = [v_1, v_2, \ldots, v_c]$.
4: **repeat**
5:     $t = t + 1$
6:     Compute $v_j = \frac{\sum_{i=1}^{n} \mu_{ij}^m}{\sum_{i=1}^{n} \mu_{ij}^m} x_j, \forall j, 1 \leq j \leq c$
7:     Compute $\mu_{ij}^{(t)}, \forall i, 1 \leq i \leq n, 1 \leq j \leq c$

$$\mu_{ij}^{(t)} = \frac{1}{\sum_{k=1}^{c} \left(\frac{d_{ij}}{d_{ik}} \right)^{\left(\frac{2}{m-1}\right)}}, d_{ij} = ||x_j - v_i||^2$$

8: **until** $\max_{i,j}(|\mu_{ij}^{(t)} - \mu_{ij}^{(t-1)}|) < \epsilon$

3.2 Analysis of FCM Algorithm

In this section, we focus on the analysis of the fuzzy membership function of a particular example to a specific cluster.

Analysis of the Estimation of μ_{ij}. We analyze the function used to calculate the degree of membership μ_{ij}, and show that the term $d_{ij}^{\frac{2}{m-1}}$ plays an essential role in the estimation of μ_{ij}. Also, we show the behavior of μ_{ij}, by using limits when $d_{ij}^{\frac{2}{m-1}}$ tends both to infinity and to zero. For doing so, we take the Eq. (8) and obtain that:

$$
\begin{aligned}
u_{ij} &= \frac{1}{\sum_{k=1}^{c}\left(\frac{\|x_j - v_i\|}{\|x_j - v_k\|}\right)^{\frac{2}{m-1}}} \\[2ex]
&= \frac{1}{\left(\frac{d_{ji}}{d_{j1}}\right)^{\frac{2}{m-1}} + \left(\frac{d_{ji}}{d_{j2}}\right)^{\frac{2}{m-1}} + \cdots + \left(\frac{d_{ji}}{d_{jc}}\right)^{\frac{2}{m-1}}} \\[2ex]
&= \frac{1}{d_{ji}^{\frac{2}{m-1}}\left[\left(\frac{1}{d_{j1}}\right)^{\frac{2}{m-1}} + \left(\frac{1}{d_{j2}}\right)^{\frac{2}{m-1}} + \cdots + \left(\frac{1}{d_{jc}}\right)^{\frac{2}{m-1}}\right]} \\[2ex]
&= \frac{1}{d_{ji}^{\frac{2}{m-1}}\left[\dfrac{\dfrac{\prod_{k=1}^{c} d_{jk}^{\frac{2}{m-1}}}{d_{j1}^{\frac{2}{m-1}}} + \dfrac{\prod_{k=1}^{c} d_{jk}^{\frac{2}{m-1}}}{d_{j2}^{\frac{2}{m-1}}} + \cdots + \dfrac{\prod_{k=1}^{c} d_{jk}^{\frac{2}{m-1}}}{d_{jc}^{\frac{2}{m-1}}}}{\prod_{k=1}^{c} d_{jk}^{\frac{2}{m-1}}}\right]} \\[2ex]
&= \frac{\prod_{k=1}^{c} d_{jk}^{\frac{2}{m-1}}}{d_{ji}^{\frac{2}{m-1}}\left[\dfrac{\prod_{k=1}^{c} d_{jk}^{\frac{2}{m-1}}}{d_{j1}^{\frac{2}{m-1}}} + \dfrac{\prod_{k=1}^{c} d_{jk}^{\frac{2}{m-1}}}{d_{j2}^{\frac{2}{m-1}}} + \cdots + \dfrac{\prod_{k=1}^{c} d_{jk}^{\frac{2}{m-1}}}{d_{jc}^{\frac{2}{m-1}}}\right]} \\[2ex]
&= \frac{\dfrac{\prod_{k=1}^{c} d_{jk}^{\frac{2}{m-1}}}{d_{ji}^{\frac{2}{m-1}}}}{\dfrac{\prod_{k=1}^{c} d_{jk}^{\frac{2}{m-1}}}{d_{j2}^{\frac{2}{m-1}}} + \cdots + \dfrac{\prod_{k=1}^{c} d_{jk}^{\frac{2}{m-1}}}{d_{jc}^{\frac{2}{m-1}}}} \\[2ex]
&= \frac{\prod_{k=1, k\neq i}^{c} d_{jk}^{\frac{2}{m-1}}}{\prod_{k=1, k\neq 1}^{c} d_{jk}^{\frac{2}{m-1}} + \cdots + \prod_{k=1, k\neq c}^{c} d_{jk}^{\frac{2}{m-1}}} \\[2ex]
&= \frac{\prod_{k=1, k\neq i}^{c} d_{jk}^{\frac{2}{m-1}}}{\underbrace{\prod_{k=1, k\neq i}^{c} d_{jk}^{\frac{2}{m-1}} + \prod_{k=1, k\neq 1}^{c} d_{jk}^{\frac{2}{m-1}} + \cdots + \prod_{k=1, k\neq c}^{c} d_{jk}^{\frac{2}{m-1}}}_{\text{all the terms include the factor } d_{ji}^{\frac{2}{m-1}}}}
\end{aligned}
\tag{10}
$$

$$= \frac{\displaystyle\prod_{k=1,k\neq i}^{c} d_{jk}^{\frac{2}{m-1}}}{\left[\displaystyle\prod_{k=1,k\neq i}^{c} d_{jk}^{\frac{2}{m-1}}\right] + d_{ji}^{\frac{2}{m-1}}\left[\displaystyle\sum_{g=1}^{c}\left(\displaystyle\prod_{k=1,k\neq i,k\neq g}^{c} d_{jg}^{\frac{2}{m-1}}\right)\right]} \qquad (11)$$

We define a as,

$$a = \prod_{k=1,k\neq i}^{c} d_{jk}^{\frac{2}{m-1}}; \qquad (12)$$

then, by replacing a in u_{ij}, we obtain that

$$u_{ij} = \frac{a}{a + d_{ik}^{\frac{2}{m-1}}\left[\displaystyle\sum_{g=1}^{c}\left(\displaystyle\prod_{k=1,k\neq i,k\neq g}^{c} d_{jg}^{\frac{2}{m-1}}\right)\right]}. \qquad (13)$$

Through the mathematical analysis of the membership function, we can determine the limits for the different values of u_{ij}. To determine the influence of the term a, we will analyze the behavior of the Eq. (13) when the term $d_{ji}^{\frac{2}{m-1}}$ tends to zero and when it tends to infinity, as shown below.

When $d_{ji}^{\frac{2}{m-1}} \to 0$ we obtain that,

$$O(u_{ij}) = \lim_{d_{ji}^{\frac{2}{m-1}}\to 0} \frac{a}{a + d_{ji}^{\frac{2}{m-1}} * \sum_{g=1}^{c}\left(\frac{\prod_{k=1}^{c} d_{jk}^{\frac{2}{m-1}}}{d_{jg}^{\frac{2}{m-1}}}\right)} = 1. \qquad (14)$$

In Eq. 14, we found the upper bound of the membership function when $d_{ji}^{\frac{2}{m-1}}$ tends to 0 then $O(u_{ij}) = 1$.

On the other hand, when $d_{ji}^{\frac{2}{m-1}} \to \infty$ we get that,

$$\Omega(u_{ij}) = b = \lim_{d_{ji}^{\frac{2}{m-1}}\to\infty^{+}} \frac{a}{a + d_{ji}^{\frac{2}{m-1}} * \sum_{g=1}^{c}\left(\frac{\prod_{k=1}^{c} d_{jk}^{\frac{2}{m-1}}}{d_{jg}^{\frac{2}{m-1}}}\right)} = 0, \qquad (15)$$

i.e. the lower bound of u_{ji} when it tends to ∞^{+} equals 0.

Then, by using the definition of limit, we see that there is a value ε_b, small enough such that $\|u_{ij} - b\| < \varepsilon_b$. Following Eqs. (14) and (15), we see that the function is upper bounded by $O(u_{ij})$ and lower bounded by $b = \Omega(u_{ij})$, respectively. The existence of this numerical value allows us to show the influence of the $d_{ji}^{\frac{2}{m-1}}$ in the calculation of the degree of membership. Figure 1 can be interpreted as the value assigned to each of the elements, being the existence of ε_b the main cause of the values assigned to u_{ji} and also shows the existence of ε_b and its influence on the membership function.

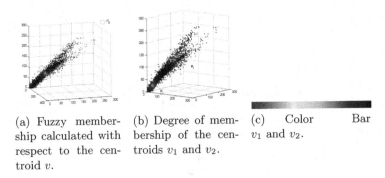

(a) Fuzzy member-   (b) Degree of mem-   (c)   Color   Bar
ship calculated with   bership of the cen- v_1 and v_2.
respect to the cen-   troids v_1 and v_2.
troid v.

Fig. 1. This image shows graphically the scattering elements in a multispectral image within a three-dimensional space and we add the information concerning the degree of membership using color. (Color figure online)

In other words, we can say that there exists u_{ij} that complies with $\|u_{ij} - b\| > \varepsilon_b$, which results in the value assigned to $u_{ij} \simeq u_{mi}, j \neq m = 1, 2, \ldots, n$, where $i \in c$.

For a better understanding of the implications of the existence of these limits in the calculation of the degree of membership, we plot, in Fig. 1, a dataset and two centroids with their respective membership value assigned to each of the clusters. From this, we can say that the number of elements that influence mostly on an estimation of u_{ij} is smaller in comparison with the other elements.

Finally, as part of the analysis, we show the implications of the different values assigned to m. The degree of belonging was calculated for one of the centroids, then a color was assigned by taking the color bar shown in the Fig. 2(r). Each of the images shows the degree of belonging of the elements to the centroid when the exponent m changes. We can state that when $m = 2$ the variation of the degrees of belonging between two close elements is small and that it follows a Gaussian dispersion of the probability values.

4   Proposal

The Gaussian distribution is a probability distribution extensively used by the scientific community for modeling purposes, not only because it provides a good approximation for many processes in nature, but also because it follows the central limit theorem, which states that the sampling distribution of the mean for a particular variable approximates a Gaussian distribution irrespective of the original distribution in the population as long as we are given a large enough sample size.

From the previous analysis of the membership function, we conclude that if the sum of $\left(\frac{\|x_j - u_i\|}{\|x_j - u_k\|} \right)^{\frac{2}{m-1}}$ exceeds (is greater or is lower) the lower bound of the membership function then there will be no distinction between the calculated

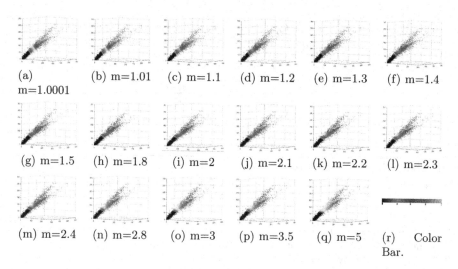

(a)   (b) m=1.01   (c) m=1.1   (d) m=1.2   (e) m=1.3   (f) m=1.4
m=1.0001

(g) m=1.5   (h) m=1.8   (i) m=2   (j) m=2.1   (k) m=2.2   (l) m=2.3

(m) m=2.4   (n) m=2.8   (o) m=3   (p) m=3.5   (q) m=5   (r)   Color
                                                                      Bar.

Fig. 2. Images obtained by computing the degree of membership for one centroid. The color assignment was carried out according the color bar presented in 2(r). (Color figure online)

values for different elements. As a solution to this problem, we propose to weight each value $\left(\frac{||x_j-u_i||}{||x_j-u_k||}\right)^{\frac{2}{m-1}}$, such that the difference of the elements is increased.

For this purpose, we used the Gaussian function, which allows to estimate the contribution factor of each value calculated in the overall sum, avoiding that the equation reaches its lower level. We used the Eq. (16), which estimates the probability density at point k, where k is replaced by the value calculated for $\left(\frac{||x_j-u_i||}{||x_j-u_k||}\right)^{\frac{2}{m-1}}$, that is,

$$f(x_j, v_i, v_k) = \frac{\frac{1}{\sigma\sqrt{2}}e^{-\left(\frac{\left(\frac{||x_j-v_i||}{||x_j-v_k||}\right)^2}{2\sigma^2}\right)}}{\sum_{l=1}^{c}\frac{1}{\sigma\sqrt{2}}e^{-\left(\frac{\left(\frac{||x_j-v_i||}{||x_j-v_l||}\right)^2}{2\sigma^2}\right)}}, \quad l \neq i; \quad (16)$$

where, is the standard deviation σ, defined as:

$$\sigma = \sqrt{\frac{\sum_{k=1}^{c}\left(\frac{||x_j-v_k||}{||x_j-v_i||}\right)^2}{c}}, \quad k \neq i \quad (17)$$

Finally, we include the new term f in the fuzzy membership equation as a weighting factor. So, the line 7 in the Algorithm 1 is replaced by Eq. (18).

$$u_{ij} = \frac{1}{\sum_{k=1}^{c} f(x_j, v_i, v_k) * \left(\frac{||x_j - v_i||}{||x_j - v_k||} \right)^{\frac{2}{m-1}}}. \tag{18}$$

Finally, the proposed Algorithm is presented as follows.

Algorithm 2. Gaussian Fuzzy C-Means (GFCM)

Input: c is the number of clusters, $c > 1$, n is the number of examples of the dataset X, and ϵ is the error defined by a user, $\epsilon > 0$.

1: Set $t = 0$.
2: Initialize randomly $\mu_{ij}^{(0)}, \forall_{ij}, 1 \le j \le n, 1 \le i \le c$ ▷ The superindex in $\mu_{ij}^{(0)}$ indicates the value of μ_{ij} computed in time $t = 0$.
3: Initialize randomly $V = [v_1, v_2, \ldots, v_c]$.
4: **repeat**
5:     $t = t + 1$
6:     Compute

$$v_j = \frac{\sum_{i=1}^{n} \mu_{ij}^m}{\sum_{i=1}^{n} \mu_{ij}^m} x_j, \forall_j, 1 \le j \le c$$

7:     Compute $\mu_{ij}^{(t)}, \forall_i, 1 \le i \le n, 1 \le j \le c$

$$u_{ij} = \frac{1}{\sum_{k=1}^{c} f(x_j, v_i, v_k) * \left(\frac{||x_j - v_i||}{||x_j - v_k||} \right)^{\frac{2}{m-1}}}.$$

8: **until** $\max_{i,j}(|\mu_{ij}^{(t)} - \mu_{ij}^{(t-1)}|) < \epsilon$

---

5 Experiments and Results

5.1 Dataset and Parameter Setting

For conducting the experiments, we used a dataset of 16 multispectral images of 500×500 pixels with 5 bands. In Fig. 3, we show a graphic representation of

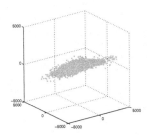

Fig. 3. Graphic representation in the three-dimensional space of the dispersion of the pixels within the test images.

the dispersion of the pixels in one of the test images is shown. The equivalent distribution of the elements was generated using the PCA algorithm. This image shows a general overview of the dispersion of the elements within the image. However, the density of the elements have a greater influence on the clustering process, this phenomenon has the greatest relevance.

The algorithms were implemented using the Julia v1.0 language, on a computer with Intel Core (TM) i5-4200H, 2.80 GHz, and 8 GB memory. The experiments confirm the existence of the upper and lower bounds in the fuzzy membership equation and its influence on the clustering algorithms. To compare the different structures generated by the clustering algorithms, we used the internal validation indices. Each of the algorithms was executed over a number of clusters comprised between the range [2, 6], for each of the images. Besides, the initial matrix of fuzzy membership was the same for each of the algorithms. By doing so, both algorithms were provided with the same initial conditions.

5.2 Experimental Results and Discussions

The analysis of the results obtained from each of the algorithms begins by organizing the data relative to each index (Partition Coefficient (PC), Modified Partition Coefficient (MPC), Partition Entropy (PE), Fuzzy Hypervolume (FHV), Fukuyama and Sugeno (FS) and Xie-Beni (XB)). For this, the results are summarized in the Tables 1, 2. Each one is referred to each of the two algorithms. In addition, each table consists of 6 rows, which present the results obtained for the

Table 1. Results obtained using the FCM algorithm, with clusters between [2, 6] and the set of test images.

c	PC	PCM	PE	FS	FHV	XieBeni
2	0.780864	0.561728	0.51198	−3.01663e8	4.18728e13	0.285753
3	0.686266	0.529399	0.80249	−3.54486e8	2.79487e13	0.292027
4	0.618501	0.491335	1.03491	−4.71458e8	2.07936e13	0.3004
5	0.586959	0.483698	1.17584	−5.14159e8	1.75036e13	0.284291
6	0.539916	0.447899	1.35479	−5.29014e8	1.67295e13	0.283133

Table 2. Results obtained using the GFCM algorithm, with clusters between [2, 6] and the set of test images.

c	PC	PCM	PE	FS	FHV	XieBeni
2	0.901084	0.802169	0.241928	−4.28989e8	5.33099e13	0.310064
3	0.910211	0.865317	0.366916	−4.70885e8	5.83018e13	0.373774
4	0.912296	0.883061	0.467469	−6.88955e8	6.10213e13	0.408728
5	0.908239	0.885298	0.518834	−7.50304e8	7.91679e13	0.418227
6	0.900885	0.881062	0.595458	−8.69357e8	1.04626e14	0.440777

algorithm executed with a certain number of clusters. Each of the rows contains the average of the calculated indexes for the 16 test images.

Finally, the data collected in the previous tables are presented in Fig. 4. As can be seen, the main advantage of the proposed modification is a better organization of the objects in the clusters. In addition this is evidenced in the Fig. 5, in this it can be seen that the smaller the entropy, the greater similarity that the pixels present and consequently more regular areas are observed.

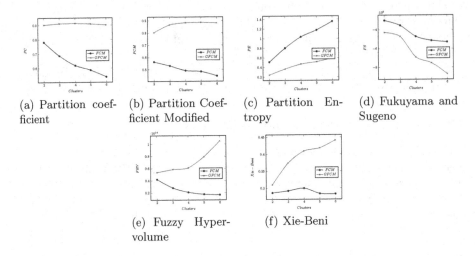

(a) Partition coefficient

(b) Partition Coefficient Modified

(c) Partition Entropy

(d) Fukuyama and Sugeno

(e) Fuzzy Hypervolume

(f) Xie-Beni

Fig. 4. Graphs of the values obtained for each of the indices, with reference to each of the algorithms.

As we can see there are numerous ways in which the results of the algorithms can be affected, among them we have; the distribution of the data will have a great impact on the groups to be generated, in the same way the equations that minimize the mean square error have an impact on the groups formed. Finally, a phenomenon not studied in this article is the influence of the intersections of the clusters formed in the final results.

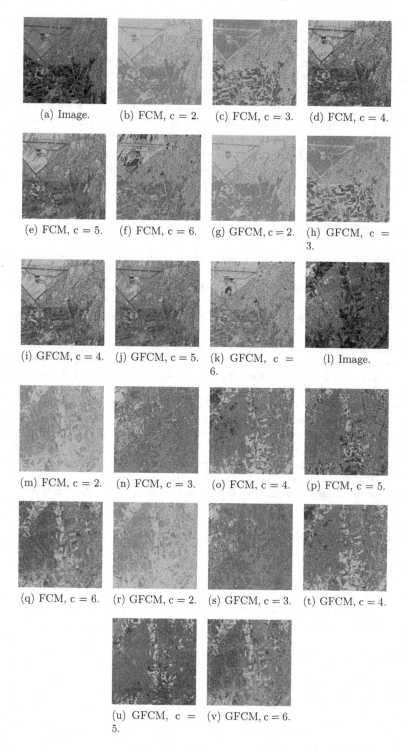

(a) Image.   (b) FCM, c = 2.   (c) FCM, c = 3.   (d) FCM, c = 4.

(e) FCM, c = 5.   (f) FCM, c = 6.   (g) GFCM, c = 2.   (h) GFCM, c = 3.

(i) GFCM, c = 4. (j) GFCM, c = 5.   (k) GFCM, c = 6.   (l) Image.

(m) FCM, c = 2.   (n) FCM, c = 3.   (o) FCM, c = 4.   (p) FCM, c = 5.

(q) FCM, c = 6.   (r) GFCM, c = 2.   (s) GFCM, c = 3.   (t) GFCM, c = 4.

(u) GFCM, c = 5. (v) GFCM, c = 6.

Fig. 5. Resulting images obtained from the segmentation process over the test images using the GFCM algorithm with [3, 7] clusters.

6   Conclusions

The present study sought to know the influence of the limits of the equations used in the FCM algorithm that minimizes the mean square error, as a result of the analysis it was possible to know that the analysis of the upper bound and the lower bound is essential in the clustering process, because they have an influence into the FCM equation. It is also necessary to know the distribution and scale of the elements because they have an influence on the minimization process of the mean square error. Finally, it is necessary to develop new models capable of not only increasing the difference between elements of different groupings, but also proposing models that do not have influence of their bounds.

References

1. Bezdek, J.C.: A convergence theorem for the fuzzy ISODATA clustering algorithms. IEEE Trans. Pattern Anal. Mach. Intell. **1**, 1–8 (1980)
2. Bezdek, J.C.: Pattern Recognition with Fuzzy Objective Function Algorithms. Springer, Heidelberg (2013)
3. Dunn, J.: Some recent investigations of a new fuzzy partitioning algorithm and its application to pattern classification problems (1974)
4. Feng, Y., Yin, H., Lu, H., Cao, L., Bai, J.: FCM-based quantum artificial bee colony algorithm for image segmentation. In: Proceedings of the 10th International Conference on Internet Multimedia Computing and Service, ICIMCS 2018, pp. 6:1–6:7. ACM, New York (2018)
5. Ganesan, P., Rajini, V.: YIQ color space based satellite image segmentation using modified FCM clustering and histogram equalization. In: 2014 International Conference on Advances in Electrical Engineering (ICAEE), pp. 1–5. IEEE (2014)
6. Kalist, V., Ganesan, P., Sathish, B., Jenitha, J.M.M., et al.: Possiblistic-fuzzy C-means clustering approach for the segmentation of satellite images in HSL color space. Procedia Comput. Sci. **57**, 49–56 (2015)
7. Kannan, S., Ramathilagam, S., Pandiyarajan, R., Sathya, A.: Fuzzy clustering approach in segmentation of T1-T2 brain MRI. Int. J. Recent Trends Eng. **2**(1), 157 (2009)
8. Khan, W.: Image segmentation techniques: a survey. J. Image Graph. **1**(4), 166–170 (2013)
9. Krinidis, S., Chatzis, V.: A robust fuzzy local information C-means clustering algorithm. IEEE Trans. Image Process. **19**(5), 1328–1337 (2010)
10. Mantilla, L., Yari, Y., Meza-Lovón, G.: A novel fuzzy probabilistic clustering algorithm for satellite image segmentation. In: 2018 IEEE International Conference on Fuzzy Systems (FUZZ-IEEE), pp. 1–7. IEEE (2018)
11. Pham, D.L., Prince, J.L.: An adaptive fuzzy C-means algorithm for image segmentation in the presence of intensity inhomogeneities. Pattern Recogn. Lett. **20**(1), 57–68 (1999)
12. Singh, P., Garg, R.D.: Classification of high resolution satellite images using spatial constraints-based fuzzy clustering. J. Appl. Remote Sens. **8**(1), 083526 (2014)
13. Zadeh, L.A.: Fuzzy sets. Inf. Control **8**(3), 338–353 (1965)

Echo State Network Performance Analysis Using Non-random Topologies

Diana Roca[1]([⊠])[iD], Liang Zhao[2][iD], Alex Choquenaira[1][iD], Daniela Milón[1][iD],
and Roselli Romero[1][iD]

[1] Instituto de Ciências Matemáticas e de Computação, Universidade de São Paulo,
São Carlos, SP, Brazil
{dianaroca,alexanderchf,danielafe7,rafrance}@usp.br
[2] Faculdade de Filosofía, Ciências e Letras, Universidade de São Paulo,
Ribeirão Preto, SP, Brazil
zhao@usp.br
https://www.icmc.usp.br/, https://www.ffclrp.usp.br/

Abstract. Echo State Network (ESN) has been widely studied and applied to many problems due to the simplicity of its training phase. This is because since in this network only the output weights are trained, avoiding to deal with the gradient's vanishing problem presents in most of the recurrent neural networks. However, this technique has been criticized recently because of the echo property limitation and its random topology that may cause chaotic activity in the reservoir layer. In this paper, we present an application of the classic ESN model modifying the reservoir topology to a non-random approaches: clustered and complex networks, as an alternative solution to the chaotic activity problem. Further, the modified and classical models are compared considering two study cases: Rössler and Lorenz systems. Numerical experiments show that the proposed model has a better performance than the classical model.

Keywords: Echo State Network · Reservoir Computing · Dynamics systems · Time series · Network complex

1 Introduction

Artificial Neural Networks are powerful techniques inspired by biological neural networks. At first, McCulloch and Pitts introduced an artificial neural network with simple threshold units called *perceptrons*, which can solve simple classification tasks in linearly separable datasets [2]. Later, feed-forward neural networks have been proposed to face more complex tasks that the *perceptron* network can not solve, like XOR function. Since then, more complex networks structures have been developed like, well-known, recurrent neural network (RNN) which differs, with the already mentioned networks, on having at least one cyclic pathway of synaptic connections. RNNs work well for non-linear dynamical system approximation however they have some disadvantages such as hyperparameters settings

© Springer Nature Switzerland AG 2021
A. D. Orjuela-Cañón et al. (Eds.): IEEE ColCACI 2020, CCIS 1346, pp. 133–146, 2021.
https://doi.org/10.1007/978-3-030-69774-7_10

and, mainly, the training phase, where all network weights need to be trained [4]. As an alternative solution to these, Reservoir Computing (RC) technique was proposed.

RC is a type of RNN, that is aroused as result of several approaches unification in literature work for time series prediction. Their main characteristic relies on the simplicity of its training phase because only the output weights are trained [15]. Liquid State Machines (LSMs), Backpropagation Decorrelation Neural Networks, and Echo State Network model (ESN) are types of RC. This model has one hidden layer that is called reservoir. It is built with sparse and random connections using a big number of neurons. ESN model is suitable for non-linear approximation problems such as: Identification Systems [5], Time Series Prediction [7], Pattern recognition [12], Modeling Neural Plasticity for Classification and Regression [20], among others.

The reservoir of ESN model is used as a processing layer and is not modified during its training phase. The reservoir state is determined by the history of its inputs and outputs. For good performance, this reservoir must satisfy a condition about its dynamics state (echo property). The dynamic state of the reservoir is influenced by the spectral radius, the highest eigenvalue of a matrix, which is a parameter that has a high impact over the performance model and the capacity of good estimations [3,18]. Although the ESN model inherits the main benefit of RC techniques (simple training phase), they have been criticized because the reservoir connections and the internal units are generated randomly. In consequence, when the tasks turn more difficult, the stability of the trained dynamics becomes a critical issue for the ESN training phase [6]. Besides, an optimal configuration about the reservoir settings is not guaranteed because of its lack of information about how the reservoir works. This is the main reason that has motivated the development of this work.

As an alternative to face the mentioned issue, modifications to the reservoir topology are being studied, such as [1,13] that proposed the implementation of complex networks to the reservoir topology of the classical ESN model, like Small World and Scale Free. In [10], it was proposed the incorporation of clusters to the reservoir topology. These changes were inspired in order to imitate some forms and learning mechanisms from the human brain which have hierarchical and distributed structure [8]. In the present work, we present an application of the classic ESN model modifying the reservoir topology to a clustered and complex networks topology as an alternative solution to the chaotic activity problem. Additionally, we compare the proposed and classical models in two study cases: Rössler and Lorenz systems.

The remaining sections are organized as it follows. In Sect. 2, it is presented some related works. A description of ESN is summarized in Sect. 3. Then, in Sect. 4, the results of experiments with the modify architecture of ESN model are presented. Finally, in Sect. 5, the conclusions and future works are presented.

2   Literature Review

As a solution to the randomness problem in the classical ESN model, several studies have been proposed, finding two main approaches: modification of weights [17] and modification of the reservoir's structure such as Multiple Loops Reservoir structure (MLR) model [14]. This last one is compared with the Adjacent-feedback loop Reservoir (ALR) model which strengthens connections within the reservoir and improves the skills of the classic model for the non-linear problems. The work also analyzes the influence of the parameters of the proposed model based on the prediction accuracy.

According to [4], the effectiveness of the ESN is strongly influenced by the size of the reservoir. For this reason, evolutionary algorithms have been used [11] to find an optimal number of neurons for the reservoir. The disadvantage is the computational cost, experience, and skill abilities that are required for those who use them. Attending to the same objective, a new ESN model known as Simple Cycle Reservoir Network (SCRN) [16] was introduced, where the reservoir was constructed deterministically. Initially, the proposed model considered a reservoir with a larger size than required using a pruning algorithm (Sensitive Iterated Pruning Algorithm) to optimize the numbers of neurons in the reservoir. So, the less sensitive neurons are turned off to optimize the number of required neurons to reach a good approximation.

Some references show a better performance of the ESN model than classical when modified the reservoir topology [1,10,13,19]. In [1,13], networks complex like Scale Free and Small World were used instead random connections as reservoir topology. In [10], three types of clustered networks were proposed using three clustering algorithms to generate the clusters. Finally, a clustered echo state network was formulated for the forecast of mobile communications traffic using the Fourier spectrum as prior knowledge to generate the functional clusters in [19].

3   Echo State Network Model

The Echo State Network (ESN) model is a new and robust type of recurrent neural network that has a hidden layer called reservoir with a fixed number of neurons known as reservoir units, where only the weights of the output layer are trained. We are going to consider an ESN constituted by K inputs units $\mathbf{x} = (x_1, x_2, x_3, \ldots, x_K)$, one hidden layer that consists of a reservoir with N internal units, $\mathbf{r} = (r_1, r_2, r_3, \ldots, r_N)$, where $\mathbf{r}$ represents the system state vector for some time t, and one output layer with L units, $\mathbf{y} = (y_1, y_2, y_3, \ldots, y_L)$.

The weights of the connections between the neurons are stored in the adjacency matrices: $W_{in}, W, W_{out}, W_{back}$ (the last one only exists is there is feedback), where W is the reservoir matrix which stores the weights of the units. These matrices have respectively the following dimensions: $N \times K, N \times N, L \times (K + N + L), N \times L$, respectively. Figure 1 is shown an example of an ESN classical model architecture.

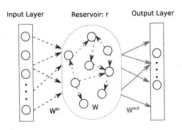

Fig. 1. Basic architecture of Echo State Network model [9].

For the ESN model to work, the dynamics of the reservoir must be damped. This condition is possible when the reservoir matrix satisfies the echo state property. According to Jaeger (2002) [4], we define the previous assumption in the next definition.

Echo State Property: A network has the echo state property if the current state of the network is only determined by the values of the past inputs and outputs. In other words for each internal unit of the reservoir, r_i, there is a e_i function, which is known as an echo function, which maps the input/output pair (x_i, y_i) of its history to the current state. Thus the current state for one reservoir's unit $r_i(n)$ in the time instance n is given by the Eq. (1)

$$r_i(n) = e_i((x(n), y(n)), (x(n-1), y(n-1)), \dots) \tag{1}$$

The echo state property is connected to algebraic properties of the reservoir matrix. In the practice is more difficult to guarantee the echo state property in a neural network, instead is useful to know when this property is not satisfied. In [4], Jaeger proposed a sufficient condition for the non-existence of echo states. This condition is based on the fact that if the corresponding reservoir matrix of an ESN model has a spectral radius greater than unity, the neural network does not have the echo states. The spectral radius of a matrix A, described in Eq. 2, is defined as the highest eigenvalue of a matrix.

$$\rho(A) := \max_i(|\lambda_i|), \quad \lambda_i \text{ is eigenvalue of } A \tag{2}$$

In consequence, the choice of the spectral radius ρ is very important for the success of ESN training. Small values of ρ means a fast dynamic reservoir, large values of ρ (close to the unity) mean slow dynamic reservoir. The model proposed here is inspired by the ideas and the network designed in [7]. The activation function for the internal units of the reservoir is given by:

$$\mathbf{r}(n+1) = (1-\alpha)\mathbf{r}(n) + \alpha f(W\mathbf{r}(n) + W_{in}\mathbf{x}(n) + \zeta) \tag{3}$$

where $0 < \alpha \le 1$ is the "leakage rate" which causes the reservoir to evolve more slowly as $\alpha \longrightarrow 0$, ζ represents the bias and the function $f = tanh$. The output of the network is given by:

$$\mathbf{y}(n) = W_{out}\mathbf{r}(n) + c \tag{4}$$

In the next section, we show the results of the experiments with the implementation of the clusters and complex networks in reservoir topology.

4   Experiments and Results

In this section, we show the results obtained based on the modifications proposed. For this, the classical ESN model is compared with clustered and complex reservoir topology, considering two study cases: Rössler and Lorenz systems to predict time series. Initially, the study cases for the prediction task are described and details of the preparation and implementation of the model are shown. The numerical results are summarized in tables and graphics.

4.1   Problem Statement

Lets consider two dynamic systems defined in (5) and (6). The input and output vectors of the system: $x(t)$, $y(t)$, $z(t) \in \mathbb{R}$, $\mathbf{s}(t) \in \mathbb{R}^2$ are known during the interval of time $[0, T]$ para $T \in \mathbb{R}$. The main objective is to estimate the values of $\mathbf{s}(t) = (\mathbf{y}(t), \mathbf{z}(t))$ for a time $t > T$, from knowledge of variable x.

– Rössler System

$$\begin{cases} dx/dt = -y - z, \\ dy/dt = x + ay, \\ dz/dt = b + z(x - c) \end{cases} \tag{5}$$

where $a, b, c > 0$ are constants known as bifurcation parameters.
– Lorenz System

$$\begin{cases} dx/dt = r(y - x), \\ dy/dt = x(s - z), \\ dz/dt = xy - pz \end{cases} \tag{6}$$

where $r, s, p > 0$ are constants known as bifurcation parameters and they are system parameters proportional to the Prandtl number[1], Rayleigh number[2], and certain physical dimensions of the layer itself.

In this work, we have chosen the parameter values according to those found in the literature because the system exhibits chaotic behavior for these.

---

[1] https://www.sciencedirect.com/topics/chemistry/prandtl-number.
[2] https://www.sciencedirect.com/topics/engineering/rayleigh-number.

4.2 Dataset Preparation

For the implementation model, we created two sampling datasets by the implementation of 4th Runge Kutta (using MATLAB):

– **Rossler_delta_0.1.csv**
– **Lorenz_delta_0.1.csv**

In the Rössler case we used the Eq. 5 where $a = 1/2$, $b = 2$ and $c = 4$. For the Lorenz case we used the Eq. 6 where $r = 10$, $s = 28$ and $p = -8/3$. The time step used for both implementations was $delta = 0.1$ over the interval $[0, 500]$, resulting in 5000 samples without the initial condition for each dataset. Both datasets were preprocessed (standardize) for each study case. The training and testing sets for two cases was defined as follows:

Training set: the first 1000 samples of each set are discarded in both datasets in order to make the reservoir state essentially independent of its initial state by time $t = 0$, as was made in [7]. The training set is formed for two subsets: the subset of samples of the available variable, x, and the subset of samples of the variables to predict, y, z. Regarding the x variable, we have 4000 samples as available knowledge and respect to the variables we wish to predict, 2000 samples are taken.

Testing set: the remaining 2000 samples of the variables we wish to predict are taken from each dataset.

4.3 Implementation Setup

We implemented the ESN model that consists of three layers with 1 input node and 2 output nodes. Connections of the neurons between layers are stored in W_{in}, W, W_{out} respectively. For the input layer, the ith input signal is connected to N reservoir nodes with connection weights in the ith column of W_{in}. Each reservoir node receives input from exactly one input signal. The non-zero elements of W_{in} are randomly chosen from a uniform distribution in $[-1, 1]$. The hidden layer is a reservoir of neurons, which we are interested in analyzing its configuration of connections to improve the performance of the model. For this, we incorporate topologies based on clusters and complex networks as a configuration of connections between the neurons into reservoir. The weights stored in W are randomly chosen from an uniform distribution in $[-1, 1]$. Also, we scale W matrix in order to guarantee the condition for the echo property. The activation function for the state of neurons is according to the Eq. 3 where $\alpha = 1$ and **bias** $= 1$. For the implementation, we used the same parameters for both datasets. The parameters used are defined in the Table 1. In the next section we describe the neural network architecture implemented with the proposed modifications.

Table 1. Configuration setup.

Definitions	Value
Initial condition	$[1, 1, 0]$
Number of reservoir nodes	$N = 400$
Spectral radius	$\rho = 1$
Average degree	$D = 20$
Bias constant	$\zeta = 1$
Leakage rate	$\alpha = 1$
Time step	delta $t = 0.1$
Initial time	$T_0 = 100$
Initial time of training phase	$T_1 = 260$
Final time of predicted phase	$T_2 = 500$
Grid of points $(L \times L)$	$L = 300$
Backbone connections	$nc\_inter = 1$
Local neuron connections	$nc\_intra = 2$

4.4   Methodology

The artificial neural network implemented in this work is described as follows:

1. **Input Layer:** For this network we use one neuron in the input layer corresponding to a $x-$signal in both cases (Rössler and Lorenz). This neuron is connected with all neurons in the next layer (hidden layer), and connected with the output layer.
2. **Hidden Layer:** Also known as the Reservoir Layer. In this layer, we construct the reservoir weight matrix, W, which is inserted in the network to obtain the reservoir state matrix, $\mathbf{r}$, by applying the Eq. 3. The weight matrix, W, represents the topology connections between reservoir nodes. Inspired in the modular structure of a human brain, we propose ESN using non-random topologies as reservoir. Thus, the adjacency matrix of the reservoir W is obtained through the different configurations using clusters and complex network topologies. To achieve a structure similar to biological networks, we modified the original reservoir topology of the classical ESN model to clustered and complex network topologies. The connections topologies based on complex networks used in the reservoir are: Erdös, Barabási, and Small World. These networks were generated using Networkx modules[3]. To generate the clustered networks, we proposed the next clustering algorithm: Initially, we cluster a grid of points using three classic clustering algorithms: K-Means, Partitioning Around Medoids, and Ward algorithm, based on [10], to simulate a community structure. For a cluster, we refer backbone to mean neuron

---

[3] https://networkx.github.io/documentation/networkx-1.9.1/reference/generators. html.

and local neurons for the rest. The connections topologies for clustered networks are defined as follows:

(a) Interclusters connections: These connections are between backbones. Each backbone has a limited number of connections defined by nc_inter.

(b) Intraclusters connections: These connections are between local neurons. Intraclusters connections are according the following statements:
  - All nodes in the same clusters are connected to its backbone.
  - All nodes have a limited numbers of connections defined by nc_intra (don't include backbone connection).
  - Each backbone is a hub of the current cluster.
  - Attachment rule for local neurons: if nc_intra is less than number of neighbors, the local neuron is connected to nc_intra closer neighbors, otherwise, the local neuron is fully connected to all neighbors.
  - The neighborhood of a local neuron is defined by the open ball whose radius is the distance between the local neuron to its backbone. This process is illustrated in Fig. 2a. The red point refers to backbone of a current cluster, black point refers to current node to link and gray points refer to the remaining nodes in a cluster.

Figure 2b shows an example how internal units look like after clustering, the black points refer to backbones. In the Table 2, the characteristics of clustered and complex networks used in the ESN models are presented.

3. **Training Phase:** After T_1 times, we collect the states in $\mathbf{r}$ obtaining the reservoir state matrix, a $N \times T_1$ matrix, which is used in the training phase. To train the network, we take the target training set and solve the simple linear regression task formed using sklearn modules of python[4].

4. **Output Layer:** This layer has two neurons, one neuron per signal predicted. After training phase, we take the testing set to predict the $y, z-$signals.

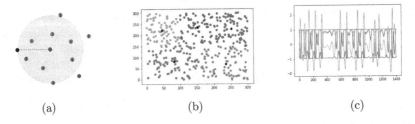

(a)   (b)   (c)

Fig. 2. (a) Illustration of a neighborhood in a clustering process. (b) Clustering internal units using kmeans. (c) Illustration of the dynamic reservoir in the ESN model.

---

[4] https://scikit-learn.org/stable/modules/generated/sklearn.linear_model.Ridge.html.

Table 2. Characteristics of complex and clustered networks used in ESN models.

Topology/Char	Size	Av. Length	Cluster Coef.
Erdös	400	2.30038	0.05041
Barabási	400	3.72219	0.04538
Small world	400	2.9852	0.60843
Cluster 1	400	4.1878	0.53963
Cluster 2	400	2.8055	0.12705
Cluster 3	400	4.1117	0.45571

5   Results

The results of this paper is divided in two parts: First, we studied the performances of the modified models compared against [7], to predict, in both study cases, the measures of the variables y, z over the interval $[T_1, T_2]$. In order to show the performance of this proposed model, we used Mean Square Error (MSE), defined in (7), like a benchmark measure.

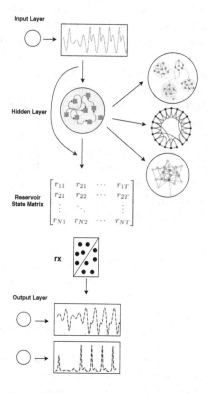

Fig. 3. Neural Network architecture implemented.

$$MSE := \frac{1}{n} \sum_{i=1}^{n} ((Y_{true}) - (Y_{esn}))^2 \tag{7}$$

where n is the number of samples entering the network, Y_{true}, Y_{esn}, are the true value and predict value of measured variables respectively. In order to compare the performance of the proposed model with the classical model, we took the values of the parameters based on [7], detailed in the Subsect. 4.3. Second, we made experimental analysis of some parameters in the proposed model. According to [3,6], the parameter with the greatest impact on the reservoir's dynamics is the spectral radius ρ. So, in this work, we performed some experiments varying ρ to visualize the error's behavior and confirm its impact on the performance of ESN models. Other parameters studied are the number of reservoir nodes, N, ridge parameter, β, leakage rate (reservoir memory capacity), α, bias term, **bias**, and number of clusters ($n\_clusters$) to check the optimal value of these parameters in the experiments. In Table 3 is shown the ESN model performance of each topology implemented. The results registered in this table, show the performance of ESN model for a mean of 30 trials in both study cases. The main approximation capability of ESN model is concentrated in its reservoir, which evokes periodic signals inside the reservoir dynamic as shown in the Fig. 2c, some reservoir states are plotted in the testing phase [260, 500]. According to the results, it is possible to observe that in both study cases, a non-random topology showed a better performance of model than classical. These results confirm that a reservoir with clustered topology could improve the performance of the ESN model. The dynamics of the reservoir is influenced by the parameters of the model, affecting the stability and accuracy of the prediction. The following is an initial experimental analysis of two important and influential parameters according to the literature on the performance of the ESN Model. In Figs. 4a–4b is shown the influence of the spectral radius in the performance of the ESN model. From the results, it possible to note that the approximation capability of this model is considerably affected by the spectral radius value. For complex network topologies, if the spectral radius is small, the reservoir dynamic is fast and if it is larger (close to unity) has a slow reservoir dynamic. For this reason, the best performance is obtained when ρ is closer than 1. An interesting result according to Figs. 4a–4b is the fact that the echo property is less influential in clustered topologies, allowing a higher range of values for this parameter.

As we mentioned before, to evaluate how much the reservoir's size can influence the performances of the ESN model we varied the number of reservoir units, N. This information can help to obtain an optimal number of reservoir units, needed to find an adequate estimation of the desired values to be predicted. In Figs. 4c–4d is shown the influence of the number of reservoir units in the performance of the ESN model. According to the obtained results, in general, it seems to be that in the experiments we can obtain a better performance for all topologies when N increase however, we can obtain good performance with a low amount of neurons in the reservoir $N \sim [250, 750]$ too. Thus, we avoid using an unnecessarily large amount of reservoir units to generate a reservoir, which could imply a higher computational cost. For the case in which we performed with

Table 3. MSE error for ESN models using network complex.

Topology/Case	Rössler	Lorenz
Erdös	4.17e−7	2.01e−5
Barabási	3.24e−7	2.12e−5
Small world	4.07e−7	1.87e−5
Cluster 1	1.06e−5	5.06e−6
Cluster 2	8.98e−6	5.890e−6
Cluster 3	1.08e−5	4.320e−6

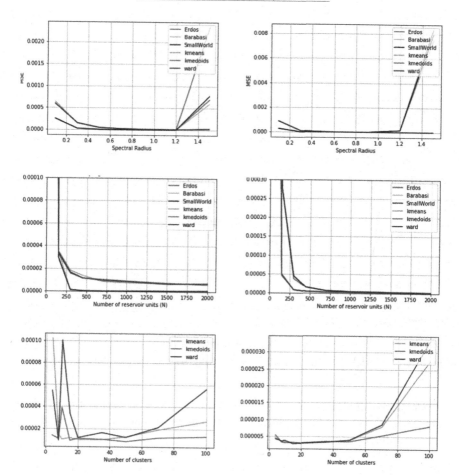

Fig. 4. ESN models performance analysis varying some parameters for study cases.

clustered topologies, Figs. 4e–4f show the error behavior of Rössler and Lorenz systems varying number of clusters. According to the results, we can observe that the network performance, in both study cases, is possible to obtain good

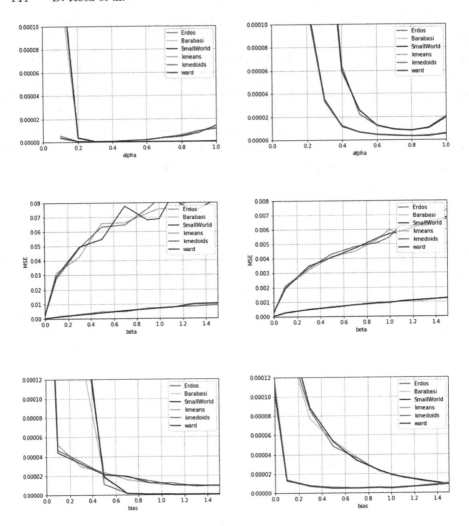

Fig. 5. ESN models performance analysis varying some parameters for study cases.

performance with a small number of clusters, avoiding as we mentioned higher computational cost in the weights reservoir matrix formation, W. Figures 5a–5f show the influence of parameters α, β, and bias term inside the proposed ESN model. From the results, we can observe that in a general way, all the parameters studied had influenced in the performance of the proposed model. In one hand, the memory capability in both cases is affected for small α values as can be seen in Figs. 5a and 5b. On the other hand, the training of the model through the solution of linear regression task obtained from the reservoir states matrix and target training set is suitable for small β values ($\beta \leq 1$) in the proposed model, as can be seen in Figs. 5c and 5d. Finally, Figs. 5e and 5f show that incorporate bias in the model improve the performance of the proposed model. According to the previous results, the influence of these parameters within the performance of the model is evidenced. The choice of these parameters can vary from one set to another and depends on the nature of the data. Finally, based on the all obtained results, We can confirm that clusters inside the reservoir improve the ESN model performance.

6   Conclusion

In this paper, we presented an application of the classic ESN model modifying the reservoir topology to clustered and complex networks. The modified and classical models were compared in two study cases: Rössler and Lorenz systems. From the results obtained in the experiments, we can conclude that a non-random topology improved the ESN model performance. Also, we confirmed the influence that the number of the reservoir units and spectral radius have in the network performance, indicating adequate results (in terms of computational cost) when $N \sim [250, 750]$, like so the others parameters in the model: $\alpha, \beta, n\_clusters$, and bias term. For future works, we believe that the network performance could be improved optimizing the clusters formed by the creation of a new algorithm, based on the distribution of the neurons in the human brain.

Acknowledgment. Research carried out using the computational resources of the Center for Mathematical Sciences Applied to Industry (CeMEAI) funded by FAPESP (grant 2013/07375-0).

References

1. Bohland, J.W., Minai, A.A.: Efficient associative memory using small-world architecture. Neurocomputing **38-40**, 489 – 496 (2001). https://doi.org/10.1016/S0925-2312(01)00378-2. Computational Neuroscience: Trends in Research 2001
2. Haykin, S.: Neural Networks: A Comprehensive Foundation, 3rd edn. Prentice-Hall Inc., Upper Saddle River (2007)
3. Jaeger, H.: The "echo state" approach to analysing and training recurrent neural networks-with an erratum note'. German National Research Center for Information Technology GMD Technical report 148, Bonn, Germany, January 2001
4. Jaeger, H.: Tutorial on training recurrent neural networks, covering BPPT, RTRL, EKF and the echo state network approach. GMD-Forschungszentrum Informationstechnik 2002, vol. 5, January 2002
5. Jaeger, H.: Adaptive nonlinear system identification with echo state networks. In: NIPS, June 2003
6. Jaeger, H., Maass, W., Principe, J.: Editorial: special issue on echo state networks and liquid state machines. Neural Netw. **20**(3), 287–289 (2007). https://doi.org/10.1016/j.neunet.2007.04.001
7. Lu, Z., Pathak, J., Hunt, B., Girvan, M., Brockett, R., Ott, E.: Reservoir observers: model-free inference of unmeasured variables in chaotic systems. Chaos Interdisc. J. Nonlinear Sci. **27**(4), 041102 (2017). https://doi.org/10.1063/1.4979665

8. MacKay, D.M.: Cerebral organization and the conscious control of action. In: Eccles, J.C. (ed.) Brain and Conscious Experience, pp. 422–445. Springer, Heidelberg (1965). https://doi.org/10.1007/978-3-642-49168-9_17

9. Mastoi, Q., Wah, T.Y., Gopal Raj, R.: Reservoir computing based echo state networks for ventricular heart beat classification. Appl. Sci. 9(4), (2019). https://doi.org/10.3390/app9040702

10. Najibi, E., Rostami, H.: SCESN, SPESN, SWESN: three recurrent neural echo state networks with clustered reservoirs for prediction of nonlinear and chaotic time series. Appl. Intell. 43(2), 460–472 (2015). https://doi.org/10.1007/s10489-015-0652-3

11. Otte, S., Butz, M.V., Koryakin, D., Becker, F., Liwicki, M., Zell, A.: Optimizing recurrent reservoirs with neuro-evolution. Neurocomputing 192, 128–138 (2016). https://doi.org/10.1016/j.neucom.2016.01.088

12. Skowronski, M.D., Harris, J.G.: Noise-robust automatic speech recognition using a discriminative echo state network. In: IEEE International Symposium on Circuits and Systems, pp. 1771–1774, May 2007. https://doi.org/10.1109/ISCAS.2007.378015

13. Stauffer, D., Aharony, A., da Fontoura Costa, L., Adler, J.: Efficient Hopfield pattern recognition on a scale-free neural network. Eur. Phys. J. B 32(3), 395–399 (2003). https://doi.org/10.1140/epjb/e2003-00114-7

14. Sun, L., Yang, X., Zhou, J.L., Wang, J., Xiao, F.: Echo state network with multiple loops reservoir and its application in network traffic prediction. In: IEEE 22nd International Conference on Computer Supported Cooperative Work in Design (CSCWD), pp. 689–694 (2018)

15. Verstraeten, D., Schrauwen, B., D'Haene, M., Stroobandt, D.: An experimental unification of reservoir computing methods. Neural Netw. 20(3), 391–403 (2007). https://doi.org/10.1016/j.neunet.2007.04.003

16. Wang, H., Yan, X.: Improved simple deterministically constructed cycle reservoir network with sensitive iterative pruning algorithm. Neurocomputing 145, 353–362 (2014). https://doi.org/10.1016/j.neucom.2014.05.024

17. Wang, H., Yan, X.: Optimizing the echo state network with a binary particle swarm optimization algorithm. Knowl. Based Syst. 86, 182–193 (2015). https://doi.org/10.1016/j.knosys.2015.06.003

18. Wang, Y., Ni, J., Xu, Z.: Effects of spectral radius on echo-state-network's training. In: 2009 Fourth International Conference on Internet Computing for Science and Engineering, pp. 102–108, December 2009. https://doi.org/10.1109/ICICSE.2009.69

19. Yu, P., Miao, L., Jia, G.: Clustered complex echo state networks for traffic forecasting with prior knowledge. In: 2011 IEEE International Instrumentation and Measurement Technology Conference, pp. 1–5, May 2011. https://doi.org/10.1109/IMTC.2011.5944078

20. Yusoff, M.H., Chrol-Cannon, J., Jin, Y.: Modeling neural plasticity in echo state networks for classification and regression. Inf. Sci. 364–365, 184–196 (2016). https://doi.org/10.1016/j.ins.2015.11.017

Deep Learning-Based Object Classification for Spectral Images

Román Jácome[1], Carlos López[1], Hans Garcia[1(✉)],
and Henry Arguello[2]

[1] Department of Electrical Engineering, Universidad Industrial de Santander,
Bucaramanga, Colombia
hans.garcia@saber.uis.edu.co
[2] Department of Computer Science, Universidad Industrial de Santander,
Bucaramanga, Colombia
henarfu@uis.edu.co

Abstract. Spectral images contain valuable information across the electromagnetic spectrum, which provides a useful tool for classification tasks. Most of the traditional machine learning algorithms for spectral images classification such as support vector machine (SVM), k-nearest neighbor, or random forest required complex handcrafted features extraction of the data, in contrast with these approaches deep learning-based methods realize the feature extraction automatically. This paper proposes a procedure to classify spectral images with a Convolutional Neural Network (CNN) approach which consists in the experimental acquisition of two datasets, medicines and honey, pre-processing of the raw data, which includes segmentation of the area of interest and a dimensionality reduction process by selecting the most informative spectral bands to reduce the computational cost of the training stage; the design of the (CNN) and finally the classification results performed by the designed CNN. Using all the spectral bands acquired the proposed CNN for the medicines dataset show accuracy in the validation set of up to 97.3% and for the honey dataset of up to 92.11% for the honey dataset compared with 86.84% ResNet-18 architecture accuracy. The dimensionality reduction method reduces the training time up to 40% by only decreasing a 10% of the test accuracy. Finally, simulations with noise show an improvement in the robustness of the CNN in the medicines dataset.

Keywords: Spectral images classification · Band selection ·
Convolutional neural network · Transfer learning · Classification

1 Introduction

Spectral imaging consists of the acquisition of more spectral bands across the electromagnetic spectrum than an ordinary image (RGB) which captures only 3 spectral bands. Spectral imaging captures wavelengths from the infrared [8], visible spectrum, ultra-violet [19], x-ray [12] and some above. The most common

© Springer Nature Switzerland AG 2021
A. D. Orjuela-Cañón et al. (Eds.): IEEE ColCACI 2020, CCIS 1346, pp. 147–159, 2021.
https://doi.org/10.1007/978-3-030-69774-7_11

optical systems for spectral images acquisition are scanning devices such as push-broom cameras [16] or imaging Fourier transform spectrometer [17] and compressive coded measurements such as coded Aperture snapshot spectral image [2] or single-pixel architecture [13].

With the recent advances in optics, spectral images record simultaneously high quality spectral and spatial scene information which is widely use in art conservation [11], remote sensing applications [25], medical applications [23] among others. Most of these applications require classification of different objects and materials, for that purpose, many algorithms have been used such as Spectral Angle Mapper (SAM) [21,29] which looks for the spectral similarity by calculating the angle between the spectral signature of a pixel with a reference signature, the reference signature corresponds to a determined signature of a dictionary with all reference signatures for each class, this method will be performed in Sect. 3 as a comparison with the proposed method. There are also machine learning algorithms such as Support Vector Machines (SVM), k-Nearest Neighbor (kNN), or Random Forest (RF) [27], these methods require complexly handcrafted of the extraction and selection of features from the data for the learning process [22].

The design of the handcrafted features extraction strategies of the machine learning methods mentioned above can be tedious and suboptimal, for this purpose deep learning provides a way to learn and extract features from the data itself, specifically convolutional neural networks (CNN) realize this features extraction by the convolutional layers. Due to this advantage and the increase of hardware resources and labeled datasets, CNNs have been strongly exploited in computer vision field tasks on RGB images such as, classification task [18,26], object detection [15], semantic segmentation [7], instance segmentation [4] and classification based in compressive acquisition [3]. With all these progress on computer vision on grayscale and RGB images, they were extrapolated on the field of spectral images bringing a very useful tool for object detection on aerial spectral images [6,30] which exploits the rich spatial-spectral features of the data, food quality [1] and food recognition [10], or in blood cell discrimination [28] among others applications.

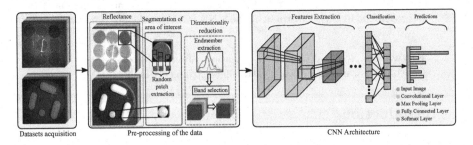

Fig. 1. Pipeline of the proposed method, which goes from the data acquisition in the laboratory, the pre-processing of the raw data and the process of classification by the CNN

The proposed method in this paper consists in the classification of two datasets; the first one is a dataset of 8 classes of medicines where there is a great color and shapes similarity which would make hard the classification with RGB images or exploiting spatial features, the second dataset is a dataset of 15 classes of honey which were extracted from different farms of Santander, Colombia where there were different environmental situation and feeding to the bees that affect the texture and the taste of the honey. It is clear that in this dataset it is not possible to use spatial features as criteria for the classification of the image. With this in mind, it was carried out a pre-processing of the raw data, then a CNN architecture was design for each dataset, subsequently, the training of the CNNs was performed and finally, the model trained was tested.

2   Method

The proposed method Fig. 1 consists in first, the pre-processing of the raw data where the spectral images were corrected by calculating the reflectance values, then in the reflectance image was applied a segmentation of the area of interest, and specifically for the honey dataset it was made a random patches extraction from the segmented images to increase the volume of the data, and balance the histogram of the data in the classes avoiding overfitting at the moment of the training process and the use band selection to reduce the dimensionality of data and reduce the computational cost of the training of the CNN, finally, it was performed the training of the designed CNN.

2.1   Data Acquisition

In the optics laboratory of the HDSP research group at Universidad Industrial de Santander de Colombia[1], two datasets were acquired using spectral scanning technique [14]. The first is a dataset of 8 classes of medicines in tablet presentation. The second one is a dataset of 15 classes of honey that come from different farms in Santander, Colombia, and where bees were fed with different food, which changes the texture and the taste of the product. These datasets were taken as a case of study since being classified from RGB images would be a complex task since there are color similarities in their RGB representation and similar spatial features in the medicines. Figure 2(a) shows the color similarities in the 8 classes of medicines, and Fig. 2(b) shows the 15 classes of honey and their respective spectral signatures in Fig. 2(c) and 2(d).

The optical architecture designed to acquire spectral images is presented in Fig. 3, which consist of the following electronic instruments: A Cornerstone 130 monochromator whose function is to select a wavelength to illuminate the scene which is transmitted by a fiber optic, also has a Stringray F-145 camera whose function is to capture images in grayscale from the wavelength that delivers the monochromator obtaining a spatial resolution of 776×1024 and a spectral resolution of 29 spectral bands within a range from 360 to 920 nm.

---

[1] http://hdspgroup.com/.

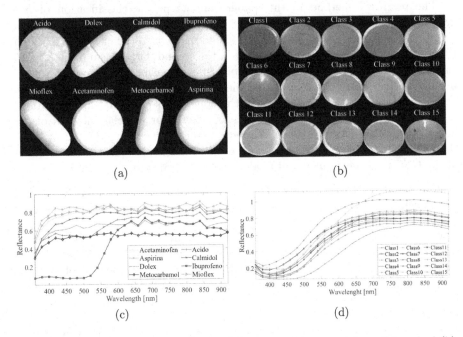

Fig. 2. False color RGB representation of the spectral images, (a) medicines and (b) honey and the spectral signatures of the different classes of (c) medicines and (d) honey.

Fig. 3. Optical architecture for the acquisition of spectral images.

2.2   Pre-processing of the Data

From the raw image acquired in the laboratory the next pre-processing of the data was realized. To avoid the variance that produces the illumination in the spectral signatures of each material, a correction of the spectral images was performed [24], for that purpose, two more spectral images were acquired, a white and black reference which consists in capturing a spectral image of a white and black surface respectively. Thus, the corrected spectral image is given by Eq. (1), where $I(x, y, k)$ is the raw image, $B(x, y, k)$ and $W(x, y, k)$ are white and black references spectral images, x, y, k are the spatial-spectral coordinates of the images and finally $R(x, y, k)$ is the reflectance values.

$$R(x, y, k) = \frac{I(x, y, k) - B(x, y, k)}{W(x, y, k) - B(x, y, k)} \tag{1}$$

Then, to reduce the spatial dimensionality of the spectral image a segmentation process was applied to extract only the area of interest. This process includes a combination of handcrafted segmentation and some techniques like edge detection, thresholding, dilatation, and more morphological processing to extract the area of interest of the spectral images. Specifically for the honey segmented images, a random patch extraction was applied to increase the data volume and balance the number of samples per class, which is useful to avoid overfitting at the training stage (high training accuracy but low validation accuracy). Thus, the medicines dataset is composed of 191 segmented spectral images and the honey dataset, originally, was composed of 107 segmented spectral images, but with the patch extraction, it ended with 1161 samples. Then a data augmentation was applied over the training and validation data to improve the learning process, this process consisted of random rotation and translation images.

Due to the high correlation of the spectral information bands, it is useful to extract only the most informative spectral bands for a dimensionality reduction of the data and therefore, reducing the computational cost without affecting significantly the performance of the classification for both datasets.

For this purpose, first, it is necessary to extract determining features of the images as criteria for the band selection. Here it was used the endmembers as criteria for the band selection, where an endmember is defined as an idealized pure signature for an object. The extraction of these features was made by the FIPPI (Fast Iterative Purity Pixel Index) algorithm [5]. This method is based in the projection of the sample vectors onto a set of vectors called skewers and the candidates for the endmembers set are those sample vectors whose projection appears most times in the extreme positions of the skewers set, these vectors are the endmembers of the spectral images.

After the characteristic endmembers of the scene were extracted, the algorithm proposed in [9] was used to select the most informative bands. This method is an unsupervised algorithm based on band similarity. It takes only 10% of the total pixel of the image to reduce computational complexity and it tries to find the most dissimilar subset of bands by minimizing a linear prediction error.

2.3   CNN Architecture

The datasets described in the previous section were split into 3 sets: training, validation, and test sets, in which the first two sets were used to train the network, and the last one is used to check the model created in the training of the network.

The architecture of the CNN is based on convolutional layers to realize the feature extraction of the data, followed by a batch normalization to increase the stability of the data through the network, and a max-pooling layer is used to reduce the dimensionality of the data, these block of layers realize the feature extraction on the spectral images. After this, fully connected layers were set to apply the classification stage ending in a softmax layer which sets the predictions of the model. In Fig. 4 the CNN architectures for both datasets are shown, the difference between them is that there are fewer max-pooling layers in CNN-Honey due to the spatial dimension of the data is small, therefore, it is not necessary to use as many max-pooling layers as they were used in CNN-Med.

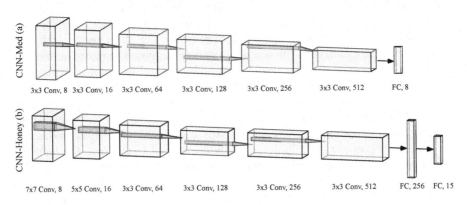

Fig. 4. Proposed CNN architecture for medicines dataset (a) and honey dataset (b)

3   Results

This section evaluates the performance of the proposed approach for the classification of spectral images with all the acquired bands and with a reduced number of bands using the band selection process described above. We compare the results of our network with state-of-art architectures by applying transfer learning to the ResNet-18 [18] and AlexNet [20] pre-trained architectures. To do this, the input layer is modified to match the dimensions of our datasets, the first convolutional layer is also modified to match the dimensions of the previous layer and finally, the last layer is modified with the number of classes we have in our dataset, then the remaining layers are frozen in order to reuse the pre-trained weights of from each model. Also, it was performed training with Gaussian noise in the images, and finally, using the spectral responses of the RGB colors the CNN was trained with the RGB representation of the spectral image.

3.1 Simulation with 29 Spectral Bands

The proposed CNN of the Fig. 4 was trained on a Dell computer with dual Intel(R) Xeon(R) CPU ES- 2697 v3 @ 2.60 GHz, which has a 192 GB RAM memory and a 12 GB NVIDIA Quadro K6000 GPU.

The dataset is divided into training, validation, and testing, which were done in two simulations, in the first simulation the training datasets were formed with 76% of the dataset, 19% was used to form the validation dataset, and the remaining 5% to form the test dataset. The dataset was divided in this way because the best results were obtained for the classification task, for the second simulation the training dataset was formed with 47% of the dataset, 12% was used to form the validation set, and the remaining 41% to form the test dataset, the dataset was divided with a smaller amount of training data, trying to determine the effect of the reduction of the spectral image set on the model.

To perform the training of the proposed model with the dataset of the medicines was made with 99 epochs as they were sufficient for the network to generalize with satisfaction the training dataset. The Table 1 shows the results for two different distributions of the data in the training, validation, and test datasets.

Table 1. Accuracy in training, validation, and testing for the two simulations of the proposed model

CNN-Med	Dataset	Number of samples	Accuracy
Simulation 1	Training	149	100%
	Validation	37	97.3%
	Testing	8	87.5%
Simulation 2	Training	89	95.5%
	Validation	22	72.7%
	Testing	80	75%

The Table 2 shows the results obtained for the proposed model and the pretrained models, the model that presents the best results is CNN-Med obtaining 97.3% of accuracy in the validation dataset.

For the honey dataset, we created 5 datasets with 5 different patch size 10×10, 40×40, 50×50, 60×60, and 80×80, these values were chosen to evaluate the performance of the network at small patch size which accelerates the training process but reduce the performance, until an optimal patch size between time-consuming training process and high performance. This patch extraction produces, not only an increase in the data volume but also an equalization of the number of samples per class. For this dataset, we employ the CNN architecture Fig. 4(b) and it was used the algorithm Stochastic Gradient Descent with Momentum (SGDM) with a momentum of 0.985, a regularization factor of

Table 2. Accuracy in training, validation, and testing with our proposed network, ResNet-18 and AlexNet.

Model	Dataset	Accuracy
CNN-Med	Training	**100%**
	Validation	**97.3%**
	Testing	**87.5%**
ResNet-18	Training	**100%**
	Validation	94.6%
	Testing	**87.5%**
AlexNet	Training	93.8%
	Validation	89.2%
	Testing	**87.5%**

0.005, and 500 epochs, and the dataset was divided in 90% training, 5% validation and 5% test. Also, the ResNet-18 architecture was retrained completely as a comparison. According to this, the Table 3 shows the obtained results.

From the Table 3, it can be observed that the proposed CNN obtained the highest accuracy level on the validation set with a 92.11%, this shows that the proposed CNN can create a better generalization model for this type of data. The simulation without patches is an exception, however, ResNet-18 performed

Table 3. Training, validation and testing results with our proposed network and ResNet-18.

Patch size	Dataset	Accuracy	
		CNN-Honey	ResNet-18
10 × 10	Training	87.5%	**88.67%**
	Validation	53.15%	**58.77%**
	Testing	**66%**	50.00%
40 × 40	Training	99.22%	**99.61%**
	Validation	**76.32%**	72.81%
	Testing	**78.8%**	75.4%
50 × 50	Training	**99.61%**	99.22%
	Validation	79.82%	**82.4%**
	Testing	**85.6%**	81.4%
60 × 60	Training	99.61%	99.61%
	Validation	**85.96%**	78.95%
	Testing	**86.84%**	79.7%
80 × 80	Training	100%	100%
	Validation	**92.11%**	86.84%
	Testing	**90.7%**	89.9%
Without patches	Training	97.65%	96.88%
	Validation	55.56%	**80.95%**
	Testing	54.5%	**62.7%**

a low accuracy compared with the other cases. Another factor is the time that ResNet-18 simulations consume for the training stage because of the depth of this network which is composed of 71 layers while the proposed CNN is only composed of 26 layers.

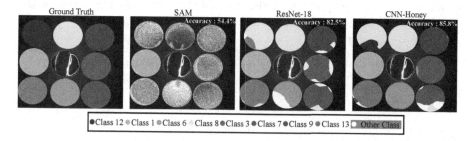

Fig. 5. Comparison of a ground truth image (a) with the performance of SAM algorithm (b), ResNet-18 architecture (c) and our proposed architecture (d).

Then it was performed the following test to measure the precision of the network: The net with the best performance on the training stage (the 80×80 patch size net), and a test spectral image which was not used in the training process is used to classify each pixel of the image by introducing into the net an 80×80 patch centered in determined pixel, the process is applied to all pixels of interest (those who belongs to any sample of honey). As one pixel is classified several times, the mode of the total predictions realized over that pixel was taken as the final prediction. According to the mentioned process an 85.84% accuracy was obtained with our CNN proposal Fig. 5(c), with ResNet-18 it was performed an 82.52% Fig. 5(d) subject to the ground-truth Fig. 5(a). Also, the SAM algorithm was applied to perform the classification of the pixel of the test image where an accuracy of 54.4% was obtained Fig. 5(b).

The low accuracy of the SAM algorithm is caused by the similitude between the spectral signatures Fig. 2(d), which differences are due to the changes in the feeding of the bees, the places where they were raised. For example, there is a big similitude between class 12 and class 8 which explains the inaccuracy at the moment of classifying the sample corresponding to class 12 in Fig. 5(c) and in the case of class 1, class 6, and class 9 they are the most different signatures among the classes which are shown in an almost 100% in the predictions. Due to this low-performance, the SAM algorithm was not employed in the simulations of Table 2 and Table 3. It is to clarify that the sample of the middle of the image was not used to the test due to the saturation produced by the spectral illumination in the image.

3.2 Dimensinality Reduction

To analyze the performance of the CNN for a dimensionality reduction of the spectral images of both datasets two methodologies were used; the first one was using the spectral responses of the RGB colors to create an RGB representation of the spectral images and do classification with these images. The second one was using the band selection method described in the previous section.

For the first type of simulations, it was used the 80 size patch dataset for the honey dataset, and for the medicines dataset, it was used the same condition of simulation with 29 spectral bands. In Table 4 are shown the results of the average of 10 experiments under the conditions previously mentioned.

Table 4. Results of the classification using the RGB representation

Dataset	Accuracy	
	Validation	Test
Medicines	81.69%	79.7%
Honey	81.08%	78.4%

The accuracy of the classification of the RGB representation is lower than the ones obtained with all the spectral information of the 29 spectral bands images in Table 2 and 3 showing in this way that the more spectral information used the better will be the classification of the different objects due to the similarities in the color visualization and also in the shape of the different classes of medicines

For the second type of simulations, 10 experiments were carried out using the, 10, 15, 20, and 25 most informative spectral bands for the classification, with 150 epochs for each dataset and a learning rate of 0.0005.

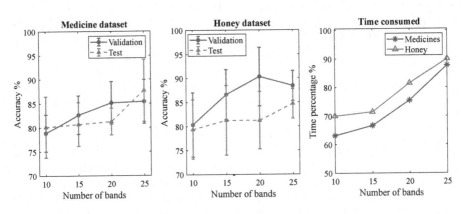

Fig. 6. Accuracy of medicines and honey dataset using the 10, 15, 20, and 25 most informative bands and the time consumption respect the 29 bands simulation.

In Fig. 6 the plots show the average and the standard deviation of the accuracy in the 10 experiments, showing that using more spectral bands helps the training of the CNN to generalize in a better way the dataset since the highest mean accuracy is obtained in the 25 spectral bands simulation, although, the highest mean values in the validation set was obtained in the 20 spectral bands simulation. Also, in Fig. 6 is shown the time used for training in percentage respect to the time consumed for the training of the 29 bands spectral images for both datasets, it can be observed that the 10 bands simulation reduces the time in 30% for the honey dataset and almost a 40% for the medicines dataset and only decreasing the accuracy of the test by a 10%.

3.3   Simulation Applying Different Levels of Gaussian Noise

Since the spectral images were taken in a laboratory, which has a controlled environment to reduce as much as possible the noise in the images, some experiments were realized adding an additive white gaussian noise (AWGN) to test the robustness of the CNN with the presence of this noise. The AWGN was used with a signal to noise ratio (SNR) of 10, 15, 20, and 25 dB. The results for these simulations are shown in Fig. 7.

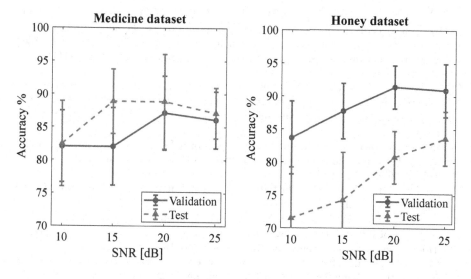

Fig. 7. Accuracy for the medicine and honey datasets with AWGN

In Fig. 7, for the medicines dataset, it can be appreciated that using a 15 and 20 dB in the SNR of the AWGN improves the robustness of the classification because it achieved higher accuracy than the noiseless classification in Table 2. The classification honey datasets showed to be more sensitive to the presence of noise because the test accuracy was reduced but the validation accuracy was not reduced, in other words, the CNN lost robustness because of the noise.

4   Conclusions

In this work was demonstrated that it is possible to design and implement an optical architecture to acquire spectral images, it was also possible to create a model of convolutional neural networks for the classification of the acquisition of spectral images, with the proposed models it was to classify medicines and honey that had similar RGB visualization, obtaining accuracy in the validation of up to 97,3% for the medicines dataset and accuracy in the validation set of 92.11% for the classification of the honey dataset, evaluated by patches, both cases outperformed the results of ResNet-18 architecture. Training with a reduced number of bands shows that the training time could be reduced up to 40% of the original 29 bands simulation by selecting only a third of the total number of bands reducing just 10% of the accuracy in the test dataset. Training with noise shows an improvement of the robustness in the medicines dataset classification improving up to 8% in the test accuracy, but for the honey dataset, the accuracy was reduced.

References

1. Al-Sarayreh, M., Reis, M., Yan, W., Klette, R.: Detection of red-meat adulteration by deep spectral-spatial features in hyperspectral images. J. Imaging **4**, 63 (2018)
2. Arce, G.R., Brady, D.J., Carin, L., Arguello, H., Kittle, D.S.: Compressive coded aperture spectral imaging: an introduction. IEEE Sig. Process. Mag. **31**(1), 105–115 (2014)
3. Bacca, J., Correa, C.V., Vargas, E., Castillo, S., Arguello, H.: Compressive classification from single pixel measurements via deep learning. In: 2019 IEEE 29th International Workshop on Machine Learning for Signal Processing (MLSP), pp. 1–6 (2019)
4. Bai, M., Urtasun, R.: Deep watershed transform for instance segmentation. In: 2017 IEEE Conference on Computer Vision and Pattern Recognition (CVPR), pp. 2858–2866 (2017)
5. Chang, C.-I., Plaza, A.: A fast iterative algorithm for implementation of pixel purity index. IEEE Geosci. Remote Sens. Lett. **3**(1), 63–67 (2006)
6. Chen, Y., Jiang, H., Li, C., Jia, X., Ghamisi, P.: Deep feature extraction and classification of hyperspectral images based on convolutional neural networks. IEEE Trans. Geosci. Remote Sens. **54**(10), 6232–6251 (2016)
7. Cordts, M., et al.: The cityscapes dataset for semantic urban scene understanding. In: 2016 IEEE Conference on Computer Vision and Pattern Recognition (CVPR), pp. 3213–3223 (2016)
8. Dam, J.S., Tidemand-Lichtenberg, P., Pedersen, C.: Room-temperature mid-infrared single-photon spectral imaging. Nat. Photonics **6**(11), 788 (2012)
9. Du, Q., Yang, H.: Similarity-based unsupervised band selection for hyperspectral image analysis. IEEE Geosci. Remote Sens. Lett. **5**(4), 564–568 (2008)
10. Esfahani, S.N., Muthukumar, V., Regentova, E.E., Taghva, K., Trabia, M.: Complex food recognition using hyper-spectral imagery. In: 2020 10th Annual Computing and Communication Workshop and Conference (CCWC), pp. 0662–0667 (2020)
11. Fischer, C., Kakoulli, I.: Multispectral and hyperspectral imaging technologies in conservation: current research and potential applications. Stud. Conserv. **51**(sup1), 3–16 (2006)
12. Fröjdh, C., Norlin, B., Fröjdh, E.: Spectral X-ray imaging with single photon processing detectors. J. Instrum. **8**(02), C02010 (2013)

13. Garcia, H., Correa, C.V., Arguello, H.: Multi-resolution compressive spectral imaging reconstruction from single pixel measurements. IEEE Trans. Image Process. **27**(12), 6174–6184 (2018)
14. Garini, Y., Young, I.T., Mcnamara, G.: Spectral imaging: principles and applications. Cytometry Part A J. Int. Soc. Anal. Cytol. **69**(8), 735–747 (2006)
15. Girshick, R., Donahue, J., Darrell, T., Malik, J.: Region-based convolutional networks for accurate object detection and segmentation. IEEE Trans. Pattern Anal. Mach. Intell. **38**(1), 142–158 (2016)
16. Hartley, R.I., Gupta, R.: Linear pushbroom cameras. In: Eklundh, J.-O. (ed.) ECCV 1994. LNCS, vol. 800, pp. 555–566. Springer, Heidelberg (1994). https:// doi.org/10.1007/3-540-57956-7_63
17. Harvey, A.R., Fletcher-Holmes, D.W.: Birefringent Fourier-transform imaging spectrometer. Opt. Express **12**(22), 5368–5374 (2004)
18. He, K., Zhang, X., Ren, S., Sun, J.: Deep residual learning for image recognition. In: 2016 IEEE Conference on Computer Vision and Pattern Recognition (CVPR), pp. 770–778 (2016)
19. Huang, W., Xu, X., Wang, G.: Detection of latent fingerprints by ultraviolet spectral imaging. In: Culshaw, B., Zhang, X., Wang, A. (eds.) 2013 International Conference on Optical Instruments and Technology: Optical Sensors and Applications, vol. 9044, pp. 236–245. International Society for Optics and Photonics, SPIE (2013)
20. Krizhevsky, A., Sutskever, I., Hinton, G.E.: ImageNet classification with deep convolutional neural networks, pp. 1097–1105 (2012)
21. Li, Q., Wang, Y., Liu, H., Chen, Z.: Nerve fibers identification based on molecular hyperspectral imaging technology. In: 2012 IEEE International Conference on Computer Science and Automation Engineering (CSAE), vol. 3, pp. 15–17 (2012)
22. Li, S., Wu, H., Wan, D., Zhu, J.: An effective feature selection method for hyperspectral image classification based on genetic algorithm and support vector machine. Knowl.-Based Syst. **24**(1), 40–48 (2011)
23. Lu, G., Fei, B.: Medical hyperspectral imaging: a review. J. Biomed. Opt. **19**(1), 010901 (2014)
24. Monteiro, S.T., Kosugi, Y., Uto, K., Watanabe, E.: Towards applying hyperspectral imagery as an intraoperative visual aid tool, pp. 483–488 (2004)
25. Pajares, G.: Overview and current status of remote sensing applications based on unmanned aerial vehicles (UAVs). Photogram. Eng. Remote Sens. **81**(4), 281–330 (2015)
26. Szegedy, C., et al.: Going deeper with convolutions. In: 2015 IEEE Conference on Computer Vision and Pattern Recognition (CVPR), pp. 1–9 (2015)
27. Thanh Noi, P., Kappas, M.: Comparison of random forest, k-nearest neighbor, and support vector machine classifiers for land cover classification using Sentinel-2 imagery. Sensors **18**(1), 18 (2018)
28. Li, X., Li, W., Xu, X., Hu, W.: Cell classification using convolutional neural networks in medical hyperspectral imagery. In: 2017 2nd International Conference on Image, Vision and Computing (ICIVC), pp. 501–504 (2017)
29. Yang, C., Everitt, J.H., Bradford, J.M.: Yield estimation from hyperspectral imagery using spectral angle mapper (SAM). Trans. ASABE **51**(2), 729–737 (2008)
30. Zhao, W., Du, S.: Spectral-spatial feature extraction for hyperspectral image classification: a dimension reduction and deep learning approach. IEEE Trans. Geosci. Remote Sens. **54**(8), 4544–4554 (2016)

Transfer Learning for Spectral Image Reconstruction from RGB Images

Emmanuel Martínez[(✉)], Santiago Castro, Jorge Bacca, and Henry Arguello

Computer Science, Universidad Industrial de Santander,
Bucaramanga 680002, Colombia
emmanuel2162134@correo.uis.edu.co
http://www.hdspgroup.com

Abstract. Spectral image reconstruction from RGB images has emerged as a hot topic in the computer vision community due to easy-access and low-cost acquisition compared with traditional spectral imaging acquisition methods. With the growth of the available spectral data-sets, this reconstruction problem has been effectively addressed using deep convolutional neural networks (CNN). The goal is to learn a non-linear mapping from 3-RGB bands to L spectral bands. However, these methods demand many spectral images to train the CNN to obtain a good recovery. In contrast, the proposed process consists of a pre-training step where the weights of a convolutional neural network fit with a large number of RGB image data sets available without its corresponding ground-truth spectral images, taking into account the RGB spectral response of the camera which is modeled as a non-trainable layer. Then, some layers of this pre-trained network are frozen to retrain it with the available spectral data-set to generate a spectral image with L bands. The proposed training scheme can be used with any pre-existing deep network that maps RGB to spectral images, and it is here evaluated with a "U-net" architecture. The RGB sensing is based on the Bayer filter pattern from a Nikon D90 DSLR camera. The simulated and experimental data demonstrate the effectiveness of the proposed approach compared to training without transfer learning, showing a gain of up to 4 dB, with less spectral data.

Keywords: Spectral and RGB images · Convolutional neural network · Transfer learning

1 Introduction

Spectral imaging captures spatial information across different ranges of the electromagnetic spectrum by forming cubes of 3D images [5,15]. Due to the great wealth of spectral information present in these images, they allow different objects and materials to be distinguished accurately and consistently [17]. Therefore, spectral images have been used in various applications such as

© Springer Nature Switzerland AG 2021
A. D. Orjuela-Cañón et al. (Eds.): IEEE ColCACI 2020, CCIS 1346, pp. 160–173, 2021.
https://doi.org/10.1007/978-3-030-69774-7_12

medicine [17,21,23], food quality [20,27], remote sensing [22,32], and environmental monitoring [26]. Traditional methods for acquiring this type of images are based on spatial scanning methods [18], which capture the spectrum pixel by pixel (whisk-broom) by lines (push-broom) to generate a spectral data cube [11,14]. However, they are time-consuming systems, and therefore, their usage in dynamic scenes is prohibited [25].

More recently, different alternatives have been proposed to solve the time-consuming problem, such as the single snapshot cameras which used compressive sensing theory [9,12,19,31]. This new sensing protocol involves a recovery process to obtain the spectral image [4]. Although these technologies allow solving the time-consuming sensing process, these acquisition devices are costly both to purchase from a company and to produce them [4,8].

Spectral image reconstruction methods with only RGB images have become a hot topic due to their easy access and low cost. State of the art methods use deep neural networks to obtain this reconstruction; learning a non-linear mapping from RGB to a spectral image, for instance, [29] uses Deep space-spectral correlations, [30] uses a modified U-net, [1] employs Gaussian processes. Even in the NTIRE 2018 and 2020 challenges, [2,3] some CNN architectures were developed to learn this reconstruction mapping. The problem with many of these architectures lies in the large number of spectral images required to learn optimal non-linear mappings. Besides, there is the restriction of going from only three bands (RGB) to a higher number of bands for a successful reconstruction.

Since the RGB cameras map the incoming spectral light into three channels, using an RGB filter response physically presented in the CCD-sensors, the RGB images can be seen as a spectral degradation of the spectral images. Therefore, the proposed process takes advantage of available RGB data-sets without spectral ground-truth but with the filter response of the camera to first pre-train a convolutional network without any spectral information. In particular, the proposed approach consists of a two-step procedure to train a CNN architecture, (in this work, we focus on the U-net [24]). The first step learns a first step learns a CNN in which input is the RGB images and map to 31-band spectral image, where then, the Bayer filter response of the NikonD90 camera is added as the last layer of the model to obtain again RGB images. This network is trained with a broad set of RGB data where its input and output are the same. After pre-training the net, the last layer is removed, and a new learning process begins with spectral images, where some already trained net weights freeze, and the trainable weights do not start with random values, which makes training more efficient, showing gains of up to 4 dB in PSNR.

2   RGB Acquisition

Traditional RGB cameras use 3 color filters on the sensor to map the incoming light into three channels according to human perception of colors [6]. These three filters have their spectral response matching the human perceptual vision (Red, Green, Blue) wavelengths. The spatial distribution of the filters is based on the

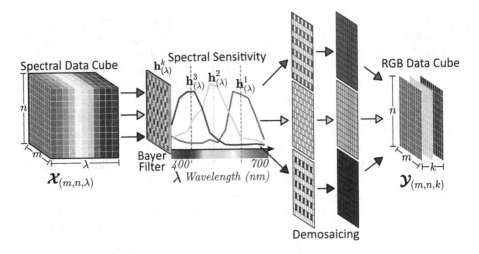

Fig. 1. Visual representation of the impulse response implemented in the proposed architecture. (Color figure online)

Bayer RGB pattern and uses demosaicing to obtain the final image [28]. Figure 1 represents the RGB acquisition. Assuming that the RGB image is obtained under the same atmospheric and illumination conditions; the RGB image can be approximated as a linear spectral degradation of the spectral image as

$$\mathcal{Y}_{(m,n,k)} = \sum_{\lambda=1}^{L} \mathbf{h}_{(\lambda)}^{k} \mathcal{X}_{(m,n,\lambda)}, \qquad (1)$$

for $k = 1, 2, 3$, where $\mathcal{X} \in \mathbb{R}^{M \times N \times L}$ represents the spectral image, with $M \times N$ pixels and L spectral bands; $\mathcal{Y} \in \mathbb{R}^{M \times N \times 3}$ is the RGB image, and $\{\mathbf{h}^{k} \in \mathbb{R}^{L}\}_{k=1}^{3}$ represents the spectral response for the red, green and blue filter, respectively. Equation (1) can be written in a matrix form as

$$\mathbf{Y} = \mathbf{HX}, \qquad (2)$$

where $\mathbf{H} = [\mathbf{h}^{1}, \mathbf{h}^{2}, \mathbf{h}^{3}]^{T}$ represents the sensing matrix and $\mathbf{X} \in \mathbb{R}^{L \times MN}$ stands for the vectorization of the spectral image where each column represents a spectral signature and $\mathbf{Y} \in \mathbb{R}^{3 \times MN}$ is the matrix form of the RGB image.

3   Transfer Learning Strategy

Deep neural networks have been used as spectral image generators, where the goal is to learn a non-linear mapping f_{θ} from $\mathbf{Y}$ to $\mathbf{X}$, i.e., $\mathbf{X} = f_{\theta}(\mathbf{Y})$ [7]. The structure of this mapping is usually a filtering operator, such as convolution, up and down sampling, followed by a non-linear activation where the trainable

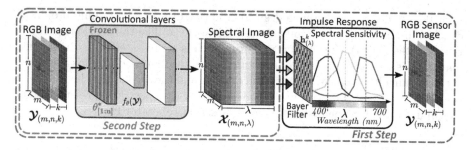

Fig. 2. Proposed architecture. This scheme is divided into two steps. The first step consists of pre-training a convolution model using RGB images as an input. The sensing process **H** is applied to the output of the final convolutional layer to train with the same RGB image. The second step consists in learning the same model using RGB as input and spectral image as output, where the convolutional layers will contain the trained $[1:n]$ parameters of the first step model. (Color figure online)

parameters are denoted by θ [13]. The proposed method uses the sensing model and the generator network as

$$\mathbf{Y} = \mathbf{H}f_\theta(\mathbf{Y}). \tag{3}$$

With the purpose to take advantage of the RGB images without full spectral information, the proposed method only uses the RGB image of a big dataset, where the weights of the net (θ) can be learned or initialized, solving the following optimization problem

$$\theta^* = \arg\min_\theta \sum_{l=1}^{T} ||\mathbf{Y}_l - \mathbf{H}f_\theta(\mathbf{Y}_l)||_F^2, \tag{4}$$

where θ^* are the learned network parameters, and $\mathbf{Y}_l$ is the l-th RGB element of a dataset of T images without spectral ground-truth. The last layer of the neural network f_θ produces an image with L bands from $\mathbf{Y}$, and finally, the sensor response $\mathbf{H}$ gives us the equivalent RGB images as illustrated in Fig. 2 with the green dotted rectangle labeled as the first step.

After solving the optimization problem described in Eq. (4), the θ^* parameters are used to create the following TL model

$$\widetilde{f}_{\theta_{[1:n]}} = f_{\theta^*_{[1:n]}}, \tag{5}$$

which freezes the already learned parameters $\theta^*_{[1:n]}$, and fit some weights of the model using a new spectral dataset. This freeze is based on the fact that deep features in the first layers can be preserved for RGB to RGB as for RGB to Spectral. Finally, this network is tuned for the trainable parameters $\theta^*_{[n:end]}$ which is described with the following optimization problem

$$\theta^*_{[n:end]} = \arg\min_{\theta_{[1:end]}} \sum_{l'=1}^{W} ||\mathbf{X}_{l'} - \widetilde{f}_\theta(\mathbf{Y}_{l'})||_F^2, \tag{6}$$

with $W \ll T$ data, which includes the ground-truth $\mathbf{X}$. This tuning process is denoted in Fig. 2 with the orange dotted rectangle. Unlike the previous problem raised in the Eq. (4), the sensing process, which is represented with the sensing matrix $\mathbf{H}$, is removed. In terms of network design, the first model builds a network with the same RGB image as input and output, and the second has the RGB and the spectral image. However, both models recover the spectral representation of the input image, but the first just before the sensing operator $\mathbf{H}$.

Raise Nikon D90 RGB images   ARAD HS spectral images

Fig. 3. Visual representation of the dataset used (a) RAISE dataset obtained with Nikon D90 and (b) false RGB mapping of the ARAD HS spectral images.

4   Simulations and Results

4.1   Datasets

Two datasets were used in this work: The first is the RAISE [10], which contains 2276 standard RGB images corresponding to different natural landscapes obtained with the Nikon D90 camera; this dataset was augmented, generating a total of 6828 images, each image is resized to 512×512 and normalized to a $[0,1]$ intensity range. The second is the ARAD HS dataset [3], which contains 450 normalized spectral images to train the model, and 10 spectral images to test; the RGB mappings were calculated using the spectral response of Nikon D90 camera obtained from [16]. Furthermore, each spectral image is resized to 512×512 in spatial resolution, and they have 31, spectral bands.

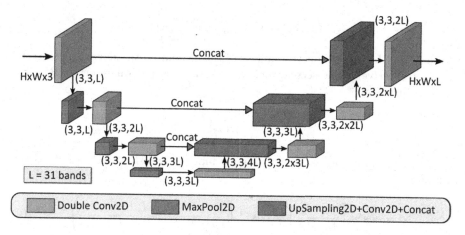

Fig. 4. Convolutional layers specified. This is a U-net based scheme that takes an image with $H \times W \times 3$ dimensions and obtains a reconstruction of $H \times W \times L$ images.

4.2 Models

The proposed scheme can be used with any CNN used for the RGB to spectral recovery task. Therefore, our experiments are performed using a UNet-based architecture with skip-connections [30], as shown in Fig. 4, since some of the state-of-the-art methods used variations of this network. This architecture is composed of three main blocks (Fig. 3):

- **Double Conv2D:** Consists of two convolutions with 3×3 filters in spatial resolution and a variety of scalar numbers of L filters in-depth, with zero padding and a RELU activation function.
- **MaxPool2D:** This layer reduces the feature map in spatial resolution.
- **UpSampling2D + Conv2D + Concat:** This block performs three operations, which consist of expanding the feature map in the spatial domain, followed by a 3×3 convolution and multiple filters of L, and finally, generating a skip connection between the encoder and decoder in the same depth level.

It is essential to highlight that the two main steps of the proposed scheme are based on the same network architecture, as illustrated in Fig. 2, the main difference is the loss function where in the first training takes into account the sensing model. The second step inherits the information acquired from the previous step, experimentally freezing some weights that are considered optimal for the current state of the model. Finally, with the second dataset, the desired spectral images are recovered more efficiently using the retrained weights.

4.3 Metrics and Configurations

Three metrics were used to measure the quality of the reconstruction. The first metric is the peak signal-to-noise ratio (PSNR), it is described in the following equation

$$PSNR = 10 \log_{10} \frac{||I_n||_\infty NM}{||I_e - I_n||_F^2}, \tag{7}$$

where I_n and I_e are the spectral images of the ground-truth images and the estimated, respectively. The second metric is the root mean square error (RMSE), and it is given by

$$RMSE = \sqrt{\frac{1}{n} \sum_{i=1}^{n} (I_n^i - I_e^i)^2}. \tag{8}$$

Finally, the last metric is a spectral angle mapper (SAM) and it is follows the equation

$$\alpha = cos^{-1} \left(\frac{I_n \cdot I_e}{|I_n||I_e|} \right) = cos^{-1} \left(\frac{\sum_{i=1}^{n} I_n^i I_e^i}{\sqrt{\sum_{i=1}^{n} (I_n^i)^2} \sqrt{\sum_{i=1}^{n} (I_e^i)^2}} \right), \tag{9}$$

where α is the spectral angle between I_n and I_e.

The results shown are the mean of the test dataset. All simulations were implemented in python 3.6.9 and using the TensorFlow 2.0 library on Google Colaboratory with its GPU runtime environment. The first step of the training strategy was carried out with the RGB dataset applying 10 epochs using the initial weights of the traditional spectral reconstruction network [23] and, Adam optimizer, where the learning rate was settled through cross-validation. The second step for the proposed strategy and the traditional method without transfer learning (Without TF) was carried out for 100 epochs, also using Adam optimizer with the best learning rate obtained.

4.4 Results

In this section, the efficiency of the proposed strategy, denoted as *With TL* is evaluated and compared with the results of the trained network without using TL denoted as *Without TL*. For this, two main tests are evaluated; the first test with the full dataset, i.e., 450 images for training, and 10 images for testing. The second test using a quarter of the dataset, i.e., (120 images for training, and the same 10 for testing), these networks are denoted as *With TL 25%* and *Without TL 25%*, this last experiment aims to show the effectiveness of the proposed method when the available data is limited. Additionally, in the second test, the weights of the first four convolutional layers were frozen.

Tables 1, 2 and 3 summarize the reconstruction quality for the four methods measured in PSNR, RMSE, and SAM, respectively. There, the optimal value of each image is shown in bold, and the second-best result is underlined. From the tables, it can be seen that the proposed approach obtained a lower RMSE and SAM and a higher PSNR, which expresses a better quality in the reconstruction of the spectral images for all cases. In particular, the proposed method outperforms the traditional method is up to 4 dB. Additionally, notice that when the dataset decreases, the quality is preserved in which shows the advantage of the weights already trained in the first step of the proposed method.

Furthermore, Fig. 5 and 6 shows a visual representation of three spectral image reconstructions for the different methods. There, it can be seen that the proposed method preserve more the intensity value in all the pixel compared with the other approach.

Table 1. PSNR values for each image in the test dataset.

Image	PSNR			
	With TL	Without TL	With TL 25%	Without TL 25%
Image 1	**33.75338**	27.93111	<u>32.48454</u>	26.28385
Image 2	**35.35452**	29.71847	<u>30.98698</u>	24.97993
Image 3	33.37145	**34.12948**	<u>33.07933</u>	31.58570
Image 4	**39.87241**	<u>35.56417</u>	35.07691	33.52659
Image 5	**31.42445**	29.42103	<u>31.18411</u>	27.48576
Image 6	**32.48617**	28.09273	<u>31.02556</u>	26.78852
Image 7	**31.70981**	25.35291	<u>28.73195</u>	25.42376
Image 8	**39.57919**	38.42656	<u>39.17162</u>	36.15251
Image 9	**37.83101**	<u>34.39092</u>	31.91504	29.27065
Image 10	**34.83979**	30.72731	<u>33.03563</u>	28.98412
Mean	**35.02222**	31.37547	<u>32.66917</u>	29.04814

Table 2. RMSE values for each image in the test dataset.

Image	RMSE			
	With TL	Without TL	With TL 25%	Without TL 25%
Image 1	**0.02018**	0.03839	<u>0.02318</u>	0.04411
Image 2	**0.01661**	0.03127	<u>0.02680</u>	0.05168
Image 3	<u>0.02099</u>	**0.01926**	0.02144	0.02611
Image 4	**0.00947**	<u>0.01614</u>	0.01729	0.02023
Image 5	**0.02651**	0.03331	<u>0.02731</u>	0.04177
Image 6	**0.02229**	0.03730	<u>0.02709</u>	0.04151
Image 7	**0.02589**	0.05257	<u>0.03599</u>	0.05082
Image 8	**0.01017**	0.01148	<u>0.01084</u>	0.01468
Image 9	**0.01251**	<u>0.01846</u>	0.02498	0.03409
Image 10	**0.01738**	0.02862	<u>0.02159</u>	0.03492
Mean	**0.01821**	0.02868	<u>0.02365</u>	0.03599

Table 3. SAM values for each image in the test dataset.

Image	SAM			
	With TL	Without TL	With TL 25%	Without TL 25%
Image 1	**0.04632**	0.07546	<u>0.06423</u>	0.07682
Image 2	**0.07123**	0.13371	<u>0.11269</u>	0.16092
Image 3	**0.08833**	0.09742	<u>0.08999</u>	0.09249
Image 4	<u>0.10821</u>	0.11338	**0.09978**	0.11693
Image 5	0.06931	0.06684	**0.05479**	<u>0.06275</u>
Image 6	**0.07321**	0.11217	<u>0.09693</u>	0.12639
Image 7	**0.05641**	0.09603	<u>0.08842</u>	0.10495
Image 8	<u>0.08166</u>	0.09398	**0.08085**	0.10035
Image 9	<u>0.03832</u>	0.04255	0.03929	**0.03665**
Image 10	0.04265	**0.03691**	<u>0.03884</u>	0.03958
Mean	**0.06756**	0.08684	<u>0.07658</u>	0.09178

Some features maps of the four frozen convolutional layers are shown in Fig. 7. Notice that this map preserved deep features such as texture and color, which help to reconstitution images in the second step of the proposed approach even when the data are limited.

Finally, to see the spectral behavior, three spectral signature of the three recovered images were randomly chosen and shown in Fig. 8 and also include the ground-truth signature. Notice that with the full dataset and with a quarter of the spectral dataset, the spectral signatures obtained by the proposed method closely resemble the ground-truth. Furthermore, when the training data is decreased, the proposed method provides an improved spectral composition compared to the methodology without TL.

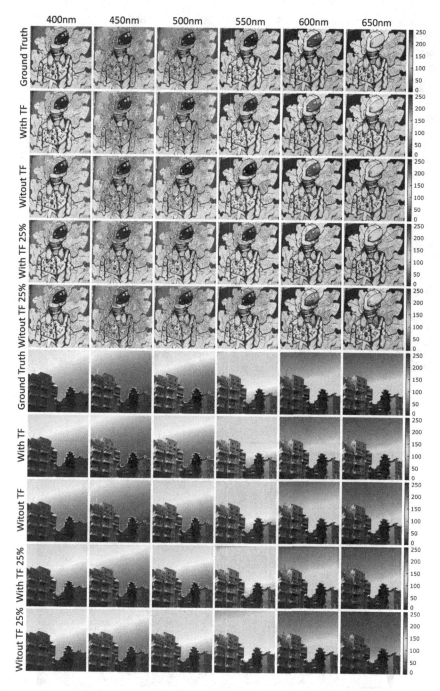

Fig. 5. Spectral image comparison and visualization of two recovered images for each of the trained models, comparing the proposed *With TF* strategy against the traditional *Without TF* method. Five spectral bands can be observed corresponding to 400, 450, 500, 550, 600, and 650 nm, respectively.

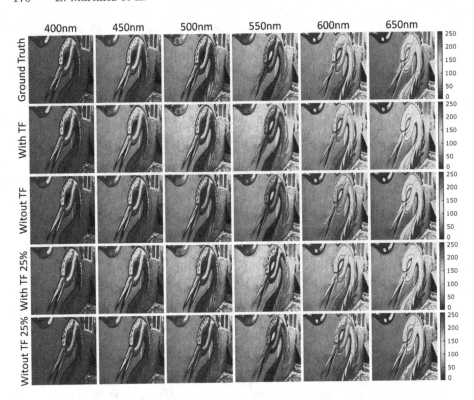

Fig. 6. Spectral image comparison of an additional test image.

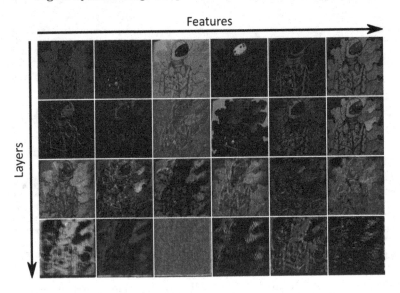

Fig. 7. Some feature maps extracted from the first step of the proposed method.

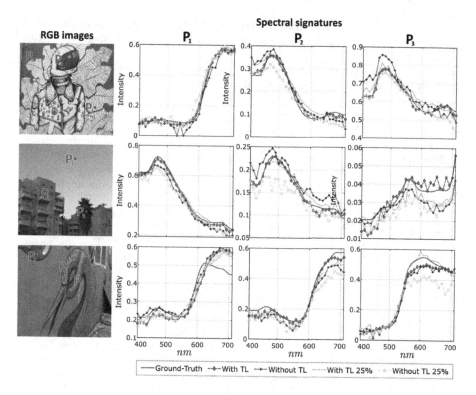

Fig. 8. Spectral signature results for testing images.

5   Conclusions

A training methodology was proposed to reconstruct spectral images using RGB images based on the TL of a network that was trained only with RGB images and then refined using the available spectral dataset. According to the results obtained through experimentation, we can see that the objective of this architecture is achieved by offering a gain of up to 4 dB even with a small training dataset.

References

1. Akhtar, N., Mian, A.: Hyperspectral recovery from RGB images using Gaussian processes. IEEE Trans. Pattern Anal. Mach. Intell. **42**(1), 100–113 (2018)
2. Arad, B., Ben-Shahar, O., Timofte, R.: NTIRE 2018 challenge on spectral reconstruction from RGB images. In: Proceedings of the IEEE Conference on Computer Vision and Pattern Recognition Workshops, pp. 929–938 (2018)
3. Arad, B., Timofte, R., Ben-Shahar, O., Lin, Y.T., Finlayson, G.D.: NTIRE 2020 challenge on spectral reconstruction from an RGB image. In: Proceedings of the IEEE/CVF Conference on Computer Vision and Pattern Recognition Workshops, pp. 446–447 (2020)

4. Arce, G.R., Brady, D.J., Carin, L., Arguello, H., Kittle, D.S.: Compressive coded aperture spectral imaging: an introduction. IEEE Sig. Process. Mag. **31**(1), 105–115 (2013)

5. Bacca, J., Arguello, H.: Sparse subspace clustering for hyperspectral images using incomplete pixels. TecnoLógicas **22**(46), 6–19 (2019)

6. Bacca, J., Correa, C.V., Arguello, H.: Noniterative hyperspectral image reconstruction from compressive fused measurements. IEEE J. Sel. Top. Appl. Earth Obs. Remote Sens. **12**(4), 1231–1239 (2019)

7. Bacca, J., Galvis, L., Arguello, H.: Coupled deep learning coded aperture design for compressive image classification. Opt. Express **28**(6), 8528–8540 (2020)

8. Boldrini, B., Kessler, W., Rebner, K., Kessler, R.W.: Hyperspectral imaging: a review of best practice, performance and pitfalls for in-line and on-line applications. J. Near Infrared Spectrosc. **20**(5), 483–508 (2012)

9. Correa, C.V., Arguello, H., Arce, G.R.: Snapshot colored compressive spectral imager. JOSA A **32**(10), 1754–1763 (2015)

10. Dang-Nguyen, D.T., Pasquini, C., Conotter, V., Boato, G.: RAISE: a raw images dataset for digital image forensics. In: Proceedings of the 6th ACM Multimedia Systems Conference, pp. 219–224 (2015)

11. Fowler, J.E.: Compressive pushbroom and whiskbroom sensing for hyperspectral remote-sensing imaging. In: 2014 IEEE International Conference on Image Processing (ICIP), pp. 684–688. IEEE (2014)

12. Gehm, M.E., John, R., Brady, D.J., Willett, R.M., Schulz, T.J.: Single-shot compressive spectral imaging with a dual-disperser architecture. Opt. Express **15**(21), 14013–14027 (2007)

13. Goodfellow, I., Bengio, Y., Courville, A.: Deep Learning. MIT Press, Cambridge (2016)

14. Gupta, R., Hartley, R.I.: Linear pushbroom cameras. IEEE Trans. Pattern Anal. Mach. Intell. **19**(9), 963–975 (1997)

15. Hinojosa, C., Bacca, J., Arguello, H.: Coded aperture design for compressive spectral subspace clustering. IEEE J. Sel. Top. Sig. Process. **12**(6), 1589–1600 (2018)

16. Jiang, J., Liu, D., Gu, J., Süsstrunk, S.: What is the space of spectral sensitivity functions for digital color cameras? In: 2013 IEEE Workshop on Applications of Computer Vision (WACV), pp. 168–179. IEEE (2013)

17. Li, J., et al.: Multispectral detection of skin defects of bi-colored peaches based on vis-NIR hyperspectral imaging. Postharvest Biol. Technol. **112**, 121–133 (2016)

18. Lim, H.T., Murukeshan, V.M.: Spatial-scanning hyperspectral imaging probe for bio-imaging applications. Rev. Sci. Instrum. **87**(3), 033707 (2016)

19. Liu, L., Yan, J., Guo, D., Liu, Y., Qu, X.: Undersampled hyperspectral image reconstruction based on surfacelet transform. J. Sens. **2015**, 11 (2015)

20. Liu, Y., Pu, H., Sun, D.W.: Hyperspectral imaging technique for evaluating food quality and safety during various processes: a review of recent applications. Trends Food Sci. Technol. **69**, 25–35 (2017)

21. Lu, G., Fei, B.: Medical hyperspectral imaging: a review. J. Biomed. Opt. **19**(1), 010901 (2014)

22. Ma, A., Zhong, Y., Zhao, B., Jiao, H., Zhang, L.: Spectral-spatial DNA encoding discriminative classifier for hyperspectral remote sensing imagery. In: 2015 IEEE International Geoscience and Remote Sensing Symposium (IGARSS), pp. 1710–1713. IEEE (2015)

23. Martinez, E., Castro, S., Bacca, J., Arguello, H.: Efficient transfer learning for spectral image reconstruction from rgb images. In: 2020 IEEE Colombian Conference on Applications of Computational Intelligence (IEEE ColCACI 2020), pp. 1–6. IEEE (2020)

24. Ronneberger, O., Fischer, P., Brox, T.: U-Net: convolutional networks for biomedical image segmentation. In: Navab, N., Hornegger, J., Wells, W.M., Frangi, A.F. (eds.) MICCAI 2015. LNCS, vol. 9351, pp. 234–241. Springer, Cham (2015). https://doi.org/10.1007/978-3-319-24574-4_28

25. Shaw, G.A., Burke, H.K.: Spectral imaging for remote sensing. Lincoln Lab. J. **14**(1), 3–28 (2003)

26. Stuart, M.B., McGonigle, A.J., Willmott, J.R.: Hyperspectral imaging in environmental monitoring: a review of recent developments and technological advances in compact field deployable systems. Sensors **19**(14), 3071 (2019)

27. Su, W.H., Sun, D.W.: Fourier transform infrared and Raman and hyperspectral imaging techniques for quality determinations of powdery foods: a review. Compr. Rev. Food Sci. Food Saf. **17**(1), 104–122 (2018)

28. Teranaka, H., Monno, Y., Tanaka, M., Ok, M.: Single-sensor RGB and NIR image acquisition: toward optimal performance by taking account of CFA pattern, demosaicking, and color correction. Electron. Imaging **2016**(18), 1–6 (2016)

29. Wang, L., Sun, C., Fu, Y., Kim, M.H., Huang, H.: Hyperspectral image reconstruction using a deep spatial-spectral prior. In: Proceedings of the IEEE Conference on Computer Vision and Pattern Recognition, pp. 8032–8041 (2019)

30. Yan, Y., Zhang, L., Li, J., Wei, W., Zhang, Y.: Accurate spectral super-resolution from single RGB image using multi-scale CNN. In: Lai, J.-H., et al. (eds.) PRCV 2018. LNCS, vol. 11257, pp. 206–217. Springer, Cham (2018). https://doi.org/10.1007/978-3-030-03335-4_18

31. Yu, A., Jiang, T., Chen, W., Tan, X.: A hyperspectral image fusion algorithm based on compressive sensing. In: 2012 4th Workshop on Hyperspectral Image and Signal Processing: Evolution in Remote Sensing (WHISPERS), pp. 1–4. IEEE (2012)

32. Zhong, Y., et al.: Mini-UAV-borne hyperspectral remote sensing: from observation and processing to applications. IEEE Geosci. Remote Sens. Mag. **6**(4), 46–62 (2018)

Author Index

Alckmin e Silva, Ludmila   103
Almeida, Pamela   60
Archila, Juan Sebastian Ramírez   77
Arguello, Henry   147, 160
Arias-Londoño, Julián D.   88
Arroyo, Rodrigo   16
Augot, Denis   31

Bacca, Jorge   160
Baroncini, Virgínia Helena Varoto   103
Benítez, Diego S.   3, 16, 31, 45, 60

Castro, Santiago   160
Choquenaira, Alex   133
Corrêa, Fernanda Cristina   103

Dávalos, José   60
Dedini, Franco Giuseppe   103
Duitama M., John Freddy   88
Duque, Adrián   3

Eckert, Jony Javorski   103

Garcia, Hans   147
Gonçalves, Cristhiane   103
González, Kevin   3
Gutiérrez, Sebastián   31

Hearn, Alex   45

Jácome, Román   147

López, Carlos   147

Mantilla, Luis   119
Martínez, Emmanuel   160
Martins, Marcella Scoczynski Ribeiro   103
Medina-Pérez, Pablo   60
Milón, Daniela   133
Moyano, Ricardo Flores   60

Orjuela-Cañón, Alvaro D.   77

Peña, Alvaro   45
Pérez, Noel   3, 16, 31, 45, 60

Riofrío, Daniel   60
Roca, Diana   133
Romero, Roselli   133

Salazar, Aaron   16
Santana-Velásquez, Angelower   88
Santiciolli, Fabio Mazzariol   103

Yari, Yessenia   119

Zapata, Sonia   31
Zhao, Liang   133

Printed in the United States
By Bookmasters